Weighing Lives

Weighing Lives

John Broome

OXFORD
UNIVERSITY PRESS

Great Clarendon Street, Oxford OX2 6DP

Oxford University Press is a department of the University of Oxford.
It furthers the University's objective of excellence in research, scholarship,
and education by publishing worldwide in

Oxford New York

Auckland Bangkok Buenos Aires Cape Town Chennai
Dar es Salaam Delhi Hong Kong Istanbul Karachi Kolkata
Kuala Lumpur Madrid Melbourne Mexico City Mumbai Nairobi
São Paulo Shanghai Taipei Tokyo Toronto

Oxford is a registered trade mark of Oxford University Press
in the UK and certain other countries

Published in the United States
by Oxford University Press Inc., New York

© John Broome 2004

The moral rights of the author have been asserted
Database right Oxford University Press (maker)

First published 2004

British Library Cataloguing in Publication Data

Data available

Library of Congress Cataloging in Publication Data

Data available

ISBN 0–19–924376–X

1 3 5 7 9 10 8 6 4 2

Typeset by the author
Printed in Great Britain
on acid-free paper by
Biddles Ltd.
Kings Lynn, Norfolk

Preface

This book completes my work on the value of life, which has occupied me, off and on, for a very long time. As I came to see the complexity of the issues, I realized they could not be dealt with in a single book. There were too many general questions about the aggregation of value that needed to be tackled even before I could come to the value of life. So I was first of all delayed by the need to write my earlier book *Weighing Goods*, which tackles those general questions and constitutes the background for the more particular arguments of *Weighing Lives*.

Something else held me up for a long time. I find it hard to believe one of the main conclusions of this book; it offends my intuition. This is not a happy position for an author to be in. An account of value that is like mine in many respects appeared as long ago as 1984, in 'Social criteria for evaluating population change' by Charles Blackorby and David Donaldson. This account violates what I call in chapter 10 'the intuition of neutral existence', an intuition that still grips me strongly. Because of that, it took me a long time to accept the Blackorby–Donaldson theory. This book records a few of my time-consuming attempts to find a way of preserving the intuition. I have now grudgingly concluded it has to be abandoned. In the meantime, Blackorby and Donaldson, in cooperation with Walter Bossert, have extended their theory and presented it in their *Population Issues in Social Choice Theory, Welfare Economics and Ethics*. The formula for value developed in this book is very similar to theirs.

The influence of the published writings of these three authors is too pervasive through this book to be sufficiently registered by individual citations. The same is true of Derek Parfit's pioneering writing on population ethics. Parfit's *Reasons and Persons* first showed me the difficulties of the subject. My thinking about it was so much shaped by Parfit that I often forget how much of my thinking was originally his.

A vast amount has been written about the value of life by other authors while this book has been undergoing its slow gestation. If I had tried to do full justice to all this writing, I would never have finished my own. I have developed my own argument, and now it will have to sink or swim with the competition. Of course, I mean no slight to the many authors I have not been able to respond to.

During the writing of this book, I was immeasurably helped by discussions with very many people, and by the written comments I received from many. I very much appreciate the contribution of each of them. I am sorry to say that so much time has passed I cannot remember everyone who has helped me. I apologize to everyone I omit to mention; please do not feel I did not value your contribution. Those I do remember include: Charles Blackorby, Walter Bossert, Geoffrey Brennan, Roger Crisp, David Donaldson, Nir Eyal, Susan Hurley, Frank Jackson, Frances Kamm, Lewis Kornhauser, Jeff McMahan, Adam Morton, Thomas Nagel, Jan Odelstad, Lars Paulsson, Derek Parfit, Wlodek Rabinowicz, and Hans-Peter Weikard. I must express special thanks to Erik Carlson and Richard Cookson, who each took the trouble to read a draft of the whole book and send me comments. Richard Bradley also gave me a particularly valuable set of comments. Special thanks too to those who sat through the seminars I gave on the book in Oxford. Some of them read the whole book and made very many valuable comments. They include Gustaf Arrhenius, Krister Bykvist, Oswald Hanfling and Mozaffar Qizilbash. I think I have spent more time talking about weighing lives with Arrhenius than with anyone else. It includes the time I spent as the opponent at his defence of his important doctoral thesis, *Future Generations*.

The Hägerström Lectures I gave in Uppsala in 1994 were an early version of part of this book. The book's writing was supported by grant number L32027301097, and some preparatory work by grant number R000233334, both from the UK Economic and Social Research Council. I thank the ESRC for its generosity and patience while awaiting results. The University of Bristol and later the University of St Andrews were both kind enough employers to tolerate my long absences, and allow me leave to take up these grants. Some of my work on the book was supported by a Visiting Fellowship at the Research School of Social Sciences at the Australian National University. I appreciate the generosity of the RSSS too.

John Broome

Contents

Contents

1

Weighing lives

Very often we are faced with decisions that require us to weigh lives against other lives, or lives against other things. This book aims to develop a theoretical basis for helping us think about these difficult practical problems.

I need first to describe the sort of practical problems I have in mind. This is best done by means of examples, so section 1.1 contains a series of practical examples. Section 1.2 presents the problem of weighing lives in general terms.

1.1 Examples

First some examples from medicine.

When a person has a terminal disease, there is often a choice to be made between alternative ways of treating her. One option may be palliative care, which aims to reduce her suffering but not to prolong her life. Alternatively, she might be given a more aggressive treatment that aims to prolong her life, but at some cost to her in suffering. These alternatives pose a dilemma for the patient and her doctors. What determines the right treatment for her to have? How should one choose between prolonging the person's life and improving the quality of her life while it lasts?

I start with this example because many people are at first horrified by the whole idea of weighing people's lives against other lives or against other things. They think a person's life is in some way sacrosanct and should not be weighed in this way. This example reminds us, first, that saving a person's life is only extending her life: making it longer than it would otherwise have been. It is a matter of quantity, then. Given that, we should not think it has an order of importance that makes it inappropriate for weighing.

The example also reminds us that we ought not always prolong life. In cases like this, when we weigh quantity of life against quality of life, it is not always right to choose quantity. Palliative care is sometimes the right choice.

Finally, the example reminds us that choices like this, though terribly difficult, are familiar and inevitable. We need to face up to them. No doubt the choice should very often be left to the patient herself. But that does not mean we have no practical need to answer the question of which alternative should be chosen. After all, the patient herself needs to know which she should choose. Moreover, in many cases she is not able to choose herself; she may be unconscious or not in her right mind.

Furthermore, decisions like this often have to be made from a distance, not for an actual patient but on behalf of patients who will face death in the future. For example, the health service has to decide what treatments it should make available to patients with a terminal disease. Should it give priority to building hospices that offer palliative care, or to the resources that are needed for more aggressive treatment?

So it is an inescapable practical problem to try and judge which is the right treatment to choose. I shall use diagrams of a particular sort to illustrate one aspect of problems like this. Figure 1 is the first of them. In all these diagrams, time is measured in the horizontal direction, and a vertical dotted line marks the present. A person's wellbeing at each time is measured on the vertical axis. The graph of wellbeing begins at the person's birth and ends at her death. Generally my diagrams will show two alternatives. Figure 1 shows the two I have just described: the alternatives that face a person who has a terminal disease. Up to the present, her life is the same in each alternative, because the past cannot be changed. But from the present onwards the alternatives diverge. *A* is the option of palliative treatment. It shows the person's life continuing for a relatively short time, but relatively well. In *B*, her life continues for longer, but less well.

Figure 1. Treatments for a terminal disease

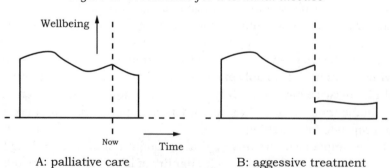

A: palliative care   B: aggressive treatment

Do no attach too much significance to the vertical scale in the diagram, or to the zero level of wellbeing. The scale and the zero will be up for discussion at several points in this book. For the time being, I hope the diagrams will make some rough intuitive sense, and that is good enough for now.

My diagrams are not intended to depict every aspect of the practical problems I shall describe, or even every aspect that may be relevant to determining which is the right choice to make. They depict only people's wellbeing, and the right choice may depend on many considerations besides wellbeing. This book has a limited aim; it will examine only one type of consideration: goodness. In any particular choice, I aim to investigate which of the options is better than which. Chapter 3 considers how restrictive this limitation is.

Figure 1 is not meant to suggest any particular answer to the question of which of the two options is the better. My diagrams present questions, not answers. For instance, I am not suggesting the better option is the one that has the greater area under its graph. Answers come later.

The problem described in figure 1 is unrealistic. In practice, choices are never as clear cut as this. For one thing, all the contingencies of life mean it is never certain what the results of any treatment will be. In some medical problems, uncertainty is a quite central feature. One example is a dilemma that sometimes faces a surgeon whilst removing a brain tumour. The tumour may enclose a blood vessel. If the surgeon tries to cut out the whole tumour, there is a substantial chance of rupturing the blood vessel, and that is likely to cause the patient to die. However, if the surgeon manages to remove the whole tumour successfully, the patient will live to enjoy a full and normal life. On the other

Figure 2. Brain surgery

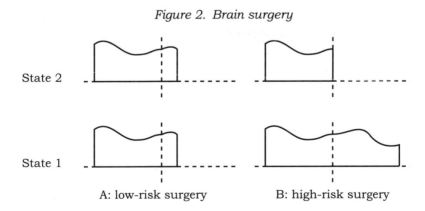

A: low-risk surgery   B: high-risk surgery

hand, if, for safety, the surgeon decides to leave a part of the tumour in place, a new tumour will eventually grow, and the patient will die in five or ten years' time.

Figure 2 is a schematic depiction of this choice. I shall always represent uncertainty by a number of 'states of nature'. One of them is the actual state, but we do not know which. Figure 2 shows just two states. Either nature is such that if the surgeon tries to cut out the whole tumour, the patient will survive, or it is such that she will die. State 1 represents the first possibility; state 2 the second. At the time of the operation, the surgeon does not know which is the actual state, though she may be able to attach a probability to each. For each option, the diagram shows what will result in either state. In the diagram, *A* is the safer option of leaving part of the tumour in place; if the surgeon chooses *A*, the state of nature makes no difference. *B* is the option of trying to remove the whole tumour, and here the state of nature makes the difference between life and death.

In the two examples I have given so far, I implicitly assumed the decision affects the life of a single person only. In practice, other people are nearly always affected, besides the patient herself. For instance, a person with a brain tumour may have young children who need her care, and that will make a tremendous difference to the choice between sorts of surgery. Furthermore, if one treatment costs more than the other, and the cost is not paid by the patient, there will be an effect on taxpayers, or on whoever does pay the cost. It helps to start with the least complicated cases, and that is why in these examples I ignored the effects on other people. But now I come to some choices, still medical, that involve more than one person.

For a single person, I have already said there is sometimes a question whether to prolong her life or make her life better while it lasts. For the

Figure 3. Heart replacement versus hip replacement

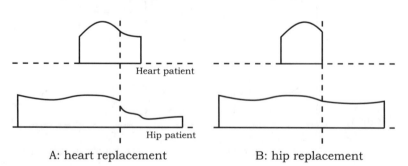

A: heart replacement   B: hip replacement

medical service as a whole, there is a corresponding question of how to divide resources between treatments that prolong lives and treatments that improve lives without prolonging them. Sometimes treatments of both types might be available to a single patient, but more often they will be available only to different patients, with differing needs. For instance, there is the question of how resources should be divided between heart replacements and hip replacements. Heart replacements prolong the lives of people with heart failure; hip replacements improve the lives of the different group of people who have arthritic hips. Figure 3 is a schematic illustration of a choice of this sort. It shows the lives of two people. One has a bad heart; the other a bad hip. Alternative *A* is to replace the first person's heart; *B* to replace the second person's hip. Each half of this diagram shows the life-charts of both people, stacked up one above the other.

This example raises the new, crucial issue of fairness. In this example, one person's life is weighed against benefits to someone else; a life is weighed against a different sort of good. In other examples, some people's lives are weighed against other people's lives. Fairness will be an issue in any problem that involves more than one person.

Next consider a choice between saving old people and saving young people. Some life-saving treatments in medicine tend to prolong the lives of older people; others the lives of younger people. For instance, money can be spent on screening for breast cancer, which generally attacks older women, or on screening for cervical cancer, which generally attacks younger women. Figure 4 is a schematic illustration of this choice.

At least, it seems an appropriate illustration at first, but actually it is not very representative. Most people who are now young will at some future time in their lives have a child, or several children. Their children

Figure 4. The old versus the young

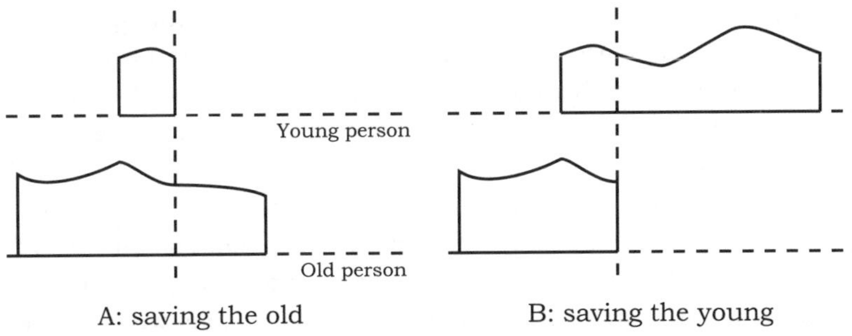

A: saving the old   B: saving the young

Figure 5. The old versus the young, more realistically

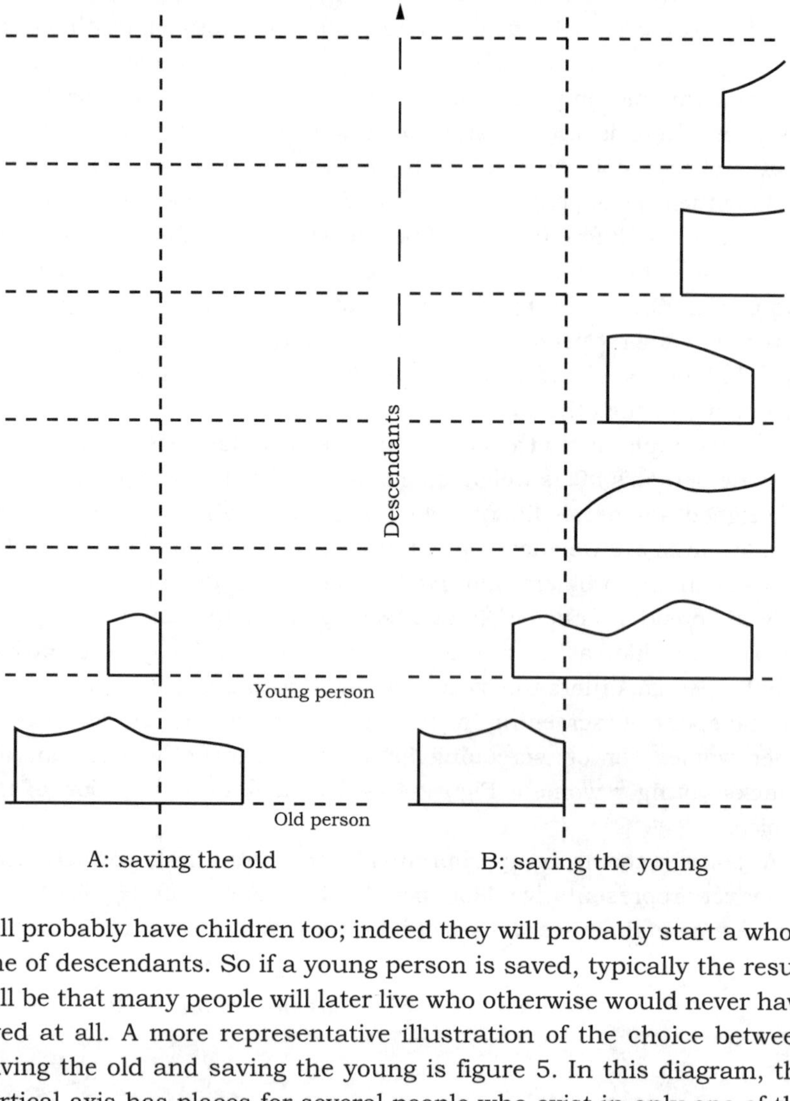

A: saving the old   B: saving the young

will probably have children too; indeed they will probably start a whole line of descendants. So if a young person is saved, typically the result will be that many people will later live who otherwise would never have lived at all. A more representative illustration of the choice between saving the old and saving the young is figure 5. In this diagram, the vertical axis has places for several people who exist in only one of the alternatives: the one in which the young person is saved. In the other alternative, these people appear as blank spaces in the diagram.

Now I turn to some examples from outside medicine. All of us regularly make decisions that influence the lengths of our lives. Generally we do so in a context of great uncertainty; almost no one knows the span of her life for certain, or how it will be changed by her actions. So our decisions appear to us as choices about the risks we bear; we can

Figure 6. Diet

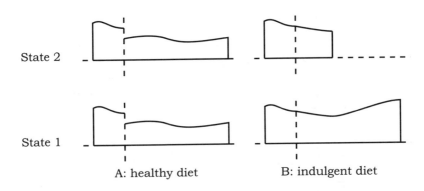

State 2

State 1

A: healthy diet   B: indulgent diet

alter our chances of dying older or younger. We make choices between safe jobs or risky ones, safer sports or more risky ones, healthy or unhealthy styles of life. The risks are too complex to be adequately depicted in a simple diagram. Nevertheless, in figure 6 I have tried to illustrate the question of whether to cut down on fatty foods. I include this example to emphasize that this book is concerned with the ordinary problems of individuals, as well as with public morality. All of us face choices that involve the weighing of lives – in this case alternative possible lives that we might lead – and all of us need to judge which is the best choice to make.

Individuals influence the risks they are exposed to, and so do governments. They do so through the medical service and in many other ways. For instance, any government has to decide how much money to spend on making roads safer. The more money goes on safety, the less is available for other purposes. This is a classic example of the question that concerns economists interested in the value of life: how much is it worth spending on safety?[1]

To produce a schematic illustration of this problem, let us imagine the society contains only two people at present. If the roads are made safe, both will survive to old age and let us assume that both will produce children and in due course a line of descendants. (In my illustration, reproduction is parthenogenetic.) Making the roads safe costs money, and they might alternatively be left in their present dangerous condition. If they are, one or the other person will soon die in an accident. It is uncertain which one it will be; that depends on the state of nature. However, the person who survives will be better off than she would have been if the roads had been improved, because the cost of the improvements will have been saved, and be available for her

Figure 7. Road safety

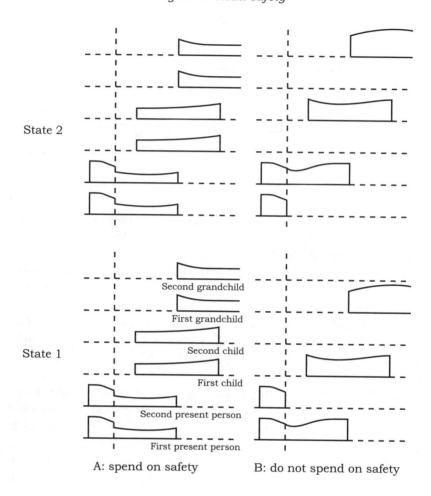

benefit. Her descendants will be better off too. All this is shown in figure 7.

Of course, this example is unrealistic in many ways. It is unrealistic to suppose that, if the improvements are not made, one person will certainly die whatever happens, and it is unrealistic to suppose that the people's risk of death is so high. Still, figure 7 shows some important features of the problem of road safety.

My next example is the question that faces a couple wondering whether to have a second child. Suppose they already have one, and the arrival of a second will make life a little less good for the first than it would have been, because the parents will have to divide their limited

Figure 8. A second child

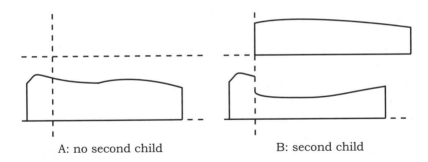

A: no second child   B: second child

resources. Figure 8 shows the problem. I could have put the lives of the parents into the diagram. But for simplicity I am assuming that these lives are made neither longer nor shorter, better nor worse, by the change. So I have left them out to save space. Would it be better if the parents had the second child? Can the good life that the second child will enjoy if she is born in some way make up for the first child's loss?

A similar question can arise for public policy, too. Governments can influence the choices couples make about having children. A government can provide free contraceptives, or it can design a tax scheme that encourages large families. What is the right population policy for a government? Figure 8 could serve as a schematic illustration of that problem too.

For comparison with this one, I want to mention a medical problem once more. What resources should be used for saving young, perhaps premature, babies? Let us suppose, implausibly, that a particular baby can be saved at the cost of reducing her sibling's standard of life. The choice is shown in figure 9. Figure 9 differs from figure 8 only in the

Figure 9. Saving a child

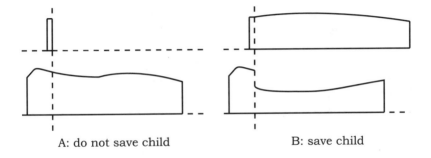

A: do not save child   B: save child

second child's very short existence before the present. Many people would be inclined to think this small blip in the diagram makes all the difference to the problem. The value of prolonging the life of an existing person seems quite different from the value of creating a new person. I shall come back to these two examples at the end of this book, on page 259.

My last example is on a very large scale. Serious global warming, caused by the emission of greenhouse gases, is now inevitable. Within a century, greenhouse gases will warm the world by several degrees Celsius. What will the consequences be? How bad will they be? Indeed, will they necessarily be bad at all? The good and bad effects of global warming on human life are extremely hard to predict. But one bad effect

Figure 10. Global warming

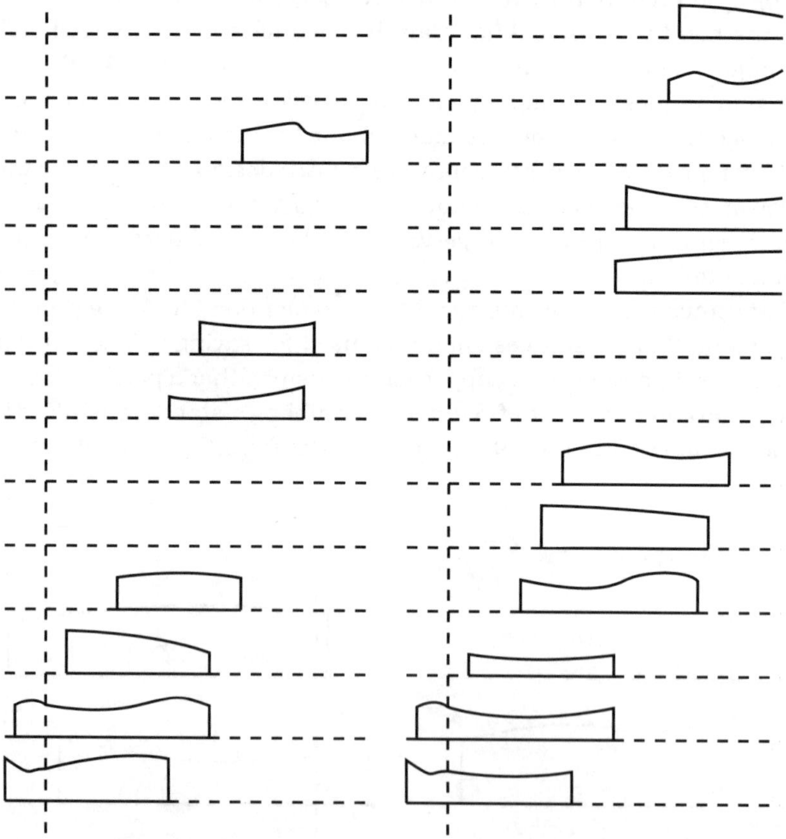

A: business as usual   B: respond

can be predicted reliably: global warming will kill millions of people. It will kill some by extreme weather and flooding, some in frequent heatwaves, and some by extending the range of tropical diseases. So a major predictable harm of global warming – perhaps the most predictable harm – is killing.[2] But most of this killing will be far in the future. So most of the people who will be killed by global warming have not yet been born.

As well as killing, global warming will force movements of population on an unprecedented scale, as some parts of the world become uninhabitable and others become more habitable. It is inconceivable that these movements could occur without large effects on the size of the world's population. Global warming is bound to affect the world's population, though at the moment even the direction of this effect is unpredictable.

It is possible to reduce the speed of global warming, and mitigate its effects. The cost may be large – a major sacrifice made now for the sake of future generations – and we have to decide how big a sacrifice we should make. This problem is illustrated in figure 10. Alternative *A* shows what will happen if we do nothing; *B* if we take action. If we do nothing, our own lives will be better, because we shall be spared the sacrifice, but some of the people who live in the future will live shorter lives. The number of people who live in the future will also be different. In the diagram I have shown it as a smaller number, but I do not insist that the difference will be in that direction.

The diagram illustrates a complicating factor. Not only will our decision about global warming affect the number of people who live in the future; it will affect the identities of those who do live. To respond to global warming, people will have to change their patterns of life. They will have to travel less, for example. This will influence who meets whom, and who marries whom. It will affect the times when people have children. The result will be that, if we respond, the people who will be alive in a century or so will mostly be different people from those who would have been alive had we not responded.

Look at the person who is eighth from the bottom of figure 10. Unless we respond to global warming, this person will live a comparatively short life. But responding to global warming will not lengthen her life; it will cause her not to live at all. Responding to global warming will cause people's lives to be longer in the future, and this is intuitively beneficial. But it may not have many beneficiaries. This particular person will not be one, for example. So there seem to be benefits without beneficiaries, and this can be puzzling.[3]

1.2 The general problem

Section 1.1 presented a number of practical problems. They are problems about how to act: what should a surgeon, or a government, or an individual patient do? But I presented them as choices between alternatives that I described in a particular way, and depicted in diagrams of a particular sort. With each alternative, I concentrated on people's wellbeing and how it is distributed across time and between people. In fact, I treated the alternatives simply as distributions of wellbeing. I presented each problem as a choice between distributions, and more specifically as a question of deciding which distribution is better. In treating the practical problems this way, I was implicitly making a number of assumptions, which I shall discuss in chapter 3. But first, in this section, I shall describe distributions of wellbeing in general terms.

Figure 11. Typical distribution

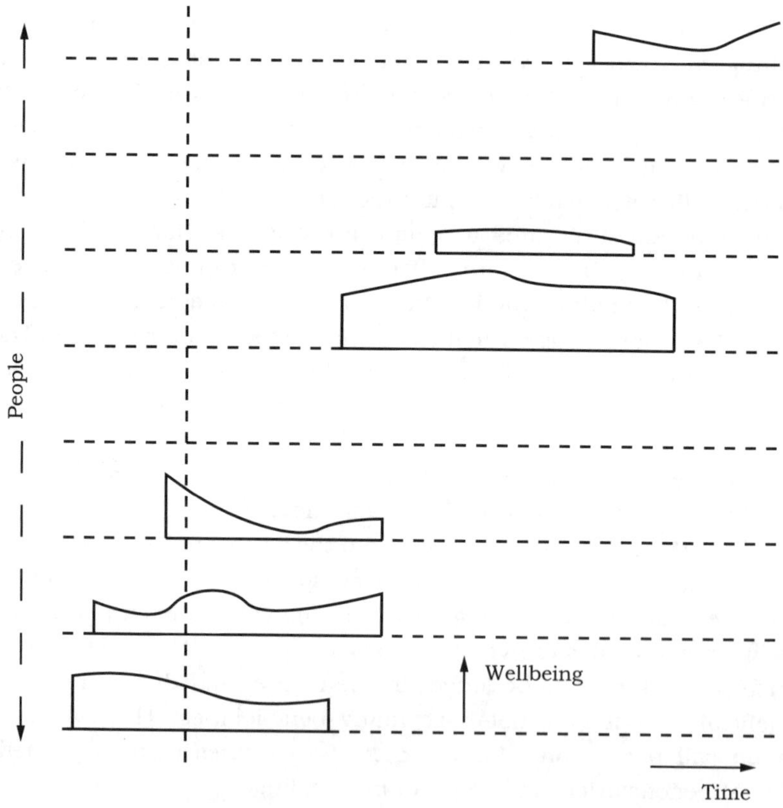

Figure 11 shows a typical distribution of wellbeing. In this diagram as before, the horizontal dimension represents time, and the present is marked with a vertical dotted line. Each person's wellbeing from birth to death is shown by a little graph. Each graph has its own horizontal axis shown as a horizontal dotted line. The diagram shows wellbeing distributed across a sort of two-dimensional grid, where one dimension is time and the other people.

I need to make some observations about this diagram. The first is that it implicitly makes some large assumptions about wellbeing. It assumes there is such as a thing as a person's wellbeing at each time she is alive. I call this the person's *temporal* wellbeing at the time, to distinguish it from her *lifetime* wellbeing, which we shall also be concerned with. Furthermore, it assumes temporal wellbeing is sufficiently like an arithmetic quantity to be sensibly represented in a graph, and that different people's wellbeings can be sensibly compared. I shall be examining the idea of a quantity of wellbeing carefully in chapters 5 and 6; I shall not baldly assume that quantities of wellbeing make obvious sense. But for the time being I shall take them for granted, for the sake of an intuitive introduction to the problems.

The second observation is that the diagram has a lot of blank space in it. For one thing, each person's graph of wellbeing extends only across the times when the person is alive. The remainder of her axis – before she is born and after she dies – is blank. So every axis is blank to a large extent.

Moreover, there are also some completely blank axes. The reason is that the diagram has an axis for each person we are interested in. The examples in section 1.1 show that we frequently need to compare distributions of wellbeing that contain different populations of people: some of the people who exist in one distribution do not exist in another. Since we have to compare distributions that contain different people, and since the identities of the people may matter, I allocate a particular axis in the diagram to a particular person. In each of the distributions that are compared, the corresponding axis belongs to the same person. A person's axis will be blank in any distribution where she does not exist. So I have to allow for blank axes.

Metaphysical matters

Because of the blank axes, some of the expressions I shall use in this book may have a paradoxical air. For instance, I shall sometimes say that *p* does not exist in a particular distribution, where '*p*' refers to a person. How can I refer to a person who does not exist? Indeed, how is there such a person to refer to?

Questions like these have led some authors to speak of a 'possible person' as though it is a special sort of entity, which exists in the place of a person in distributions where that person does not exist. But we should not be so metaphysically extravagant. These questions do indeed raise significant metaphysical issues. However, I think it is safe to set them aside. In this particular case, I think common sense will carry us through.

Suppose history had gone differently. Suppose San Marino had joined Italy, for example. If this event had occurred, some different couples would have got together and married, and some different children would have been born. So some people who exist as things are would not have existed. Also, if this event had occurred, some people would have existed who do not exist as things are. The distribution of wellbeing that would have obtained would not have included some people who exist as things are. Also, our actual distribution of wellbeing does not include some people who would have existed had this event occurred.

On grounds of common sense, I think we can take all these conditional statements to be indubitably true. To be sure, they raise metaphysical questions. The quantifier 'some' seems to range over people who do not exist in the actual world, and a quantifier whose scope seems to include actually nonexistent entities is metaphysically troubling.[4] Nevertheless, since the statements are indubitably true, they evidently make sense. The metaphysical questions must be about how they make sense, not about whether they make sense. So we can safely set those questions aside.

In the distribution of wellbeing that would have obtained had San Marino joined Italy, some people would have existed who do not exist in the actual distribution. Using other words, I shall sometimes say that some people exist in that distribution who do not exist in the actual distribution. Here I use the indicative rather than the subjunctive mood, but I mean to express the very same proposition. The shift of mood is simply a stylistic variation. I cannot avoid making it, because I have long arguments to pursue, and the subjunctive cannot be sustained in English for very long.

Once we have an existential statement that says some people who exist in one distribution do not exist in another, I can arbitrarily pick one of those people and assign the name '*p*' to her. Then I can say that *p*, who exists in one distribution, does not exist in the other. This device of arbitrary naming is a standard part of the logic of quantification. It is used in the standard rule of existential elimination, and is required for making derivations from existential statements. It should be uncontroversial.

Since the name 'p' is assigned arbitrarily, I do not need any prior means to pick out one particular individual rather than another, in order to give her this name. Then, once the name is assigned, I can use it to refer to the person it is assigned to. So there is no real problem over reference.

There may be a different metaphysical problem. I have been discussing how a person who exists in one distribution may not exist in another. There may also be a problem over how a person who exists in one distribution may also exist in another. I have been taking it for granted that people may exist in more than one distribution; that is implicit in my diagrams. But David Lewis argues that the very same person cannot exist in more than one possible world.[5] Instead, a person in one world has at most a counterpart in another world.

If there is a metaphysical problem here, I think we can rely once again on common sense to carry us through. Some people who exist as things are would also have existed had San Marino joined Italy; this is probably true of many Javanese, for instance. I think we may take this as another indubitably true statement. As Lewis agrees,[6] if there is a metaphysical problem, it is about how this statement is true, not about whether it is true. If Lewis is right, counterparthood can substitute for identity.

To summarize, we should not be troubled by the metaphysical questions, and we certainly should not imagine there are such things as possible people. The term 'possible person' is harmless and useful, but we must remember it refers to an ordinary person who might not exist, rather to a special sort of a thing that does exist.

Uncertainty

Having set aside the metaphysical issues, I can return to observations on figure 11. Whenever a person has a life-and-death choice to make, each of the alternative acts available to her will bring about a particular distribution like the one shown in this diagram. Each will determine which people live, when each of these people is born and when she dies, and what each person's wellbeing is at each time she is alive.

But there is a complication. Each act will bring about a particular distribution, but at the time a person acts she rarely knows what that distribution will be. We are nearly always uncertain what the results of our acts will be. I shall continue to model uncertainty as I did in section 1.1, by means of states of nature. There is a range of possible states of nature. One of them will turn out to be the actual state, but at the time of decision we do not know which.

An act together with a state of nature determines what the distribution of wellbeing will be. To put it another way, an act determines a distribution for each state. Each is a two-dimensional distribution like the one shown in figure 11. We can treat the states as constituting a third dimension; we can stack up all the two-dimensional distributions, one for each state, to make up a three-dimensional distribution. We can say that overall an act determines a three-dimensional distribution of wellbeing. Wellbeing is distributed across the three dimensions of time, people, and states of nature. Because the results of an act are in practice always uncertain, it is really three-dimensional distributions we are interested in for practical purposes.

I shall not try to draw three-dimensional diagrams. Instead, when I need to, I can draw a separate two-dimensional distribution for each state of nature, and print these separate diagrams one above the other. I have already done that for some of the examples in section 1.1. Figures 2, 6, and 7 each show a three-dimensional distribution, illustrated that way.

Aggregation

The problem I have set myself in this book is to compare distributions of wellbeing and look for principles that determine which is better than which. For practical purposes, these need to be three-dimensional distributions. We need to discover how bits of wellbeing distributed across a three-dimensional grid together determine the overall goodness of the distribution.

This can be thought of as a problem of aggregation: how is wellbeing aggregated across a grid? We can also consider the aggregation of wellbeing across the three dimensions individually. How does the wellbeing that comes to a person at different times in her life go together to determine how good her life is as a whole? – that is a matter of aggregation across the dimension of time. How does the wellbeing of different people together determine overall good? – that is aggregation across the dimension of people. How does the goodness of an act's various possible results, one for each state of nature, together determine how good is the overall outlook that the act leads to? – that is aggregation across the dimension of states.

Throughout this book, I use the term 'aggregation' in a broad sense. It includes any way of putting together wellbeing at different points on the grid. One way of aggregating is simply to add up. Another is to take the average, and there are many other ways too.

The aggregation problem I have described is a generalization of the problem I investigated in my previous book *Weighing Goods*. In that book too, I considered how to compare the goodness of three-dimensional distributions of wellbeing. But in that book I did not consider problems of existence. I did not consider decisions that affect which people come into existence, nor decisions that affect the times when people exist – the lengths of their lives. In effect, I ignored the possibility of blank spaces in a distribution of wellbeing. The purpose of this book is to take account of blanks. In a way, the large blank areas of figure 11 are its most important feature.

In this book, I shall concentrate primarily on two-dimensional distributions. How is wellbeing aggregated across time and across people? The third dimension of uncertainty will take up little space. The reason is that I believe in *expected utility theory*, which is a particular theory about aggregation across the dimension of uncertainty. It is described in section 5.1. I have discussed the grounds of expected utility theory at length in *Weighing Goods*, and I shall not do so again in this book. I shall simply take it for granted, and I do not need to dwell on it.

Though it will mostly be in the background, uncertainty will have an important place in this book all the same. Surprisingly perhaps, it provides some very useful theoretical leverage. Aggregation across the dimension of states of nature can tell us something about aggregation across the other two dimensions, in ways that will appear later in the book.[7]

Extending life and creating life

This book brings together two topics that have generally been treated separately. One is the topic commonly known as 'the value of life'. What is the value of continuing to live, or the value of saving a person's life? To put the same question another way: what harm does death do? Both economists and philosophers have written extensively on this subject. The second topic is the value of changes in population. How do we judge whether it is good or bad to add new people to the population of the world? Economists and philosophers have written extensively on this subject too.

The two topics are obviously connected in principle. Extending a person's life and adding a new person to the population are both ways of bringing it about that more life is lived by someone. So in one sense they both do the same thing. Of course, there is a crucial difference too. In one case the extra living is done by someone who already exists, and in the other case it is done by someone who would otherwise not exist at all. Nevertheless, it must be a mistake to deal with the two problems in complete isolation from each other.

Furthermore, the two are commonly connected in practice. Many acts in practice have effects of both sorts. As I said in section 1.1, saving the life of a young person will generally have the extra effect that people – her descendants – will live who otherwise would not have lived. So this act extends an existing life, and adds some new lives.

Furthermore again, the borderline between extending an existing life and creating a new life is not a clear one. Sometime between conception and adulthood, a person comes into being. Just when this happens is hotly disputed. It may not even be at a single moment; the creation of a person may be gradual. If a zygote, fetus or baby dies before it becomes a person, one person fewer comes into existence than otherwise would have done. If it dies after that time, one person lives a shorter life than she otherwise would have done. It is not at all clear how we should distinguish one of these eventualities from the other.

'Population'

A note about my use of the term 'population' in this book. By the 'population' of a distribution, I mean the collection of all the individual people who, at some time or other, are alive in that distribution. I do not mean the *number* of those people; I shall call that the 'size' or the 'number' of the population. So in my terminology, two different populations may have the same size.

A population is eternal: it consists of all the people who are ever alive. However, in sections 4.3 and 11.3 I shall also speak of the *temporal* population of the world at a particular time, meaning the collection of all the individual people who are alive at that time.

Notes

1 See M. W. Jones-Lee, *The Economics of Safety and Physical Risk.*
2 The killing is predictable, but predictions for the numbers of deaths are very hard to make. The 2001 report of the Intergovernmental Panel on Climate

Change – see the chapter on 'Human health' in that report, by Anthony McMichael and Andrew Githeko – contains no specific figures. But it gives grounds for thinking global warming will kill hundreds of thousands of people per year, and no grounds for expecting any end to the killing for centuries ahead.

3 This is the 'nonidentity problem' identified by Derek Parfit in *Reasons and Persons*, chapter 16. See p. 136 in this book.

4 See David Lewis, *On the Plurality of Worlds*, for example.

5 Lewis, *On the Plurality of Worlds*, pp. 198–202.

6 *On the Plurality of Worlds*, p. 198.

7 In chapters 5, 6, and 9.

2

Some technical matters

Chapter 1 illustrated the problem of weighing lives and described it informally. This chapter formulates the problem more precisely, and sets up some of the apparatus we shall need to tackle it. Section 2.1 develops the idea of the betterness ordering amongst distributions, and makes some assumptions about its structure. Section 2.2 describes distributions in algebraic terms. Section 2.3 explains how an ordering may be represented by means of a mathematical function. Specifically, it explains how the betterness ordering may be represented by a value function.

2.1 The betterness ordering

I said in chapter 1 that the problem is to discover, amongst distributions, which is better than which. Betterness – comparative goodness – is all that matters in this book; we need not concern ourselves with any other aspect of goodness. We need not worry whether some distributions are absolutely good or bad in any sense. Nor need we worry about the amount by which one distribution is better or worse than another.

Indeed, in so far as either of these worries goes beyond questions about betterness, I doubt it even makes good sense. I doubt there is anything more to the idea of goodness than betterness. If we knew which things are better than which, we would have nothing more to know about the goodness of things. But at any rate, whether or not there are further questions to be asked about goodness, this book is concerned with betterness only. I use 'goodness' in a sense that can be defined in terms of betterness; the definition appears on page 27.

Between distributions there is a *betterness relation*:

(2.1.1)   ... is better than __.

The betterness relation may hold between things of many different sorts:

things of many sorts may occupy the blanks in (2.1.1). For example, the betterness relation may hold between states of the weather: we may say that sunshine is better than rain. In this book, I shall discuss betterness amongst lives, amongst ways of life, and amongst things of other sorts. But I am ultimately concerned with betterness amongst distributions of wellbeing. So for the moment, the blanks in (2.1.1) are to be filled in with distributions. The project of this book is to investigate the form of the betterness relation (2.1.1) amongst distributions of wellbeing.

I can say a few things from the start about the form of this relation, just because it is a relation of betterness. First, the betterness relation is transitive: that is to say, if *A* is better than *B*, and *B* is better than *C*, then *A* is better than *C*. Second, it is asymmetric: if one thing *A* is better than another *B*, then *B* is not better than *A*. Third, it is irreflexive: nothing is better than itself. (This follows directly from asymmetry.) A transitive and asymmetric relation is a sort of ordering; technically, it is a *strict partial ordering*. So betterness is a strict partial ordering.

The betterness relation is transitive, asymmetric and irreflexive simply in virtue of the meaning of 'better'. It has these properties analytically. Any comparative relation, such as 'hotter than', 'more conceited than', 'further than', and so on, must have these same three properties. They are implied by the very idea of a comparative. We may think of these properties as part of the very general logic of comparatives.

Despite all this, some arguments have been raised against the transitivity of betterness. Section 4.1 discusses them, and for the time being I shall take its transitivity for granted.

As well as the betterness relation, I shall inevitably need to mention some other axiological relations too. (I use 'axiological' to mean to do with goodness.) These are not independent; they can be defined in terms of betterness. One is the worseness relation: '*A* is worse than *B*' means that *B* is better than *A*. This is obviously the right definition, but my definition of equality of goodness is less obvious. When I say '*A* is equally as good as *B*', I mean that *A* is neither better nor worse than *B*, and that any third thing *C* is better or worse than *A* if and only if it is correspondingly better or worse than *B*.

Why is this the right definition? To be adequate, a definition of equality of goodness must ensure that 'equally as good as' is an equivalence relation. That is to say, it must be reflexive, symmetric and transitive. Otherwise the definition would not be true to the idea of equality. My definition satisfies this requirement. It obviously follows from the definition that 'equally as good as' is symmetric: that is to say,

A is equally as good as *B* if and only if *B* is equally as good as *A*. Less obviously, it also follows that the relation is transitive: that is to say, if *A* is equally as good as *B* and *B* equally as good as *C*, then *A* is equally as good as *C*. The proof is not difficult and I shall not spell it out.

The transitivity and symmetry of 'equally as good as' are consequences of the definition alone. Reflexivity depends also on the fact that 'better than' is irreflexive, which I mentioned above. Given this fact, the reflexivity of 'equally as good as' follows obviously from the definition. So this is indeed an equivalence relation.

That partly justifies my definition. But there are other equivalence relations I could define on the basis of betterness, so why is this the appropriate one? It is because it makes the right distinction between cases where *A* and *B* are equally good and cases where *A* or *B* are incommensurate in value. I define '*A* is incommensurate with *B*' to mean that *A* is not better than *B*, and *B* is not better than *A*, and *A* is not equally as good as *B*. The point of the distinction will appear in chapter 12; here I shall say no more about it. Chapter 12 is also the place where I shall consider the plausible idea that the betterness relation must be vague or indeterminate to some extent. Till chapter 12 I shall assume the relation is precise, and I shall make an assumption that rules out incommensurateness.

To state this assumption, I need first to identify the set of distributions that will concern us. Perhaps there are some distributions that are neither better nor worse than any other distribution; they do not participate in betterness, we might say. If there are any non-participating distributions, we can ignore them. The *field* of the betterness relation is the set of distributions that do participate, in that they are either better or worse than some other distribution; these are the ones that will concern us. My assumption is that, if we pick any two distributions in this field, then either one of them is better than the other, or the other is better than the one, or the two are equally good. This assumption rules out incommensurateness within the field of betterness. I shall call it the assumption of *completeness*.

Completeness is just a holding assumption till chapter 12. But I also need to make real commitments to some assumptions. I shall commit myself to the assumption that we are concerned only with a finite period of time. This seems reasonable, since the universe will be habitable for only a finite time. It could be argued that a theory of value should be independent of such a contingency. If so, the betterness relation should cover infinitely long distributions, even though they will not actually occur. However, infinitely long distributions raise difficult questions that are not particularly to do with weighing lives.[1] Simply to avoid tackling too many difficult questions at once, I shall consider only finite periods of time.

I shall also commit myself to the assumption that we are concerned only with distributions that contain a finite number of people. I take it for granted that only a finite number of people will actually live, since only a finite number can live at one time and the universe will be habitable for only a finite time. Once again, this is a mere contingency, and we might want our theory of value to transcend it. But once again, I make this assumption to avoid the special difficulties raised by infinite populations.

So I assume that the population of any single distribution has a finite size. However, we shall be concerned with betterness amongst many possible distributions – perhaps infinitely many – and different distributions may contain different people. I do not assume that all these possible distributions taken together contain only a finite number of people. To put it another way, I allow that there may be an infinite number of *possible* people. However, I do assume we are concerned with at most a countable number of possible people. Arguably, this is again in line with the contingent facts. The number of possible human DNA sequences is finite, and arguably, no more than a countable number of different possible people could have a particular DNA sequence. However, once again my real reason for making this assumption is to avoid the special difficulties that would be raised by uncountable numbers.[2]

2.2 Distributions described algebraically

So far, I have described each distribution only by means of a diagram such as figure 11. It will be useful to have a symbolic description too.

I shall imagine that time proceeds in quantum steps, so we must now imagine a typical two-dimensional distribution as something like figure 12. This is a modelling assumption; I make it only for the sake of convenience and simplicity. It will ease my presentation of the theory, because I shall not need to write any integrals. I believe that all my arguments could be reconstructed in a model that has continuous time.

Still, I must acknowledge that this simplifying assumption does have one substantive effect. There is one view about value that cannot be expressed within a discrete-time model. This is the view that length of life has a value that lexically dominates quality of life. As I use the term, one value dominates another *lexically* if any increase in the quantity of

Figure 12. Typical distribution

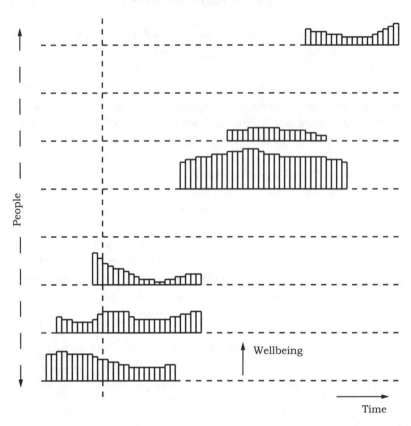

the one value, however little, is better than some particular increase in the quantity of the other value. In this case, the lexical view is that extending a person's life by any length of time, however short, is always better than improving a person's life by some particular amount, without lengthening it. To make this a little more precise: there is some improvement in a person's life – say, seeing the Northern Lights – such that extending the life by any length of time, however short, is better than this improvement. (I am assuming that seeing the Northern Lights is a genuine improvement; it makes the life better.) A discrete-time model cannot accommodate this view, because it cannot recognize any extension to life that is shorter than its quantum of time.

I think nothing is lost by ruling out the lexical view, because it is so implausible. Indeed, it is implausible that any value lexically dominates any other.[3] Since I shall soon be ruling out other lexical views, I shall use this example to emphasize their implausibility.

Suppose you believe that extending a person's life by a single hour is so valuable that it is always better than improving the life by letting the person see the Northern Lights. There is no difficulty about expressing your views in the discrete-time model; we have only to make the quantum of time an hour or less. Suppose you now change your view to a more extreme one, and substitute a minute for an hour. The discrete-time model can accommodate this view too; we must now make the quantum a minute or less. If you substitute a second for a minute, your view can still be accommodated. However brief the period of life that you value so extremely, your view is consistent with the discrete-time model.

The view that is not consistent with the discrete-time model is the view that *any* extension of a person's life, however short, is better than improving the life by letting the person see the Northern Lights. This lexical view is the extreme limit of progressively more extreme views. These views become implausible before they reach the limit, and we need give no credence to the limiting, lexical view. This is true of any view that gives lexical priority to any value.

So I shall adopt the discrete-time model. I have already assumed on page 22 that we are concerned with only a finite span of time. The result is that we have to deal with only a finite number of distinct times. Let this number be T, and let the times be numbered in temporal order from 1 to T.

I have also assumed there is only a countable number of possible people. Let them be numbered 1, 2, ... in some arbitrary order.

If a person p exists at time t, let the symbol g_t^p stand for her wellbeing at that time. In this case, g_t^p is a real number. (The measurement of temporal wellbeing is discussed in chapter 6.) But if p does not exist at t, let g_t^p have some arbitrary non-numerical value that designates nonexistence, say Ω. The value of g_t^p is therefore either a real number or Ω. This 'Ω' is nothing more than a convenient piece of notation. I shall call g_t^p p's *condition* at t. p's condition is either her wellbeing or nonexistence. For each person p there will be a vector of conditions, one for each time t:

$$(g_1{}^p, g_2{}^p, \ldots g_T{}^p).$$

(A vector is just a list.) Call this vector g^p. It will consist mostly of Ωs, but it will include a real number for each of the times when p is alive. If p never lives at all in the distribution I am describing, g^p will consist entirely of Ωs.

An entire two-dimensional distribution is a vector consisting of all the individuals' vectors strung together. This vector may be infinitely, but countably, long. Call it g:

(2.2.1) $g = (g_1{}^1, g_2{}^1, \ldots g_T{}^1, g_1{}^2, g_2{}^2, \ldots g_T{}^2, g_1{}^3, g_2{}^3, \ldots g_T{}^3, \ldots)$.

The two dimensions will appear more clearly if I write the vector on separate lines:

$$
\begin{aligned}
g = (g_1{}^1, \; g_2{}^1, & \quad \cdot \quad \cdot \quad \cdot \quad & g_T{}^1, \\
g_1{}^2, \; g_2{}^2, & \quad \cdot \quad \cdot \quad \cdot \quad & g_T{}^2, \\
g_1{}^3, \; g_2{}^3, & \quad \cdot \quad \cdot \quad \cdot \quad & g_T{}^3, \\
& \quad \cdot \quad \cdot \quad \cdot \quad \cdot \quad \cdot & \\
& \quad \cdot \quad \cdot \quad \cdot \quad \cdot \quad \cdot \;).
\end{aligned}
$$

This is a full description of a two-dimensional distribution of wellbeing. Here is an example:

$$
\begin{array}{cccccc}
(2, & 5, & -2, & \Omega, & \Omega, & \Omega, \\
\Omega, & 3, & 0, & 3, & -1, & \Omega, \\
\Omega, & 2, & 1, & 3, & \Omega, & \Omega, \\
\Omega, & \Omega, & 4, & 1, & -3, & 1, \\
\Omega, & \Omega, & \Omega, & 3, & 2, & 2, \\
\Omega, & \Omega, & \Omega, & \Omega, & \Omega, & \Omega).
\end{array}
$$

I explained on page 17 that I shall work principally with two-dimensional distributions. I have no need to describe a three-dimensional distribution algebraically.

2.3 The value function

I shall next assume that the betterness relation between distributions can be *represented* by a mathematical function. This means we can find a function $v(\cdot)$ that assigns a real number to each distribution in the field of the relation in such a way that the number $v(A)$ assigned to one distribution A is greater than the number $v(B)$ assigned to another distribution B if and only if A is better than B. Granted that the betterness relation is complete, it follows also that $v(A)$ is equal to $v(B)$ if and only if A and B are equally good. I shall call $v(\cdot)$ a *value function*, and call $v(A)$ the *value* of the distribution A.

Now we are equipped to describe a two-dimensional distribution by means of a vector, we may write a value function this way:

(2.3.1) $v(g_1{}^1, g_2{}^1, \ldots g_T{}^1, g_1{}^2, g_2{}^2, \ldots g_T{}^2, g_1{}^3, g_2{}^3, \ldots g_T{}^3, \ldots)$.

My aim in this book is to investigate the form of the betterness relation between distributions. Put differently, it is to investigate the form of a value function $v(\cdot)$ that represents this relation.

A value function represents betterness, which is an ordering. The better a distribution, the higher its value of $v(\cdot)$. But the values of $v(\cdot)$ do not tell us anything about how much better one distribution is than another. To use a term that emphasizes this point, we can say $v(\cdot)$ represents betterness *ordinally*.

The only feature a function needs to have if it is to represent better-ness ordinally is that it assigns higher numbers to better distributions. This means that many different value functions can represent the same betterness ordering. Suppose we already have a value function $v(\cdot)$. Then any other function that puts the distributions in the same order as $v(\cdot)$ does will represent their betterness equally well. For example, the function $w(\cdot) = \sqrt{v(\cdot)}$, which assigns the square root of $v(A)$ to any distribution A, also represents the order of betterness. (For this exam-ple, assume $v(A)$ is always positive.) This is because $w(A)$ is greater than $w(B)$ if and only if $v(A)$ is greater than $v(B)$, which in turn is true if and only if A is better than B.

Any function $w(\cdot)$ is called an *increasing transform* of $v(\cdot)$ if it has the property that $w(A)$ is greater than $w(B)$ if and only if $v(A)$ is greater than $v(B)$. If one function is an increasing transform of another, the other is an increasing transform of the one. If one function represents an ordering, then any increasing transform of it represents the same ordering. There is a whole family of functions that represent betterness ordinally; each is an increasing transform of the others. A value func-tion $v(\cdot)$ is just one function picked arbitrarily out of this family. In effect, it stands in for the family as a whole.

I use the word 'goodness' as synonymous with 'value', which I defined above. So goodness is defined as the value of a function that represents betterness. For the moment it is therefore only an ordinal notion. Cardinal notions of goodness will appear in chapters 5 and 6.

That betterness can be represented by a value function cannot be taken for granted; it is a significant assumption. It can be guaranteed by the assumption I have already made that betterness is a complete ordering on its field, plus a new assumption that the betterness ordering is *continuous* in a particular sense. The sense is mathematically sophisti-cated, and I shall not specify it in detail here.[4] But the rough idea is easily explained. An ordering is continuous if and only if, whenever some distribution A is better than another B, then any distribution that is very similar to A is also better than B, and any distribution that is very similar to *B* is also worse than *A*. 'Very similar' means similar *enough*. It means we can find a degree of similarity to *A* such that all distributions that are to that degree similar to *A* are better than *B*, and all distributions that are to that degree similar to *B* are worse than *B*.

I use the term 'continuity' only in this mathematically defined sense. The term has acquired various other meanings in moral philosophy. For example, James Griffin defines 'continuity' to mean 'that, so long as we have enough of *B*, any amount of *A* outranks any further amount of *B*, or that enough of *A* outranks any amount of *B*'.[5] An ordering that is continuous in the mathematical sense may not be continuous in Griffin's sense. One of Griffin's examples of discontinuity is this: fifty years living with the best Rembrandts is better than any number of years living with nothing but kitsch.[6] Take a billion-year life with only kitsch. This is worse than fifty years with the Rembrandts. It may well be that any sufficiently similar life – a billion and one years with only kitsch, or a billion years with something just a tiny bit better than kitsch – is also worse than fifty years with the Rembrandts. It may also be that any life sufficiently similar to fifty years with the Rembrandts is better than the billion-year life with kitsch. So no mathematical discontinuity is implied by Griffin's type of discontinuity.

Griffin points out that it would not be acceptable to assume continuity in his sense. But is it acceptable to assume mathematical continuity? If we were dealing with an infinite period of time, it would not be. In that context, continuity has strong and implausible consequences.[7] But I have already assumed a finite duration for time. Given that, the principal effect of continuity – though not the only one – is to rule out any lexical elements in the betterness ordering: no value can lexically dominate another. I consider this no loss because, as I said on page 24, lexical domination is implausible. So it is acceptable to assume continuity of the betterness ordering. Therefore there is a value function.

However, I must acknowledge that many popular theories of value imply lexical domination. Indeed, many imply a stronger sort of lexical domination than the one I defined on pages 23–4. For example, the so-called 'leximin' theory gives strong lexical priority to the wellbeing of the worst-off person. It claims that any improvement in that person's wellbeing, however small, is better than any improvement in anyone else's wellbeing, however big. (Unlike 'maximin', which is not lexical, it nevertheless attaches some value to other people's wellbeing. If two options are equally good for the worst-off person, it says one is better than the other if it is better for the second worst-off person or, if the two are equally good for that person, if it is better for the third worst-off person, and so on.) This and all other lexical theories are excluded by the assumption of continuity. Leximin is no more plausible than any other. It is implausible that any benefit to the worst-off person, however small it may be, is always more valuable than a great benefit to someone better off.

The context of weighing lives offers an opening to new lexical views. Here is an example. Suppose you think that, other things being equal, it is better that a woman should exist rather than a man, but this value of femaleness is lexically dominated by the value of wellbeing. More precisely, your view is this. Take two distributions that contain the same number of people and indeed exactly the same people apart from one. This one is a man in one distribution and a woman in the other. Suppose the pattern of wellbeing is the same in both distributions: each person who exists in both distributions has the same wellbeing in each, and the man who exists only in one has the same wellbeing as the woman who exists only in the other. Then your view is that the second distribution is better than the first, but if someone in the first had more wellbeing than she has in the second, however little more, then the first would be better. This view implies discontinuity and is inconsistent with the existence of a value function. I find this view as implausible as any other lexical view. I think continuity remains an acceptable assumption in the context of weighing lives.

Notes

1 A lot has been written about these problems of infinity. See Peter Vallentyne and Shelley Kagan, 'Infinite value and finitely additive value theory'.

2 The assumption is used in the proof contained in my 'Representing an ordering'. See note 3 below.

3 In *A Theory of Justice*, pp. 44–5, John Rawls recommends a lexical ordering only as an approximation. He says 'It seems clear that, in general, a lexical order cannot be strictly correct'. I agree.

4 It is defined in my 'Representing an ordering', which also proves that, given this sort of continuity, betterness can indeed be represented by a value function. See also Charles Blackorby, Walter Bossert, and David Donaldson, 'Population ethics and the existence of value functions'.

5 Griffin, *Well-Being*, p. 85. See also the discussion in John Skorupski, 'Quality of well-being; quality of being'.

6 *Well-Being*, p. 86.

7 See Peter Diamond, 'The evaluation of infinite utility streams', and the discussion in section 3.4 of my *Counting the Cost of Global Warming*.

3

Right and good

A person faced with a practical problem like the ones I described in section 1.1 has to work out what she ought to do. She has to choose between the alternative acts that are available to her, so she needs to know which she ought to choose. But the question I have posed in chapters 1 and 2 is about goodness, and specifically about the goodness of distributions of wellbeing. When a person faces a choice, each of the acts she might choose will result in a particular distribution. How far can the problem of identifying which act she ought to do be brought down to the problem of assessing the goodness of the resulting distributions? This chapter aims to answer that question.

Each act that is available to a person will bring it about that events in the world progress in a particular way. I shall say it brings about a particular *history*. A history includes the past and the future; it runs through the whole period of time we are concerned with, which I assumed on page 22 to be finite. In practice, an actor never knows for sure which history will result from one of her acts; that depends on the state of nature, which she does not know. An act together with a state of nature brings about a history. To put it another way, an act brings about a history for each state. We can say it brings about a portfolio of histories, one for each state. I shall call such a portfolio a *prospect*. So an act brings about a prospect.

A feature of a history is its distribution of wellbeing: a two-dimensional distribution of the sort I described in section 1.2. Correspondingly, a feature of a prospect is its three-dimensional distribution; as I also explained in section 1.2, it has the extra dimension of states of nature. So when a person acts, an effect of her act is to bring about a three-dimensional distribution of wellbeing.

When a person has a choice among acts, how is it determined which she ought to do? Is it fully determined by the distributions that will result from the various alternative acts available to her? Does what she ought to do depend only on the distributions that will result from her acts? Only if it does can the problem of determining how one ought to act be treated as the problem of evaluating the distributions. How far can we make the assumption that this is so?

I shall consider this question in stages. First I shall consider whether what a person ought to do is determined by the goodness of the acts that are available to her. The claim that this is so I call *teleology*. Next I shall consider whether the goodness of an act is determined by the prospect it leads to. The claim that this is so I call *consequentialism*. Finally, I shall consider whether the goodness of an act is determined more specifically by the distribution of wellbeing it leads to. The claim that this is so I call *distribution*. If it is correct, we can identify the goodness of an act with the goodness of the resulting distribution. Since a distribution of wellbeing is a feature of a prospect, the claim of distribution implies consequentialism, but is more specific. I shall discuss teleology, consequentialism and distribution respectively in sections 3.1, 3.2, and 3.3.

Only if all three claims are true can we reduce the problem of determining what one ought to do to a problem about the goodness of distributions. But even if one or other of the claims is false, the goodness of distributions is still likely to be important in determining what one ought to do; it will simply not determine it fully. This chapter will help to locate and assess the importance of goodness.

Put briefly, this chapter rejects teleology, accepts consequentialism, and gives cautious support to distribution.

3.1 Teleology

When a person faces a choice between a number of alternative acts, which ought she to do? Teleology is the view that the answer depends only on the goodness of the alternative acts: what the person ought to do supervenes on the goodness of the alternative acts. How true is this?

The answer you should give to this question depends on two things. It depends first on what normative theory you espouse, and second on what account of goodness you adopt along with your normative theory.

Normative theories and axiologies

By a normative theory, I mean a collection of 'ought' statements, which specify some things that ought or ought not to be done in particular circumstances. The 'things' must be specified in non-normative and non-evaluative terms. One example of a normative theory is that one ought to do whatever will lead to the greatest total of people's pleasure; let us call this 'hedonistic utilitarianism'. Another is that one ought not to hurt anyone, but that, within this constraint, one ought to do whatever will lead to the greatest total of pleasure for oneself; let us call this 'constrained hedonistic egoism', or 'constrained egoism' for short.

Most normative theories are associated with an account of goodness – an axiology – which specifies or at least says something about the goodness of acts. For example, hedonistic utilitarianism is naturally associated with the view that the goodness of an act is the total amount of people's pleasure it leads to. Constrained egoism may be associated with the view that the goodness of an act can only be judged from the point of view of a particular person, and it is the total amount of that person's pleasure that it leads to.

A normative theory with its associated axiology, and perhaps with some other elements too, together make up a broader ethical theory. The normative component of an ethical theory is its practical core. The axiology generally serves a practical purpose too. In practice, it is often difficult to work out what one ought to do, even given a normative theory. Many complex and competing considerations may be relevant. The idea of goodness supplies a useful organizing principle that can help guide us through the complexities, on our way to a normative conclusion about what we ought to do. It has this heuristic purpose.

A theory's axiology may also have an explanatory purpose. An ethical theory may claim that one should act in such-and-such a way *because* it promotes goodness. Alternatively, the explanation may run in the other direction: an act may count as good because it ought to be done in particular circumstances. The true direction of explanation is much disputed, and it does not matter in this book. So I shall leave this question aside.[1]

A normative theory with an associated axiology together imply a particular relationship between goodness and what one ought to do – between good and ought, to put it briefly. For instance, when hedonistic utilitarianism is coupled with the view that the goodness of an act is the total amount of pleasure it leads to, it implies that one ought to do the best of the acts that are available. This in turn implies teleology. Teleology expresses one sort of relationship between good and ought. By a *teleological theory*, I mean a theory that implies teleology.

Not just any relationship between good and ought makes sense, and consequently not just any axiology can be attached to a given normative theory. For example, constrained egoism could not have attached to it the view that pleasure is bad for a person. That would make no sense in the context of the normative theory that a person ought to do what brings her the most pleasure, within a constraint. Our ordinary concept of goodness limits the relationships between good and ought that are possible, and this is beyond the limit.

However, the concept of goodness does not rigidly determine what sort of relationship is possible. Teleology is possible, but so are other relationships. Constrained egoism, with the associated axiology I described for it, is not teleological. It implies that sometimes what one ought to do is affected by the constraint that one ought not to hurt anyone. But this constraint is not part of the axiology. So it implies that what one ought to do does not depend only on the goodness of the available acts. Yet constrained egoism makes sense. Teleology is not a conceptual or analytic truth, then.

Teleologizing a normative theory

I cannot specify fully just what relationships between good and ought are conceptually possible; I shall just mention two conceptual constraints. One is that goodness and normativity cannot be entirely independent of each other. Goodness cannot be normatively irrelevant; it must sometimes make a difference to what one ought to do. Another (which I can only express vaguely) is that, when goodness does make a difference to what one ought to do, it must do so favourably; if one act is better than another, that must not count against doing the first act.

The flexibility permitted by the concept of goodness allows some normative theories to be coupled with more than one axiology – not simultaneously but as alternatives. Take the normative theory of constrained egoism. I offered one axiology for it. But the theory is also compatible with a different axiology. Given the theory, we might say that hurting a person is a very, very bad thing to do. It is good to pursue one's own pleasure, but the badness of hurting a person lexically dominates that goodness. Any act that hurts someone is therefore worse than any that does not. Consequently, one ought not to do such an act.

Under this alternative axiology, constrained egoism is teleological. It implies that what one ought to do depends only on the goodness of the available acts, taking account of the extreme badness of hurting a person. Goodness in this axiology is relative to the person: goodness from the point of view of one person differs from goodness from the point of view of another; each includes only the person's own pleasure. But I am not ruling out relative axiologies. So a given normative theory may be nonteleological when coupled with one axiology, and teleological when coupled with another. It may be nonteleological as it is first presented, but be made teleological by means of some reinterpretation.

This example illustrates the sort of reinterpretation that may be needed. Firstly, the axiology may need to be broadened. The normative theory must in some way make what one ought to do depend on the properties of the available acts. Some of these properties may be taken as contributing to the acts' goodness; some not. Let us call the first type 'goodness properties' or just 'goods'. As I first presented constrained egoism, the pleasure an act brings one is a good, but the property of an act that it hurts no one is not a good. The latter property helps to determine what one ought to do, not through goodness but by the different means of removing a constraint. Under the reinterpretation, this latter property also counts as a good. It contributes to determining what one ought to do through its contribution to the goodness of acts. In this way, the axiology is broadened.

Secondly, the structure of the axiology may need to be made more complex. The goodness of an act may depend on its individual goodness properties in more complex ways. In the original presentation of constrained egoism, the goodness of an act, from the point of view of the actor, is given simply by the pleasure it brings her. The reinterpretation introduces the idea of one good's lexically dominating another. Lexical domination is an extra structural complexity.

Broadening the axiology and making it more complex are typical moves in the process of teleologizing a normative theory. But teleologizing a theory is not always easy; there is one major obstruction in the way. The relation of betterness is transitive, which means that a normative theory must have a transitive structure if it is to be teleologized. Suppose a normative theory implies that, when the available alternative acts are A and B, one ought to do A, and when the available alternatives are B and C, one ought to do B, and when the available alternatives are C and A, one ought to do C. This normative theory does not have a transitive structure. It cannot be the case that A is better than B, B better than C, and C better than A. So what one ought to do, according to this theory, cannot depend only on the goodness of the alternatives. This theory cannot be made teleological. It does not have what I call 'teleological structure'.[2]

At least, this theory cannot be made teleological without some more work. Actually, resources are available for teleologizing even a theory like this. We can count A when the alternative was B as a different act from A when the alternative was C, and so on. This type of move will allow us to give the theory an artificial transitive structure; I do not need to go into details.[3] It has sometimes been suggested that all plausible normative theories could be teleologized by some means or other, but I shall take no stance on this question.[4]

Teleologizing a theory is sometimes useful, when it can be done. It can serve a purpose in the theory of ethics. Goodness has a particular structure. The transitivity of betterness is one of its structural features. My book *Weighing Goods* explores more complicated structural features of goodness. Since in teleology what ought to be done depends only on goodness, when a normative theory is teleological, it inherits some structural features from goodness. So teleologizing a normative theory, or seeing how far it can be teleologized, can be a way of exploring its structure.

But there is a cost. I have already said that teleologizing a theory often involves making the axiology broader and more complex. Also, it often makes it less intuitive. To use Robert Nozick's term, it may require a 'gimmicky' axiology.[5] This can be harmful because, as I said on page 32, the axiology that accompanies a normative theory generally serves a heuristic purpose. The less intuitive the axiology, the less effectively it can serve this purpose.

Teleologizing a normative theory does not alter the theory itself; it makes no difference to what the theory says one ought or ought not to do. It merely finds an axiology to match the given theory. Moreover, when it attaches an axiology to the theory, it does not assign the axiology any explanatory role. It does not suggest that what ought to be done ought to be done *because* it is good. The notion of good that emerges from teleologizing a theory merely *represents* the theory, in a sense akin to the one I defined on page 26, in which an ordering is represented by a value function.

I am therefore using 'teleology' in a weaker sense than John Rawls's. Rawls defines a teleological theory as one in which 'the good is defined independently from the right, and then the right is defined as that which maximizes the good.'[6] In teleologizing a normative theory, 'good' is defined in terms of 'right'. I define a teleological theory as one that can be represented by an axiology. This only requires it to have a teleological structure. Principally, its structure must be transitive.

Choosing an axiology

We have some discretion. We can choose a broader or less broad axiology, including more or fewer considerations as goods. A significant aim of this book is practical; I would like it to contribute to decision making in matters of life and death. So in this book I want to stick to a reasonably intuitive, and consequently fairly narrow, axiology. The inevitable effect is to expose teleology to doubt. Some normative theories are firmly teleological; hedonistic utilitarianism is one of these. But many more plausible theories are not teleological under a narrow axiology. In determining what one ought to do, they give a place to considerations that do not fit into a narrow axiology.

To a large extent, I can remain noncommittal about teleology. I explained in section 1.2 that this book aims to examine how wellbeing that is distributed across people, times and states of nature comes together to determine the overall goodness of a distribution. Wellbeing is made up of goods, but I am interested in the aggregation of wellbeing, not in what goods constitute it. To a large extent I can leave it up to you, the reader, to decide for yourself which normative considerations you will include as goods, and which you will exclude. The theory developed in this book provides a framework, and you can decide what considerations you think can be fitted into it. Any that cannot, you will have to find a way of dealing with separately.

I hope you will find at least some use for the framework. Most normative theories give at least some place to goodness in determining what ought to be done. But it is plain by now that, because this book is about goodness only, I do not expect it to say everything there is to say about how one ought to act in matters of life and death. My ambition in this book is modest, and I do not defend teleology.

I do have some remarks to make about what considerations should be counted as goods. Some are uncontroversial. For instance, if pleasure is an ethical consideration at all, it is uncontroversially a good. For the sake of testing what is at issue, let us pick a more tricky example. What about the putative good of determining one's own future? It seems intuitively that often people ought to determine their own future, rather than have it determined for them. Is self-determination a good?

It seems not, at first. Think about a case where one person is making a decision on behalf of another; say a doctor is choosing a treatment for a cancer patient. Suppose for simplicity that no one else is affected; there are no relatives, friends or dependants to be considered. Very often, in such a case, the wishes of the person affected should determine the decision; the doctor should do what the patient wants. But people do not always want what is best for themselves. A patient may not be able to judge properly what, say, a drugged life will be like. She may have given way to despair, or she may cling to life when there is nothing left for her but pain. She may not be able to understand properly the risks of surgery, or give them proper weight. Nevertheless, even though they are not for her own good, the wishes of the person should still prevail in many cases. It seems, then, that a doctor should sometimes do something other than what would be best, in order to let a patient determine her own future. Here self-determination is contrasted with good; it is not counted as part of good.

However, self-determination has the feature that it can plausibly be weighed against other considerations in determining what is the right thing to do on a particular occasion. It is not always right to do, on behalf of a person, whatever the person herself wants. When, during a period of depression, a person wants to die, the good that will come to her in the rest of her life, if she lives, may outweigh the consideration of self-determination in favour of her dying. If that is so, it would be right to save this person's life against her own wishes.

No doubt, occasions where a person's wishes should be overridden are rare. Partly, this is because self-determination is an important good and not lightly outweighed. Partly, too, it is because people generally want what is good for themselves, so that a person's wants are generally good evidence of what is good for her. Nevertheless, though this may be rare, self-determination can sometimes be outweighed.

Intuitively, weighing is characteristic of goods. When we judge which of two options is better, we typically think that each option has some good and some bad features, which have to be weighed against each other. So we can use weighing as a criterion for what counts intuitively as a good. It is not the right criterion for the purposes of a theoretical account of good. A theoretical account might allow one good to dominate another lexically, which rules out weighing. My second interpretation of constrained egoism, which appears on page 33, contained a lexically dominating good. But when we are aiming for an intuitive axiology, we might reasonably insist on weighing.

Since self-determination can be weighed against other goods, it can be treated as a good without straining intuition. We can say it is good for a person to have her wishes respected, and that is why a doctor ought generally to do what her patient wants.

Fairness

But there is one ethical consideration that I shall not count as a good in this book, and that is fairness. My reason is purely pragmatic. As a matter of fact, from a theoretical point of view, I think fairness may indeed be considered as a good. In *Weighing Goods* I treated it that way.

Moreover, it is amenable to weighing; it can be weighed against other goods. If some act would be a little unfair to someone, but would bring large benefits to many people, it might be right to do it. Fairness may be outweighed by other goods, then.

However, in so far as it is a good, fairness is a second-order good. It is concerned with how first-order goods are distributed among people. For instance, health care is a first-order good, which may be fairly or unfairly distributed. Moreover, a distinguishing feature of fairness is that in a sense it actually opposes the weighing of first-order goods.

To explain how fairness opposes weighing, I shall take a crude example. I shall make a lot of assumptions, but that is only to keep the example simple. Suppose a quantity of serum is available, which can extend for a while the lives of either of two patients. Without the serum, both patients will die soon. For some reason, the serum works twice as well for one patient as for the other. Each small unit can add two days to the life of one patient, but only one day to the life of the other. I shall assume a day of life is as good for one as it is for the other.

Suppose we were to decide how to use the serum on the basis of weighing goods. For each unit, we would weigh the good it will bring one patient against the good it will bring the other. For each unit, giving it to the first patient would do twice as much good as giving it to the second. So on the basis of weighing, we would give each unit to the first patient. She would end up with all the serum, and the second patient with none.

Is this fair? Not as most people would see it; most people would think it unfair to refuse the second patient any share in the life-saving serum. I can add some theory to explain this thought.[7] Fairness requires proportionality. When some resource is to be distributed, fairness requires it should be distributed in proportion to people's claims on it. In the example, it is debatable what claim the two patients have on the serum. We might think their claim is given by their need for it, and there is a case for saying that the second patient needs it twice as much as the first does. Alternatively we might think claims are given by the benefit the patients will get from the serum. If so, the second patient has half the claim of the first. Or we might have some other view about claims. But at any rate, the second patient surely has some claim. Given that, according to the proportionality rule, fairness requires her to get some of the serum. Yet weighing of goods would lead to her getting none. To generalize, the rule of proportionality and the rule of weighing are different rules. So fairness conflicts with weighing.

That is not the end of the story. Many health economists believe that the demands of fairness can actually be accommodated within an axiology that is regulated by weighing. Their idea is to adjust the weight given to the benefit of each patient by means of a system of weighting factors. Benefits are weighed against each other only after the adjustments are made. Specifically, less weight is given to benefits that come to a person who already has greater benefits. This is an application of the idea of 'giving priority to the worse off', which has been used by economists for a long time as an attempt to represent the value of equality.[8] The idea is that fairness can be accounted for by means of priority.

If you are convinced by the prioritarian move, you may count fairness as a good. It will then be covered by this book's account of how goods are aggregated. But my own opinion is that prioritarianism is not an adequate way to understand fairness. The full argument is long and I shall not rehearse it here.[9] I think fairness really is inimical to weighing. For that reason, I think it is a pragmatic mistake to count it as a good when we are dealing with practical questions of weighing lives. Doing so encourages the mistaken idea that it can be adequately accounted for by weighing.

Fairness is nevertheless a vitally important issue in these practical questions. I think the only way to give it proper recognition is to account for it separately. By merging it with goodness, the methods of health economics give too little respect to fairness.

Kamm

Frances Kamm's major work *Morality, Mortality*, and particularly its first volume *Death and Whom to Save From It*, deals with a large part of the subject I call 'weighing lives'. However, Kamm founds a great deal of her work on fairness, whereas I have just excluded fairness from the subject matter of this book. Kamm, like me, sets fairness apart from goodness. Fairness she treats as an aspect of right, which she contrasts with good. Having made the division between right and good, she concentrates on right. I concentrate on good. The consequence is that our conclusions are largely incommensurable. Though our broad subject is the same, our specific questions are different, and there is not much to compare between our answers.

Kamm and I are both ultimately interested in the normative question of what one ought to do in matters of life and death. But Kamm aims to answer this question directly, and assigns little importance to goodness in answering it, whereas I aim only to assess the goodness of the alternatives. I do this because I believe goodness contributes significantly to answering the normative question. But in this book I do not answer the normative question itself.

True, Kamm is prepared to deal in goodness. For example, she thinks that, when you have a choice between saving five people from death and saving one, it is better to save the five.[10] However, as I understand her, this fact plays no role in determining what you ought to do if ever you face this choice. Fairness alone determines what you ought to do.

Here she disagrees with a common view about the problem of saving one versus saving five. The common view is that the problem displays a conflict between goodness and fairness.[11] Fairness requires you to give each person an equal chance of being saved. This can be achieved by tossing a coin to decide whether to save the one or the five; then everyone will have a one-half chance of being saved. On the other hand, so far as goodness is concerned, it is better simply to go ahead and save the five, without tossing a coin. Sometimes goodness wins this conflict, and you ought to save the five. In those cases, you ought not to do what fairness requires, which is to toss a coin.

Kamm agrees that in some circumstances you ought to save the five. But she argues that those are circumstances in which fairness itself requires you to save the five.[12] In other circumstances fairness requires you to act differently, and again, in those other circumstances, you should do as fairness requires. Goodness plays no part in determining what you ought to do.

Kamm is avowedly a deontologist. This by itself does not mean her view is not teleological in the weak sense of 'teleological' I have adopted. Teleology in my sense is not the view that goodness explains or determines what you ought to do. A normative theory is teleological in my sense if it can be represented by an axiology, and this is a matter of its structure only: it must have a teleological structure. Principally, its structure must be transitive. Whenever it says that out of two options A and B you ought to choose A, and out of B and another option C you ought to choose B, then it must also say that out of A and C you ought to choose A.

However, as it happens, Kamm's normative theory does not have a teleological structure. She explicitly insists it is not transitive.[13] For this reason it cannot be teleological even in my sense. However we look at it, good has little part to play in her theory.

Killing

In keeping with my modest ambition, I have one other exclusion to announce. In this book, I shall set aside the special questions raised by deliberate killing. This book does not deal with capital punishment, war, euthanasia, abortion or any of the other important issues that involve killing. Killing raises special ethical problems of its own, over and above the issues raised by death, and those I shall leave aside. I shall not try to incorporate the rightness or wrongness of acts of killing as a sort of good or bad within my axiology. This does not mean the book has nothing to contribute to questions involving killing. An act of killing causes a death. The goodness or badness of this effect is generally one consideration that helps to determine whether the act is right or wrong. So an account of good is likely to form a part of any ethical theory of killing. But it is far from the whole.[14]

3.2 Consequentialism

Consequentialism as I understand it is the view that the goodness of an act is determined by the prospect it leads to: it supervenes on this prospect. This is not to give 'consequentialism' its commonest meaning. For one thing, teleology is often conflated with consequentialism. If we put what I call 'teleology' together with what I call 'consequentialism', we reach the view that what one ought to do is determined by the prospects that the alternative acts will lead to. This conflated view is closer to consequentialism as it is more commonly understood.

It remains different in at least one respect. In the context of uncertainty, an act leads to a prospect, but it eventually brings about a particular history, given the actual state of nature. It is common to take the consequence of the act to be the history that actually results, rather than the prospect. Correspondingly, 'consequentialism' is often used for the view that what one ought to do is determined by the histories that the alternative acts will lead to. But I am thinking of an act's consequence as the prospect it leads to.

There is a point of substance as well as terminology here. Consequentialism as I define it excludes the view that the goodness of an act is determined by the history it leads to, rather than the prospect it leads to. G. E. Moore took that view, for example.[15] Since the history is part of the prospect, it may seem that my sort of consequentialism is more general, and should include Moore's view. But that is not so.

Which history an act leads to depends partly on which is the actual state of nature, and that fact is not a part of the prospect the act leads to. Suppose I do an act that is likely to lead to a bad outcome, but by luck it leads to a good one. According to Moore, that is a good act. According to consequentialism as I have defined it, it is a bad act. I have tried to justify this feature of my assumption of consequentialism in section 6.1 of *Weighing Goods*, and I hope I will be forgiven for passing over it here.

Setting that issue aside, should we believe consequentialism as I define it? A familiar objection to it is that an act may have value in itself, quite apart from the consequences that result from it. In a sense, no doubt that it so. Breaking a promise is no doubt often bad in itself, in a way that goes beyond whatever harm results. But as I defined a history on page 30, it includes all of the past, present and future. So when an act is performed, the act is contained in each of the histories that may, depending on the state of nature, result. The prospect the act leads to is the collection of all these possible histories. So the act is a part of the prospect. It must therefore be possible to count any intrinsically good or bad feature of the act as a good or bad feature of the resulting prospect. For some purposes, there may be a good reason to exclude an act from its own consequences. Doing so will yield a different, narrower notion of consequentialism, which may well be false. But that is no objection to my broad version.

The broad version is not idiosyncratic to me; it is common in the philosophical debate about consequentialism. For instance, Samuel Scheffler says:

When I speak of the act-consequentialist as requiring agents to produce the best overall outcomes or states of affairs, I do not mean that the act-consequentialist divides what happens into the act and the outcome, and evaluates only the latter with his overall ranking principle. Rather, the act itself is initially evaluated as part of the overall outcome or state of affairs. The act-consequentialist first ranks overall outcomes, which are understood, in this broad way, to include the acts necessary to produce them, and then directs the agent to produce the best available outcome so construed.[16]

Many serious doubts have been raised about consequentialism,[17] but they are not about consequentialism as I defined it. Some have been about teleology as I defined it,[18] and some have been to do with the relativity of good, which I shall be considering in section 4.3. So I shall take consequentialism for granted.

3.3 Distribution

The claim I call 'distribution' is that the goodness of an act is determined by the distribution of wellbeing the act leads to; it supervenes on this distribution. The distribution in question is a three-dimensional distribution of temporal wellbeing across people, times and states of nature. How far should we accept the claim of distribution?

Given consequentialism, we know that the goodness of an act is determined by the prospect it leads to. The distribution of wellbeing is a feature of the prospect. So the claim of distribution will fail if and only if the goodness of an act depends on some feature of the prospect other than the distribution of wellbeing.

There obviously are such features. They include nonhuman goods. An uncontroversial example is the wellbeing of animals, since my distributions include only the wellbeing of people. Controversial examples are the good of ecologies, beauty that is appreciated by no person, and the pleasure of God.

What to do about this? The wellbeing of animals could be brought within the scope of this book by adding animals to the dimension of people. But that would raise doubts about the assumption of impartiality that I shall make on page 135. So instead, I shall accept a further limitation on the scope of this book. In section 3.1, I limited myself to a comparatively narrow, intuitive notion of good, which excluded fairness. I now arbitrarily determine that this book will be concerned only with goods that appear within a three-dimensional distribution of people's wellbeing. That is to say, I simply adopt the claim of distribution. In doing so, I exclude nonhuman goods. All considerations other than those that appear in a distribution of wellbeing will have to be accounted for separately. The wellbeing of animals is amongst them.

I assume that people's good and nonhuman goods can be separated in this way: that people's good can be evaluated independently from nonhuman goods. This is technically an assumption of 'separability'. Separability assumptions play an important part in this book, but I shall not spend time on this one. First, I doubt there even are nonhuman goods apart from the wellbeing of animals. Second, in chapter 13 I defend an assumption I call 'separability of people', and a simple extension of this assumption implies people's good is separable from the wellbeing of animals.

The limitation I have now accepted on the scope of this book, imposed by the assumption of distribution, excludes nonhuman goods. Does it also exclude some sorts of human good? It may, but not many. Two things make it a less severe limitation than it may at first seem to be.

Pattern goods

The first is that the assumption of distribution does not require each good to show up in the wellbeing of some individual, at some time, in some state of nature. It is much, much weaker than that. The assumption is that the goodness of an act depends on the whole of a distribution of wellbeing. Many goods may show up as a pattern contained within the distribution, rather than at any particular place in it. Call these *pattern goods*. Some examples follow. I do not certify that each is a genuine good. But each might be thought genuine, and I mention them because none is excluded by the assumption of distribution.

The survival of humanity. It might be thought a good thing if the human species survives for a long time. This would be a good that is separate from the wellbeing of any particular individual. But it is a pattern good. How long humanity survives is a feature of the distribution of wellbeing, so this value is consistent with the assumption of distribution.

Longevity. It seems a good thing for a person to have a long life. But if it is, that good does not appear at any particular location in the grid. It appears only when we take many times together and see that the person is alive at all of them. Longevity is another pattern good, consistent with the assumption of distribution.

The shape of a life. We might think that a life that starts badly but improves is better than one that starts well but deteriorates and ends badly; it is better for life to go uphill rather than downhill.[19] If this is so, it identifies another good that does not appear at a particular location in the grid; it emerges only from the difference between a person's wellbeing at later times and her wellbeing at earlier times.

Equality of wellbeing. If equality is valuable, it is better for wellbeing to be equally distributed across people than for it to be unequally distributed. This feature of a distribution does not appear in one location in the distribution, but only when different people's wellbeings are compared together.

Avoiding risk. In many circumstances, risk seems a bad thing. Risk shows up in a distribution of wellbeing in the form of differences between people's wellbeings in different states of nature. If a person's wellbeing varies a lot between one state and the next, she is exposed to a lot of risk.

The assumption of distribution excludes none of these pattern goods. But I should say here that, later in this book, I shall consider and adopt various assumptions that do exclude particular pattern goods. They are assumptions of separability. They say in effect that a distribution can be evaluated by evaluating parts of it independently of other parts. For example, chapter 7 examines and rejects a separability assumption that would rule out the value of longevity. Chapter 8 examines and accepts a separability assumption that says each person's lifetime wellbeing can be evaluated independently of other people's wellbeing. Each assumption of separability rules out particular sorts of pattern goods.

How can pattern goods be formally distinguished from other goods? If distribution is a correct assumption, the goodness of an act depends only on the resulting distribution. In mathematical terms, it is a function of the vector that describes the distribution. For a two-dimensional distribution, this function is shown in (2.3.1) on page 26. The function's arguments are the individual amounts of people's temporal wellbeing that make up the vector. A pattern good is one that appears in the form of the function, rather than in one of the arguments of the function. For example, if equality is truly good, the function has a different shape from the shape it would have had if equality had not been good.

Wider notions of temporal wellbeing

There is a second way in which the assumption of distribution is less restrictive than it appears. I do not assume any particular account of temporal wellbeing. The wellbeing of a person at a time is how well her life goes at that time. It takes into account everything that is good or bad for her at the time. There are narrow accounts of temporal wellbeing, such as hedonism, and broader accounts. I am happy to accommodate any of them. This book is about the aggregation of wellbeing, and I prefer to remain as uncommitted as possible about the nature of the wellbeing that is aggregated.[20] If you think you know of some sort of good that does not appear in the distribution of temporal wellbeing, you may need to broaden your conception of temporal wellbeing. Once you have done that, the good may appear in the distribution after all.

The rest of this section considers some examples. They are all goods that, if they are really goods at all, belong to a particular person but, on the face of it, do not appear in the person's wellbeing or in the pattern of the person's wellbeing. It may be possible to accommodate them to the claim of distribution by broadening the notion of wellbeing.

Some of these examples depend on the pattern of the person's life, in a sense. One is this. Suppose it is good for a person to live a well-rounded life, containing varied experiences and achievements. This is a good that depends, in a sense, on the pattern of the person's life. But it does not depend just on the pattern of her wellbeing. Well-roundedness requires a variety of specific experiences and achievements, not just a variety of levels of wellbeing. So it is not a pattern good in my sense. On the face of it, it is excluded by the assumption of distribution.

Another example in the same class is the good of completing some worthwhile programme of activity. For example, perhaps it adds to the goodness of a person's life if she completes a book she is working on, rather than leaving it uncompleted at her death. Once again, this good depends on a certain sort of pattern in her life. But it is not a pattern in her wellbeing, so it is not a pattern good in my sense, and on the face of it, it is excluded by the assumption of distribution.

There is a way of understanding these goods that brings them within the fold of this assumption. We might think that, if a person completes a book she is writing, that throws a new light on the whole period while she is writing it. It makes her life during that time more worthwhile. So, during that whole period, her life was better than it would have been had she left the project uncompleted. In this way, her success adds to her wellbeing at a particular times. It adds wellbeing retrospectively; there is a backwards causation of wellbeing. If this is a correct way to think about goods like this, it makes them compatible with the assumption of distribution.

This understanding of goods depends on backwards causation of wellbeing, but there need be nothing wrong with that. If a person's wellbeing at a time necessarily depended only on her physical states at that time, backwards causation of wellbeing would be impossible. Hedonism excludes backwards causation, therefore. But wellbeing is not necessarily so restricted in its nature. We must anyway recognize that a good may be caused by an event that is not simultaneous with the existence of the good. If a letter gives you pleasure, the posting of the letter causes the pleasure, but the pleasure occurs at a different time from the posting. Some goods may not exist at any specific time at all; pattern goods are examples. Nevertheless, these atemporal goods may be caused by an event that occurs at a particular time. Given that atemporal goods may be caused by events that occur at a particular time, there seems to be no reason why some temporal goods should not be caused by events that occur later than the good.

Another type of putative good might receive a similar treatment. Some types of good for a person seem not to require the person to be alive at the time they are caused. For example, perhaps it is good for a person to be famous. If so, for some people this is a good that is caused only after they are dead. Aristotle believed a person could be benefited or harmed after her death by the fortunes of her descendants.[21] Many philosophers think it is good for a person to have her desires satisfied. If they are right, many instances of this good are caused only after the person has died, because people often have desires about what happens after they are dead. For instance, it may be good for a person to have her will properly executed.

If there are truly goods like this, we have three options. First, we might count them as atemporal goods. If we do that, they do not show up at all in the distribution of wellbeing, so for them the assumption of wellbeing will fail. Second, we might count them as occurring at the time when they are caused. This is a time when the person whose goods they are is not alive. To accommodate this possibility within the assumption of distribution would require me to change my story so far. I have always taken it for granted that a person has wellbeing only during her life, but that implicit assumption could be dropped. Still, I prefer the next option, which is to suppose there is backwards causation in these cases. An event that occurs after a person has died causes wellbeing within the person's lifetime.

The third option is only plausible if there is some time within the person's life when the person may plausibly receive the wellbeing. For a posthumously-satisfied desire there is: the time of the desire. For posthumous fame there generally is: the time when the person did whatever later led to her fame. Still, I do not insist that this sort of device can make every good compatible with the assumption of distribution. I am only showing that the assumption is less restrictive than it may seem at first.

I think it quite likely that there are some personal goods that are inconsistent with the assumption of distribution. They will have to be excluded from much of the argument in this book. But not all of it. Some of the book, starting in chapter 8, will be concerned with aggregating together the wellbeing of different people. It will turn out that aggregating wellbeing across people can be treated separately from aggregating wellbeing across time. And in aggregating across people, we can take into account all of each person's goods, even if they do not satisfy the assumption of distribution. I shall suspend this assumption from section 8.4 to chapter 14.

Notes

1 In section 1.3 of *Weighing Goods*, I defined good in terms of ought, in a way that committed me to what T. M. Scanlon calls a 'buck-passing' account of goodness (*What We Owe to Each Other*, p. 97). This gives goodness no explanatory role. However, I am now more hesitant about this type of account, because I am not sure it is consistent with every type of nonteleological theory. I prefer to leave open the possibility that goodness might play an explanatory role.

2 For more on transitive structure, see my *Weighing Goods*, section 1.3.

3 See Robert Nozick, 'Moral complications and moral structures', pp. 2–4 and Peter Vallentyne, 'Gimmicky representations of moral theories'.

4 Graham Oddie and Peter Milne make this claim in 'Expectation and the representation of moral theories'. There is a response in Erik Carlson's *Consequentialism Reconsidered*, chapter 3. In 'Gimmicky representations of moral theories', p. 255, Peter Vallentyne gives an example of a theory that he believes is not teleologizable. A discussion and some examples appear in my 'Deontology and economics', section 4.

5 Nozick, 'Moral complications and moral structures', pp. 2–4.

6 *A Theory of Justice*, p. 24.

7 My 'Fairness' presents this theory much more fully.

8 See the textbook *Lectures on Public Economics* by Anthony Atkinson and Joseph Stiglitz. So far as I know, it was not used in health economics till it was recommended by Adam Wagstaff in his 'QALYs and the equity–efficiency trade-off'. An interesting application is Alan Williams's in his 'Intergenerational equity'. The slogan 'giving priority to the worse off' comes from Derek Parfit's 'Equality or priority?', a major philosophical discussion of prioritarianism.

9 For my general reasons, see my *Weighing Goods*, chapter 9, and my 'Equality versus priority'. For their application to health, see my 'Measuring the burden of disease', sections 9 and 10.

10 *Morality, Mortality*, volume I, chapter 5.

11 I support the common view myself, and defend it against Kamm in my 'Kamm on fairness'.

12 Chapter 6.

13 See particularly *Morality, Mortality*, volume II, chapter 12.

14 Jeff McMahan, *The Ethics of Killing*, is a major new work on this subject.

15 *Principia Ethica*, particularly pp. 149–50. I am slightly misrepresenting Moore. Moore claims that one ought to do the act that, out of those available, will lead to the best history. He does not say this is the best act;

he does not speak of the goodness or badness of acts. I am implicitly imputing to him the assumption of teleology. In 'Imposing risks', Judith Thomson takes the same view as Moore.

16 Scheffler, *The Rejection of Consequentialism*, note on pp. 1–2. Scheffler's definition of consequentialism differs from mine in that he requires consequentialism to be agent neutral. See the 'Introduction' to his *Consequentialism and Its Critics*, p. 1.

17 For example, in the papers collected in *Consequentialism and Its Critics*, edited by Samuel Scheffler.

18 See *Weighing Goods*, pp. 3–6.

19 See David Velleman, 'Well-being and time'.

20 There are limits on what I can do in this respect. In section 3.1 I have already excluded fairness from wellbeing, for pragmatic reasons.

21 *Nicomachean Ethics*, book 1, chapter 10.

4

Features of Goodness

A few general issues about the nature of goodness need to be settled before we can get on with the more concrete work of this book. Section 4.1 responds to some arguments that purport to show the betterness relation may be intransitive. Section 4.2 makes the fundamental distinction between personal good – what is good for a person – and general good. Section 4.3 considers the idea that goodness might always be relative to a point of view.

4.1 The transitivity of betterness

On page 21, I assumed that the relation 'better than' is transitive. I use this assumption constantly throughout this book, regularly, unhesitatingly, and often invisibly. It is essential to my method. Fortunately, my method is soundly based in this respect: the betterness relation truly is transitive. But its transitivity has been challenged, so I need to discuss it.

Take any monadic predicate such as 'dangerous' or 'sunny in the morning'. For generality, designate it with the schematic letter 'F'. We can often form from F a dyadic predicate, or relation, designated by 'more F than'. For example, we form 'more dangerous than' and 'more sunny in the morning than'. Call this the 'comparative relation' of F. In English, when 'F' is a short adjective, 'more F than' generally has the synonym 'Fer than'. Irregularly, 'more good than' has the synonym 'better than'.

A comparative relation is necessarily transitive. This is an analytic feature of the operator 'more … than': the meaning of 'more … than' implies that 'more F than' is transitive. The more formal features of the meaning of a term are often called the 'logic' of the term. Deontic logic is the logic of 'ought', for example. In this sense, transitivity is a feature of the logic of 'more … than'.

Some authors write as though the transitivity of betterness is an issue in ethics.[1] It is not; it is an issue in semantics. But then, if it is only semantics, how can it matter for ethics? The answer is that we can only understand each other using the meanings we have. True, you could decide to use 'better than' with a nonstandard meaning that does not require it to be transitive. But then your 'better than' would not mean better than, and it would not be the comparative of any predicate 'good'. You would say some things are better than others when actually they are not. Consequently, it would be hard for us to understand your ethical conclusions.

That comparative relations are transitive is self-evident. It is an axiom that lies at the foundation of our arguments. It does not itself need to be supported by argument, and not much argument is available to support it directly. I could point out that '*A* is more *F* than *B*' means that the degree to which *A* has the property *F* is greater than the degree to which *B* has this property, and the relation 'greater than' is transitive. This is true, but it does not really support the transitivity of 'more *F* than'. The notion of 'more ... than' – that is to say, the notion of comparison with respect to a property – is prior to the notion of the degree to which something possesses a property. We are only able to attribute degrees to a property because, when we make comparisons in terms of the property, these comparisons are transitive. Moreover, the transitivity of 'greater than', which I assumed, is itself an application of the principle that 'more ... than' is transitive.

Still, I can give indirect support to the claim that comparatives are transitive, by responding to apparent counterexamples. Many situations can induce us to make comparative judgements that turn out intransitive. Indeed, our judgements are often not merely intransitive but cyclical: we judge that *A* is more *F* than *B*, *B* more *F* than *C*, *C* more *F* than *D*, and so on down to, say, *Y*, which we judge more *F* than *Z*, and we also judge that *Z* is more *F* than *A*. The existence of a cycle like this is inconsistent with transitivity. I shall describe some situations that can induce cyclical judgements, and show they are illusions. I shall show how the situation draws us into making erroneous judgements. I hope this will help persuade you that cyclical judgements are indeed erroneous.

However, if an illusion is good, it is hard to reject the judgements it induces us to make. There are trios of musical sounds such that one seems higher than the second, which seems higher than the third, which in turn seems higher than the first. In some peculiar perspective drawings, one figure seems taller than a second, which seems taller than a third, which in turn seems taller than the first. In both these cases, we are tempted to make intransitive comparative judgements. But we know these judgements cannot all be correct. So we know we have to think again. It may be hard to know what judgements to make, but it is not hard to know we should not make intransitive ones.

Football teams

You might think that, if one football team can regularly beat a second, it must be the better team. You might even think this is what it means for one team to be better than another. Yet, it might happen that one team can regularly beat a second, which can regularly beat a third, which in turn can regularly beat the first. This could lead you to think the first is better than the second, the second better than the third, and the third better than the first.[2]

This illusion is comparatively easy to dispel. Evidently the goodness of a football team is a complex matter involving the ability to do well against a variety of opponents. One team may be able to beat another regularly, not because it is a better team, but because its particular strengths happen to exploit the other's particular weaknesses. The very fact that the relation 'can regularly beat' may be intransitive amongst football teams should make you realize it is not equivalent to 'is better than'.

I imagine that, among sprinters, 'can regularly beat' is a transitive relation. Sprinting is less strategic, and it may well be that, if one sprinter can regularly beat another, she must be the better sprinter. Football is more complex.

Times of day

The next example is one of the most effective I know.[3] It is about the lateness of trains. Unfortunately, 'late' is doubly ambiguous, so I need to start by explaining how I shall use it. 'Late' in one sense means behind schedule; if the train due at 14.35 arrives at 14.43, it is late in this sense. I shall not use that sense at all.

In another sense, the train that leaves at 15.25 on 15 July 2005 is later than the one that leaves at 13.20 on 15 July 2005. 'Late' here refers to historical time; in the same sense, the Battle of Waterloo was later than the Battle of Trafalgar. When I use 'late' in this sense, I shall make the sense explicit.

There is another sense of 'late', and this one will turn out to have an apparently cyclical comparative. It is the sense that appears in 'a late breakfast'. It is contextual: a late breakfast happens earlier than a late lunch, for instance. In the context of trains, this contextual sense of 'late' is roughly equivalent to 'late in the day'. The 23.35 is a late train and the 08.23 is not.

'Train' is also ambiguous. There are token trains, such as the 15.25 on 15 July 2005, and also type trains such as the 15.25, which runs every day. My example concerns type trains, not token ones.

When we speak of type trains and contextual time, it is surely true that the 18.30 train is later than the 17.30. Likewise, the 19.30 is later than the 18.30, and the 20.30 later than the 19.30, and so on all round the clock. So there seems to be a cycle in 'later than'.

However, despite first appearances, actually there is no cycle. This can be demonstrated on the basis of the principle that, if A is F and B is more F than A, then B is F. This principle is another feature of the logic of 'more ... than', besides transitivity. It is even more indubitable than transitivity; I have never seen it challenged, and I shall take it for granted.

The 23.30 train is certainly late. Suppose the 00.30 is later than the 23.30, and the 01.30 later than the 00.30pm, and the 02.30 later than the 01.30, and so on. Then the principle I have just stated, applied repeatedly, implies first that the 00.30 is late, and consequently that the 01.30 is late, and then that the 02.30 is late, and so on. It will follow that the 07.30 is late. But the 07.30 is not late; it is early. Therefore, at least one of the suppositions is false. Either the 00.30 is not later than the 23.30, or the 01.30 is not later than the 00.30, or ..., or the 07.30 is not later than the 06.30. There must be at least one break in the cycle.

This may be hard to believe, because of two confusing factors. One is the ambiguity of 'late'. The token train that leaves at 05.30 on any particular day is certainly later in historical time than the 04.30 that leaves on that day. This makes it tempting to assume that the type 05.30 must be later in contextual time than the type 04.30, but that does not follow.

The second confusing factor is that the boundary between late trains and early ones, in contextual time, is vague. If there was a clear break so that, say, the 04.30 was definitely late and the 05.30 definitely early, it would be clear that the 05.30 could not be later, in contextual time, than the 04.30. As it is, the break in the cycle of 'later than' is concealed by the vagueness. From a theoretical point of view, we might treat the vagueness in various ways. But however we do it, there has to be a break in the cycle. Transitivity of 'later than' is not threatened.

Nevertheless, the example might still indicate a difficulty. My argument in defence of transitivity in the example depends on there being some trains in the 24-hour cycle that are late and others that are not late. In the context of trains, where 'late' roughly means late in the day, this is true. The cycle is not completely symmetrical in this respect. But the argument would not apply if we could find an example of an apparently symmetrical cycle of 'more *F* than', where no member of the cycle is *F* or no member is not *F*.

I have not been able to find one, and I think there is a good reason why not. Take a cycle of a different sort. When people are sitting in a circle, the relation 'to the left of' amongst these people is cyclical. 'To the left of' is not a comparative – it is not the comparative of a monadic predicate – and we have no comparative in English that is equivalent. We do not have 'lefter than', say. My diagnosis of why not is that, since no one in the circle is left and no one is not left, there is no temptation to think anyone is lefter than anyone else. If we did think that, we would have an intransitive comparative, which the logic of comparatives prohibits. In the cycle of generic trains, there are indeed some that are late in contextual time and some that are not. This makes us recognize some as later than others. Just as it does that, it also prevents the comparative 'later than' from being intransitive.

Attractiveness

Here is a second effective example.[4] Think about the glass balls that hang on Christmas trees. Suppose they are sold in sets of three, each containing a red ball, a blue ball and a green ball. It is plausible that the attractiveness of a set depends only on the attractiveness of its three members, and that the attractiveness of an individual ball depends only on its appearance.

Compare three sets, *A*, *B*, and *C*. Suppose the red ball in *A* looks the same as the red ball in *B*. That is to say, these balls have the same appearance. Suppose also that the blue ball in *A* has the same appearance as the blue ball in *B*. But suppose the green ball in *A* does not have the same appearance as the green ball in *B*; suppose it is distinctly more attractive. Then the set *A* is more attractive than the set *B*.

Next suppose the red ball in *B* has the same appearance as the red ball in *C*, and the green ball in *B* has the same appearance as the green ball in *C*, but the blue ball in *B* is distinctly more attractive than the blue ball in *C*. Then the set *B* is more attractive than the set *C*.

Finally suppose the blue ball in *C* has the same appearance as the blue ball in *A*, and the green ball in *C* has the same appearance as the green ball in *A*, but the red ball in *C* is distinctly more attractive than the red ball in *A*. Then the set *C* is more attractive than the set *A*. We seem to have a cycle in the comparative 'more attractive than'.

In order to construct this example, I assumed that the red ball in *A* has the same appearance as the red ball in *B*, which in turn has the same appearance as the red ball in *C*, yet the red ball in *C* is distinctly more attractive than the red ball in *A*. It seems obvious this could happen. Suppose the red ball in *C* is more attractive than the red ball in *A* because it appears slightly brighter. Suppose the red ball in *B* has a physical reflectiveness that is somewhere between the reflectiveness of *A* and the reflectiveness of *C*. The physical difference in reflectiveness between the red ball in *A* and the red ball in *B* might be so slight that the two balls look the same; they have the same appearance. For the same reason, the red ball in *B* might have the same appearance as the red ball in *C*. But there is a bigger physical difference between the red balls in *A* and in *C*. It may be enough to give them a different appearance.

It seems obvious this could happen, but actually what I have just said directly implies a contradiction. I said the red ball in *A* has the same appearance as the red ball in *B*, and the red ball in *B* has the same appearance as the red ball in *C*. It follows by the transitivity of identity that the red ball in *A* has the same appearance as the red ball in *C*. But I said it has a different appearance.

This is a paradox: something that it seems could obviously happen implies a contradiction. It is a well-known paradox. It is the basis of the phenomenal version of the sorites paradox, and it is particularly intractable. I do not feel responsible for solving it.[5] Whatever the solution turns out to be, it will also resolve the apparent intransitivity in 'more attractive than'. The example is founded on a contradiction, so it cannot be a correct demonstration that 'more attractive than' is intransitive.

Large numbers

I now come to examples that are specifically about betterness. I shall start with one of a sort described by Larry Temkin in 'A continuum argument for intransitivity' and Stuart Rachels in 'Counterexamples to the transitivity of *better than*'. Owing to a technical hitch, the conclusions these authors draw do not actually follow from their assumptions. To make the argument strictly valid, I shall have to present it in a different way from theirs.[6]

Suppose there is a finite sequence of illnesses – I shall label them

I_1, I_2, ... I_k – that has the following properties. (a) Curing a single person of I_1 is better than curing any number of people, however large, of I_k. (b) There is a sequence of numbers, 1, n_2, n_3, ... n_k, starting with 1, with the property that curing n_i people of I_i is better than curing n_{i-1} people of I_{i-1}, for any value of i from 2 to k.

If such a sequence of illnesses exists, then 'better than' is not transitive. There is a cycle in 'better than', as follows. Because of property (b), curing n_2 people of I_2 is better than curing a single person of I_1. Also, curing n_3 people of I_3 is better than curing n_2 people of I_2. And so on, till we get to: curing n_k people of I_k is better than curing n_{k-1} people of I_{k-1}. Yet property (a) implies that curing a single person of I_1 is better than curing n_k people of I_k.

Why should we suppose such a sequence exists? Temkin asks us to start by making I_1 a very severe illness, such as AIDS, and I_k a very mild one, such a mild headache for a short time. This is meant to give us property (a) since Temkin finds curing a single person of AIDS intuitively so important that it is better than curing any number of short, mild headaches. Then we set up a sequence of illnesses ranging in severity between AIDS and a short, mild headache, each one just a little bit less severe than the previous one in the sequence. Provided we make the gaps in severity small enough, we can ensure that saving some number of people from any illness in the sequence is better than saving, say, one-tenth the number from the previous illness in the sequence. So saving ten people from the second illness in the sequence is better than saving one person from AIDS. Saving a hundred people from the third illness is better than saving ten from the second, and so on. Now we have property (b). All this is supposed to be on grounds of intuition.

I am not myself at all inclined to make cyclical judgements about this example. I do indeed believe there is a sequence of illnesses linking AIDS and a short, mild headache that satisfy property (b). I believe this, not on intuitive grounds, but because it follows from arguments made later in this book. Consequently, because betterness is transitive, I believe there is some number (which is very large) such that curing that number of people of a short, mild headache is better than curing one person of AIDS. I have no inclination to believe the opposite.

However, Temkin and Rachels do believe the opposite. Rachels tells us that the opposite view 'is supported by the strong preference of competent judges'.[7] Temkin lists a number of famous philosophers who think like him.[8] The view of these competent judges and famous philosophers deserves a response.

Their view is founded on their intuitions. But we are dealing with very large numbers of people, and we have no reason to trust anyone's intuitions about very large numbers, however excellent their philosophy. Even the best philosophers cannot get an intuitive grasp of, say, tens of billions of people. That is no criticism; these numbers are beyond intuition. But these philosophers ought not to think their intuition can tell them the truth about such large numbers of people.

For very large numbers, we have to rely on theory, not intuition. When people first built bridges, they managed without much theory. They could judge a log by eye, relying on their intuition. Their intuitions were reliable, being built on long experience with handling wood and stone. But when people started spanning broad rivers with steel and concrete, their intuition failed them, and they had to resort to engineering theory and careful calculations. The cables that support suspension bridges are unintuitively slender.

Our moral intuitions are formed and polished in our homely interactions with the few people we have to deal with in ordinary life. But nowadays the scale of our societies and the power of our technologies raise moral problems that involve huge numbers of people. This book considers problems on this huge scale, as well as small-scale problems. We cannot expect our intuitions to cope successfully with such big problems. No doubt our homely intuitive morality gives us a starting point, but we have to project our morality beyond the homely to the vast new arenas. To do this properly, we have to engage all the care and accuracy we can, and develop a moral theory.

Indeed, we are more dependent on theory than engineers are, because moral conclusions cannot be tested in the way engineers' conclusions are tested. If an engineer gets her calculations wrong, her mistake will be revealed when the bridge falls down. But a mistake in moral theory is never revealed like that. If we do something wrong, we do not later see the error made manifest; we can only know it is an error by means of theory too. Moreover, our mistakes can be far more damaging and kill far more people than the collapse of a bridge. Mistakes in allocating healthcare resources may do great harm to millions. So we have to be exceptionally careful in developing our moral theory.

How can we possibly project moral theory beyond the scope of our intuitions? What means do we have for that? We have the ordinary materials of reason: logic and the other instruments of argument. One thing we must not do is rely on our intuitions outside the domain where we have grounds for thinking they are reliable. No bridge-builder has the right to rely on intuition. Similarly, no moral philosopher has the right to rely on intuitions in areas where we have no grounds for thinking they are reliable.

We have no grounds for thinking our intuitions about very large numbers are reliable. On the contrary, we have good grounds for mistrusting them. The evidence is that they are often wrong, because our imagination is not able to grasp just how big numbers can be. For example, many people's intuition tells them that the process of natural selection, however many billions of years it continued for, could not lead from primordial slime to creatures with intelligence and consciousness. But they are wrong. Four billion years will do it.

In this book, I put no weight on intuitions about large numbers. One of these intuitions has played a major part in the discussion of population ethics: the intuition that 'the repugnant conclusion' is repugnant.[9] I shall discuss this intuition in section 14.4, but I put no weight on it or other intuitions of the sort. Instead I build theory with the tools of logic and mathematics, including the principle that comparatives are transitive.

I do not deny that ethics must ultimately be founded on some sort of intuition. Moreover, many of my assumptions are supposed to apply to any number of people, however large. For example, I shall assume something I call 'the principle of personal good'.[10] This says, in part, that if we take two distributions that have the same population, and if one of them is better than the other for someone, and at least as good as the other for everyone, then it is better. I assume this for any size of population. Implicitly, then, my assumption is governed by the universal quantifier 'for any number of people'. I claim a right to this sort of principle. So how can I deny famous philosophers their right to principles with a universal quantifier such as: for any number of people, curing a single person of AIDS is better than curing that number of people of a short, mild headache?

I shall not try to formulate a general principle that distinguishes universally quantified intuitions we can rely on from those we cannot rely on. Instead, I shall identify a particular feature that makes some of these intuitions unreliable. The intuition about AIDS mentions a fixed event A and a variable event $B(n)$ that depends on the number of people. The fixed event is curing one person of AIDS; the variable event is curing n people of a short, mild headache. The intuition has the form: for all numbers n, A is better than $B(n)$. An intuition of this form is exposed to doubt because the goodness of $B(n)$ may increase with increasing n. It does so in this case. The intuition is that, although $B(n)$ gets better and better with increasing n, it never gets better than A, however large n may be. This sort of intuition particularly depends on our intuitive grasp of large numbers. So it is unreliable. The principle of personal good does not have this form.

Population

Now I come to the arguments against the transitivity of betterness that are the most troubling in the context of this book. They come from Larry Temkin's 'Intransitivity and the mere addition paradox'. They involve changes in population, so they are especially relevant to weighing lives. I particularly need to respond to them.

Temkin argues that, when we compare the goodness of two alternatives, particular criteria are relevant to the comparison, and different criteria may be relevant to different comparisons. Whether or not A is better than B depends on how A and B measure up against the criteria that are relevant to the comparison between the pair A and B. When we compare the pair B and C, different criteria may be relevant. Whether or not B is better than C depends on how B and C measure up against those criteria. Whether or not C is better than A may depend on yet different criteria again. The result may turn out to be that A is better than B, B better than C, and C better than A. Because different criteria are relevant to each comparison, nothing prevents this from happening. If it does happen, the betterness relation is cyclical.

Here is an example that is parallel to one of Temkin's.[11] Think of a couple who already have one child and are wondering whether to have a second. If they do not, their existing child will have an overall lifetime wellbeing of five units. Call this option distribution A. If the parents do have a second child, they will have a choice between two different ways to look after their family. They can distribute their attention equally, in which case both children's wellbeing will be four units. Call this option B. Alternatively, they can distribute their attention unequally, in which case the first child's wellbeing will be six units, and the second's one unit. Call this C. (I shall discuss the measurement of wellbeing in chapter 5; for the time being take these numbers for granted.)

When the parents compare alternatives A and B, they might think that the second child is neither better nor worse off in A than in B, because she does not even exist in A. Because of this, the parents might think A and B should be compared on the basis of how good they are for the first child only: that is the relevant criterion for this comparison. It leads to the conclusion that A (where the first child gets five) is better than B (where she gets four). The same criterion is the relevant one for the comparison between *C* and *A*, and it leads to the conclusion that *C* (where the first child gets six) is better than *A* (where she gets five). However, when the parents compare *B* and *C*, they will find that the second child is better off in *B*, and the first child is better off in *C*. They might conclude that the right criterion this time is a balance of interests between the children. Since *B* has more wellbeing in total than *C* (eight units compared with seven) and has it equally divided between the children, they may well conclude that *B* is better than *C*.

The parents' judgements are cyclical, and they seem to be backed by persuasive reasoning. Since this is not Temkin's own example, I do not know what his views would be about it, but he might well agree with the parents' judgement. He might think this is a genuine case where betterness is intransitive. The intransitivity seems to occur in just the way Temkin describes: different criteria figure in different comparisons.

This seems to be a case of intransitive betterness. How can I resist the parents' arguments? Surely the example shows Temkin is right to say that different criteria can be relevant to different comparisons, and that intransitivity can result. How can I deny it?

It is important to understand that we are considering the goodness of various options, and how their goodnesses are compared. We are not considering choices between options, and which one ought to choose. Cycles may occur in what one ought to choose; it may be that, given a choice between *A* and *B* one ought to choose *A*, and given a choice between *B* and *C* one ought to choose *B*, and given a choice between *C* and *A* one ought to choose *C*. Even if we insist on a teleological ethics, so one ought to choose what is best, this need not conflict with transitivity of betterness. It is often plausible that the goodness of an option depends on what the alternatives are. If so, we have to treat *A* chosen when *B* is the alternative as a different option from *A* chosen when *C* is the alternative, and recognize that these options may have different values. Then transitivity of betterness is easily maintained.

But Temkin's cases are not like that. His point is not that the available alternatives can make a difference to the value of what one chooses. It is that different comparisons raise different criteria. In the example, the question is not what the parents should do when faced with various choices. It is what their judgements of betterness should be when they make pairwise comparisons between the options. We should not suppose the actual choice they are faced with varies at all. For instance, we might assume throughout that they have a choice between all three of *A*, *B* and *C*. So I cannot resolve the apparent intransitivity by recognizing that the value of an option may vary with the available alternatives.

Temkin mentions one theory that would guarantee transitivity. He calls it 'the intrinsic aspect view'.[12] It says that the goodness of an option is an intrinsic property of that option. If it is, we can derive as follows the conclusion that the betterness relation is transitive. If *A* is better than *B* and *B* better than *C*, then according to the intrinsic aspect view *A* must be intrinsically good to a degree greater than *B* is, and *B* intrinsically good to a degree greater than *C* is. Consequently *A* must be intrinsically good to a degree greater than *C* is. So *A* must be better than *C*.

This derivation of the transitivity of betterness does not actually depend on the intrinsic aspect view. It does not require the premise that goodness is an intrinsic property. If *A* is better than *B* and *B* better than *C*, then *A* is good to a degree greater than *B* is, and *B* is good to a degree greater than *C* is, and this is so whether or not goodness is intrinsic. Consequently *A* is good to a degree greater than *C* is. So *A* must be better than *C*. I mentioned a general version of this argument on page 51, and said it adds nothing to the already self-evident fact that any comparative is transitive. For one thing, it assumes that 'greater than' is transitive. The basis of the argument is simply that 'better than' is the comparative of the monadic predicate 'good'. There is no need for goodness to be an intrinsic property. The comparative of *any* predicate is necessarily transitive. Take a transparently nonintrinsic predicate: 'distant from Edinburgh'. Its comparative 'more distant from Edinburgh than' is necessarily transitive.

The relation 'judged by me to be at least as good as' may be intransitive, since it is not the comparative of any predicate. When I make judgements of betterness, different criteria may come to my mind as I make different comparisons. The result may be intransitive judgements. The example of the parents' choice shows how this can happen. But, because 'better than' is the comparative of the predicate 'good', betterness must be transitive. Therefore, my judgements of betterness cannot possibly be *correct* unless they are transitive.

This is how I can guarantee the transitivity of the betterness relation, despite the attraction of the example. So long as my judgements are intransitive, I know I still have work to do in sorting them out. The parents in the example still have work to do.

The work may not be easy. When I work on intransitive judgements, the result may be that I come to change one of them. Or the judgements may refuse to change; it may seem to me that I have made the very best possible judgements, accurately taking into account all the right criteria, and yet these judgements may still be intransitive. If so, they cannot be judgements of betterness, whatever I may have intended. If Temkin is right that different criteria may be relevant to different comparisons, I cannot guarantee in advance that my judgements will turn out transitive. In that case, I cannot guarantee in advance that my criteria are criteria for betterness, whatever I may have thought.

Perhaps Temkin thinks betterness is not the comparative of a genuine predicate. Some of his remarks suggest this. He says goodness is 'essentially comparative'. I am not sure what he means, but here is one possibility. As a matter of grammar, the sentence '*A* is better than *B*' attributes the comparative relation 'better than' to the pair consisting of *A* and *B*. Temkin may think this piece of grammar is misleading. He may think there is no property of goodness, and so no genuine predicate 'good' for 'better than' to be the comparative of. There would then be no genuine dyadic predicate 'better than'. The sentence '*A* is better than *B*' may be parsed differently. It attributes the monadic predicate 'better than *B*' to *A*. Temkin may think that only this parsing captures the true situation. There is no single dyadic predicate 'better than', but only a plethora of monadic predicates of the form 'better than __'. On this view, '*A* is better than *B*' should be read as '*A* is better-than-*B*'. Then nothing rules out the possibility that *A* is better-than-*B*, *B* better-than-*C* and *C* better-than-*A*.

If Temkin really means to sacrifice grammar in this way, he is setting himself a difficult task in his ethical theory. Our grammar gives structure to all our talk about goodness. Without it, we shall have to reconstruct a theory of value out of nothing. For example, what rules out the possibility that *A* is better-than-*A*? If *A* is better-than-*B*, what rules out *B*'s being better-than-*A*? Without a transitive relation 'better than', we shall have no basis for a quantitative notion of goodness. Yet we regularly think of goodness in quantitative terms.

To express what he believes, I think Temkin would do better to give up the vocabulary of goodness. He might reasonably think the idea of goodness does not fit the true nature of the ethical problems we face. If the problems have an intransitive structure, they cannot be seen in terms of goodness. If Temkin took that view, I would have no complaint.[13]

There are alternatives he might find preferable. For example, perhaps he should understand the parents' views in the example as deontic rather than axiological. Perhaps the parents' thoughts are inaccurate. Instead of thinking *A* is better than *B*, perhaps they should simply think they ought to choose *A* if they have a choice between *A* and *B*. As I said on page 60, there may be a cycle in what they ought to choose. Understood this way, the example raises no questions about the transitivity of goodness.

4.2 General, personal, and temporal goodness

This book is concerned with goodness, or more accurately betterness, of various different types. This section settles a few points that are principally matters of terminology.

I set out the betterness relation in (2.1.1) on page 20. For clarity, I shall sometimes call it the *general* betterness relation. For each person p, there is also her individual or *personal* betterness relation:

(4.2.1)   ... is better for p than __.

Like the general betterness relation, a personal betterness relation may hold between things of various sorts. I am particularly concerned with betterness between ways the world might go, which on page 30 I called different 'histories'. Between histories I take (4.2.1) to be the same relation as

(4.2.2) p is better off in ... than in __.

'Better for'

However, Wlodek Rabinowicz has pointed out to me that these two formulations may not be analytically equivalent. Remember there are histories in which p does not exist. It is analytic that (4.2.2) can hold only between pairs of histories in which p exists. But it may be analytically possible for (4.2.1) to hold between two histories even if p does not exist in both of them.

Indeed, some theories of betterness imply this is so. According to one theory – call it 'preferencism' – one history is better for a person than another if and only if the person prefers the former to the latter. A person may prefer one history to another even if she does not exist in both of them. An actually existing person may have preferences among a range of histories, including many that are not the actual history. It may be that in some of these non-actual histories she does not exist. So according to preferencism, a history in which a person does not exist may be better or worse for her than some other history.

On the face of it, preferencism makes sense. The preposition 'for' in 'better for' and 'good for' allows us to treat goodness for a person as a relation that the person has to a history, rather than as a property she has in a history. So it is not ruled out by the meaning of 'good for' that a history is good for a person to some degree even if the person does not exist in that history. At least it is not obviously meaningless to use 'good for', and correspondingly 'better for', in this way.

On the other hand, (4.2.2) says that the degree to which p is well off in A is greater than the degree to which she is well off in B. The degree to which a person is well off in a history is explicitly a property of the person in the history. Consequently, (4.2.2) applies only between histories in a which a person exists. There seems, therefore, to be a difference in meaning between (4.2.1) and (4.2.2).

However, if there is indeed a difference in meaning, I am going to ignore it. By (4.2.1) I mean the same as (4.2.2); I choose to use 'better for' in this way. As I mean 'better for', a history in which a person does not exist is neither better nor worse for her than any other history. This suits my purposes. The role of personal betterness relations in this book is to define people's wellbeing; chapter 5 describes how. A person's wellbeing is the good *of* the person, or the degree to which she is well off, so (4.2.2) expresses accurately the betterness relation I require in this book. But I find the locutions 'good for' and 'better for' rhetorically unavoidable, so I shall very often use the formulation (4.2.1).

Do I lose anything by this piece of legislation? Suppose it turned out that a particular history in which a person exists was better for her than one in which she does not exist. What difference would that make? It might contribute to determining the relative value of these histories. If, say, the histories were the same in other respects, it might determine that the history in which the person exists is better than the one in which she does not exist. It might determine that, other things being equal, this person's existence is a good thing.

But, when I come to the question of whether a person's existence is a good thing, I prefer to approach it directly, and not through an analysis of 'better for'. It is the subject of a large part of this book. In answering the question, I think an analysis of 'better for' will be unproductive. We use this locution primarily to describe the comparative good of a person when the person's existence is not in question. We can use it to express our ethical beliefs about those cases. Suppose now it turns out that the grammar of the preposition 'for' allows us to extend the locution to other cases too, where existence is in question. That is no reason to think the same ethical beliefs can be extended unaltered to these other cases. We must reassess each belief *de novo*. So the extended use of 'better for' adds nothing.

Personal and general value

Granted the assumptions set out in chapter 2, the general betterness relation can be represented by a general value function. Similarly, a personal betterness relation can be represented by a personal value function, granted corresponding assumptions. The representation is ordinal, as I defined ordinal representation on page 27. However, in section 5.2 I shall find a personal value function that can actually be taken to represent degrees of goodness, and not merely the order of goodness. The values of this function are quantities of personal value. They are what I define as the person's wellbeing.

Furthermore, in section 5.3 I shall find a way to make these quantities comparable between people. For example, we shall be able to make sense of the claim that one person has more wellbeing than another, or equivalently that she is better off than the other person.

As I mean 'better for', a history in which a person does not exist is neither better nor worse for her than any other history. This means it does not belong to the field of the person's betterness relation.[14] Consequently, the person's value function will not assign any value to a history in which the person does not exist. These histories have no personal value for the person; she has no wellbeing in a history where she does not exist. The position is not that the history has zero personal value for the person, or that she has zero wellbeing. The position is that the concept of the person's personal value or wellbeing does not apply to this history.

Take two histories where a particular person exists in one but not in the other. The difference in general value between these distributions may well be affected by the person's existence or nonexistence. So her existence or nonexistence may well have a general value. It contributes to the general value of the distribution. But it has no personal value for the person. So here we have a general value without a corresponding personal value.

On the other hand, many things have both personal and general value. But even then the two values do not necessarily coincide. For example, some people believe in 'giving priority to the worse off'.[15] They believe it is better for benefits to go to worse-off people rather than to better-off ones. Suppose I am worse off than you, and suppose some nice present could be given to one or the other of us. Suppose my getting the present would benefit me equally as much as your getting it would benefit you. That is to say, my getting it and your getting it have the same personal value; they would add equally to our respective wellbeings. Because the personal value is the same, according to the priority theory, it is better for me to get the present rather than you, since I am worse off. That is to say, my getting the present is generally better than your getting it. So the general value of my getting the present is greater than the general value of your getting it. Yet the personal values of these two events are the same. The priority view implies that general value and personal value differ, therefore. In general, the amount of a person's wellbeing is not necessarily the same as the amount her wellbeing contributes to the general value of a distribution.

Temporal betterness and temporal value

As well as general and personal betterness, I shall also need to call on *temporal* betterness relations such as:

$$\dots \text{ is better for } p \text{ at } t \text{ than } \_\_,$$

where t is a time. When the blanks in this relation are occupied by histories, I make the same presumption as I did with (4.2.1). I take it to be the same relation as:

$$p \text{ is better off at } t \text{ in } \dots \text{ than in } \_\_.$$

Temporal betterness is an ordering and, like other orderings, it can be represented by a value function. In section 6.1 I shall find a function that represents degrees of temporal goodness. I define the person's wellbeing at the time t as the value of this function. This gives us a notion of temporal wellbeing for a person. When I need to emphasize the contrast between a person's temporal wellbeing and her wellbeing as a whole, I use the term 'lifetime wellbeing' for the latter.

Temporal betterness relations are limited, like personal betterness relations, by my legislation about 'better for'. A person's temporal relation for a particular time holds only between histories in which the person exists at that time. The field of this relation is more severely limited than even the field of the person's betterness relation. A person does not have wellbeing at a time when she does not exist.

A life worth living

Now, with some terminology in hand, I turn to the concept of a 'life worth living'. Many authors employ this concept, often without explaining it. But it needs explaining.

When we say a life is worth living, we are referring to the life's personal value and not its general value. A life worth living is worth living to the person whose life it is. That is to say, this person is better off living it than not. We might also be interested in whether a life is generally better lived than not, but this would be a different question. If we conclude some particular life is generally better not lived than lived, perhaps because it is the life of an evil person who does great harm to other people, we should not express our conclusion by saying the life is not worth living.

'A life worth living' is unambiguously concerned with personal value, but in another way it is ambiguous. The term 'a life' has two different senses. It may refer to the whole of a person's life or to the way a person's life is going at a particular time. 'Elizabeth's life is worth living' may mean that Elizabeth's life, taken as a whole, is worth living, or it may mean that her way of life as she is living now is worth living. It may be a comment on the overall value of Elizabeth's life – her lifetime wellbeing – or it may be a comment on the value of her life at a time – her temporal wellbeing. 'A life worth living' has a temporal and a lifetime sense.

Take the temporal sense first. Suppose Elizabeth's way of life, as she is living now, is worth living. Living it is better for Elizabeth than not living it. Dying now would be worse for her than continuing to live. This does not mean that, if she were to die now, she would then be worse off than she would be if she were to continue to live. That makes no sense. As I said, a person's temporal betterness relation holds only between histories in which the person is alive at the time concerned. Instead, it means that Elizabeth's life as a whole would be worse for her if she died than it would be if she continued to live.

So to determine whether a way of life is worth living at a time, we call on the overall value of the person's life. To make the judgement, we move up a level from the perspective of a single time to the perspective of the life as a whole. Chapter 16 considers the quality of a life worth living in this sense.

Now take the lifetime sense of 'a life worth living'. Suppose Elizabeth's life as a whole is worth living. It is better that she lives it rather than not. But what sort of betterness is this? Could it be Elizabeth's personal betterness? Could it be that Elizabeth is better off living rather than not? If so, had she not lived at all, she would have been worse off than she is. This makes no sense. As I said, a person's personal betterness relation applies only between histories in which the person lives.

We could make a move like the one we made in judging whether a life is worth living at a time. We could move up to a wider perspective. We could evaluate the life as a whole from the perspective of general good rather than personal good. But if we judged from this perspective that the life is better lived than not, that would not be to judge it is worth living. Whether it is worth living is a matter of personal, not general value.

Is there, then, any intelligible lifetime sense for 'a life worth living'? I see two possibilities. One is to revert to the idea I mentioned on page 63, that a history might be better or worse for a person than another even if she does not exist in both. Then we might say a person's life is worth living if her living it is better for her than her not living it. This would give us a lifetime sense for 'a life worth living'. However, my legislation for this book – the meaning for 'better for' I specified on page 64 – has ruled out this sense. Moreover, I argued on page 64 that it cannot be expected to be useful for ethical purposes. So I shall not use 'a life worth living' in this potential lifetime sense.

Here is the second possibility. We understand what it is for a life to be worth living at a time. Call a life 'neutral' at a time if it is just on the borderline between being worth living and not worth living at that time. Call a life 'constantly neutral' if it is neutral at every time.[16] We might say that a life as a whole is worth living if and only if it is better than a constantly neutral life.

This is indeed an intelligible lifetime sense of 'a life worth living'. But I shall not use it because I do not find it useful. Also it can be misleading because it can be confused with other possible senses. If a life is worth living in this sense, there are two things that does not mean. It does not mean that the life as a whole is personally better lived than not: that a person is better off living this life than not living it. It also does not mean that the life as a whole is generally better lived than not lived: that it is generally better that this life is lived than not. It is an open question what is the general value of a life that is worth living in this sense. That depends on the general value of a constantly neutral life, which I shall consider in chapter 18.

I therefore eschew the notion of a life worth living, in a lifetime sense.

4.3 Relativity

Some authors argue that betterness and good are relative concepts. They think there are several different *points of view*, and a betterness relation relative to each:

... is better than __ relative to the point of view __.

Different points of view may have different betterness relations, so that one thing may be better than another relative to one point of view, but worse relative to a different point of view. A point of view might be a time, for instance: the goodness of a history might depend on what time it is judged from. Or it might be a person – person-relative good has been much discussed[17] – or something else. The sort of relative good I shall be most concerned with in this book is relative to a population; section 11.3 is devoted to it. Section 17.3 considers another important sort of relativity.

All these relative sorts of good are meant to be *general* good as I defined it in section 4.2. Even person-relative good is not meant to be good for the person; it is general good as seen from the point of view of the person. I do not guarantee that the distinction between a person's own personal good and general good relative to the person can be properly maintained, but that is not my problem, since I shall not myself use the idea of relative good. To give it a fair run, let us suppose the distinction is sustainable.

In this book, I shall generally assume there is only one general betterness relation, and so only one correct answer to the question of whether one distribution is better than another. This is to adopt a nonrelativist position.[18] I am dubious about relativity, for reasons I shall explain later in this section. However, that does not mean relativists have to stop reading here. My aim is to develop a general account of the structure of betterness. It happens that this account can apply almost as well to relative betterness as to nonrelative betterness. If there are several relative betterness relations – one for each time, say – the account will apply to each. I hope it will be almost as useful to a relativist as to a nonrelativist.

It will not be quite as useful because I shall occasionally make assumptions of impartiality, which a relativist is unlikely to accept. For instance, impartiality about people means treating each person equally: giving each person the same weight in valuing a distribution of well-being, and so on. If you believe good is person-relative, you think good judged from the point of view of one person is different from good judged from the point of view of another person. But if each point of view gives each person equal weight, it is hard to see what difference there could be between the different points of view. So person-relativity seems inevitably to rule out impartiality between people. Similarly, time-relativity rules out impartiality between times, and so on.

If you are a time-relativist, you should therefore leave out the parts of this book that assume impartiality between times. A person-relativist

will have work to do after the assumption of impartiality between people
that is stated on page 135. By the time I reach that point in my argument, I shall have produced a value function that is a weighted total of
people's wellbeings (formula (9.1.1) on page 133). The impartiality
assumption turns it into an unweighted total (formula (9.1.2) on page
137). That is all it does. If you are a relativist about good, you will have
to carry the weights forward through the book. You will also have to
ignore the few conclusions that I draw from impartiality.

Relativity does play one important part in this book. It offers a
prospective solution to a major problem about population that is raised
in chapter 10. Section 11.3 examines this prospective solution.

The relation between nonrelativity and impartiality

Impartiality implies nonrelativity. Nonrelativity does not necessarily
imply impartiality. For example, the theory that the emperor's wellbeing
counts more than other people's, from everyone's point of view and not
just the emperor's, is partial but nonrelative. A more plausible example
of a nonrelative but partial view is a particular view about discounting
for time.

Some people think that wellbeing that comes later in time counts for
more than wellbeing that comes earlier. For instance, they think saving
a life is more valuable if it happens in the near future than if it happens
in the distant future. They think later wellbeing should be *discounted*
compared to earlier wellbeing.

Discounting is a sort of partiality about time, but it does not imply
time-relativity. If you believe in discounting, you may believe wellbeing
that comes earlier in history always counts for more than wellbeing that
comes later. Wellbeing in 2010 counts for more than wellbeing in 2020,
which in turn counts for more than wellbeing in 2030, and so on. You
could think this is true whatever time you look at it from. From the
perspective of 2005, wellbeing in 2020 counts for less than wellbeing in
2010, and it still counts for less from the perspective of 2015, or 2025,
or any other time. Future wellbeing is worth less than present wellbeing,
and present wellbeing is worth less than past wellbeing. This is consistent with temporal nonrelativity.

Nonrelative discounting is possible, therefore. However, it is hard to
believe. It requires later wellbeing to count for less than earlier wellbeing,
whatever date it is regarded from. Wellbeing in 2010 counts for a fraction
of wellbeing in 1910, say, and that is so from the perspective of 1920,
2010 or any other date. So major sacrifices would be worthwhile in 2010

if they could bring small benefits in 1910. This seems implausible.

It is hard to test its plausibility, because it is hard to see how sacrifices made in 2010 could possibly bring benefits in 1910. But we can invent a thought experiment. Some people think it is good for a person to be famous after her death. On page 47 I mentioned that, if this is so, we might treat it as a case of backwards causation of wellbeing. Whatever you think of this idea, imagine for a moment it is correct. Then it would be possible to benefit Thomas Hardy by propagating his fame in 2010. And if wellbeing in 1910 is worth so much more than wellbeing in 2010, it would be worth great sacrifices on our part in 2010 to propagate Hardy's fame. It would be much more valuable than propagating the fame of a contemporary author. This is hard to believe.

Think of this too. Nonrelative discounting for time means we should be much more upset to hear of some newly-discovered disaster that happened long ago, than to hear of a contemporary disaster. This is also hard to believe.

I think most people who favour discounting favour it both forwards and backwards in time. They think that wellbeing in 1910 counts much more than wellbeing in 2010 from the perspective of 1910. But wellbeing in 1910 counts much less than wellbeing in 2010 from the perspective of 2010. This view makes value time-relative. In practice, discounting and time-relativity generally go together.[19]

I do not favour discounting myself. But I recognize there are arguments for it as well as against it, and I do not want to use up space in this book debating it. So in principle I would like to allow for it. However, in practice it would complicate my arguments and formulae too much, so I shall content myself with occasional mentions, pointing out where discounting would make a difference. The principal mention is in section 8.3.

Discounting is the only sort of partiality I shall make any attempt to accommodate in my account of the structure of good. I do so only because temporal discounting can be nonrelative, even though not very plausibly. After the discussion below, I shall maintain the assumption that betterness is nonrelative throughout this book, with the exception of section 11.3.

First doubt about relativity

It is matter of debate whether betterness can really be relative. I am cautious about relativity for two main reasons.

The first is that there is a serious danger in accepting the idea of relative good too readily. An important way we make progress in ethics is by looking at problems from different points of view. We test how they look from one point of view against how they look from another. In doing this, we assume that the truth is the same however we look at it. If it looks different from different points of view, how it looks from one of them must be wrong. If we are too willing to accept that the truth viewed from one position may actually be different from the truth viewed from another, we lose the power of this type of reasoning.

Here is an example of the method. Derek Parfit considers the case of a fourteen-year-old mother.[20] This girl chooses to have a child at fourteen, but she could instead have waited to have a child later. If she had waited, that child's life would have been better than the life of the child she actually does have at fourteen. Doubtless, we can all agree it would have been better if the girl had waited. But, as Parfit says, 'We may shrink from claiming, of this girl's actual child, that it would have been better if he had never existed.'[21] Nevertheless, he says,

If we claimed earlier that it would be better if this girl waits, this is what we must claim. We cannot consistently make a claim and deny this same claim later. If (1) in 1990 it *would be* better if this girl waits and has a child later, then (2) in 2020 it *would have been* better if she had waited and had a child later. And (2) implies (3) that it would have been better if the child who existed had not been her actual child. If we cannot accept (3), we must reject (1). I suggest that, on reflection, we can accept (3). I believe that, if *I* was the actual child of this girl, I could accept (3). (3) does not imply that my existence is *bad*, or intrinsically morally undesirable. The claim is merely that, since a child born later would probably have had a better life than mine, it would have been better if my mother had waited, and had a child later.[22]

Here Parfit is testing the claim that it would be better if the girl waits and has a child later, by looking at it from the perspective of a later time, when her child actually exists. This is a tough test, which, as it happens, Parfit thinks it passes. But if he accepted that good might be relative, he would have to acknowledge that his statement (1) could be true and (2) false. It might be that, from the point of view of 1990 it would be better if the girl waits, whereas from the point of view of 2020 it would not have been better if she had waited. If good were relative in this way, Parfit's test would lose its effect. We shall lose an important method if we embrace relative good too readily. So we should be cautious about doing so.

Let me generalize a little. I think the formal structure imposed by axiology provides some useful discipline for organizing our ethical thinking. Goodness has a structure; for instance, the relation of betterness is transitive. A good way of clarifying our thinking is by working to bring it within this structure. For instance, if we think one thing *A* is better than another *B*, and *B* is better than *C*, but we do not think *A* is better than *C*, we have more thinking to do. Transitivity gives us a way of testing our opinions. Looking at our opinions from different points of view gives us another test. We should not too readily take the lazy way out by adopting relativity.

Now I have Parfit's example on the table, I can use it to introduce some more sorts of relativity, which will come up later in this section. Suppose, contrary to Parfit, we were to go relativist about the example. Two distinct types of relativity are available. Parfit considers two possible histories: one – call it *A* – in which the girl has her child at 14, and one – call it *B* – in which she delays and has a different baby later. Valuing these options from different perspectives gives us different sorts of relativity.

One relativist view is that, from the perspective of 1990, it would be better if the girl did not have her child, but from the perspective of 2020 it is better that she did have him. This would not be simple temporal relativity. What makes the difference between 1990 and 2020 is not the mere passage of time, but the existence of a particular person in 2020 who did not exist in 1990. Our relativist view is that, once we have the child among us, it is no longer the case that it would have been better if he had not been born. So the example raises the possibility of good relative to the population of people who exist at the time. I shall come back to this sort of relativity on page 75 and again in section 11.3. I call it 'temporal-population-relativity'. It takes good to be relative to the population of people who are alive at a particular time.

Alternatively, you might adopt a more radical sort of relativity about the example. It is a sort Parfit does not consider. You might think betterness is relative to the population of people who exist, not just at a particular time but at any time. This view is known as 'actualism'.[23]

In Parfit's story, the girl actually has her child at 14. So the actual population includes the child born when his mother was 14. Relative to this population, let us suppose for the sake of future argument that the distribution *A*, which includes this child, is better than *B*, which does not. Had the girl waited and had a child later, the actual population would have been different. Let us suppose that, relative to the population that would then have been actual, *B* would have been better than *A*.

Second doubt about relativity

If we are offered a concept of relative good, one thing we must be sure of is that it is genuinely a concept of *good*. It must retain much of the normal meaning of 'good'. Most importantly, as I said on pages 32–3, it must be connected in an appropriate way to how one ought to act. If you propose a relative concept of good, you should be able to specify what the connection is. You should be able to combine your relativist axiology with an account of what one ought to do. My second doubt about relativity is that it is hard to see how you can do this in a plausible manner.

Just what difficulties will come up in the attempt depend on the particular sort of relativity we are dealing with. Actualism is a good one to start with. We are interested in situations where there is a choice between various alternative distributions. I have just said that what one ought to do, which in this context means which distribution one ought to choose, must be in some way connected to the goodness of the alternative distributions. According to actualism, the goodness of these distributions is relative to which distribution is the actual one, and the actual distribution is the one that is chosen. So which distribution is chosen must affect which distribution ought to be chosen.

In the actualist account I gave of Parfit's example, since the girl chooses distribution *A*, the child she has at 14 is actual. Consequently, I supposed that *A* is better than the alternative *B*. Had she chosen *B* instead, a different child would have been actual, and I supposed that *B* would then have been better than *A*. Suppose we assume teleology, the simplest sort of connection between good and ought: one ought to choose the actually best of the options.[24] Then, since the girl chooses *A* she ought to choose *A*. However, had she chosen *B* it would have been the case that she ought to have chosen *B*. So what she ought to choose depends on what she chooses.

If we do not assume teleology, but some other connection between good and ought, actualism could similarly imply that what one ought to choose depends on what one chooses. It might require a more complicated example to display this result.

It is quite implausible that what one ought to do depends on what one does. I think this is enough to cast severe doubt on actualism.[25]

So let us set actualism aside. Relativists of other sorts might adopt a relativist teleology as their connection between good and ought: that what a person ought to do is determined by the goodness of the acts that are available to her, relative to the point of view she occupies. But this can lead to a type of incoherence when a single person is liable to occupy several different points of view in succession.

Suppose you now have a choice between two options A and B. If A is better than B relative to the present time, then relativist teleology says you ought to choose A. Suppose you do as you ought and choose A. But suppose that relative to some later time, B is better than A. Then at the later time you ought not to have chosen A. You choose rightly, but it later turns out you chose wrongly. Indeed, it may turn out that you ought later to undo what you rightly did. Moreover, you might be able to foresee even as you choose A that just this would happen. This is a most implausible sort of incoherence in your activity.

This problem for relativity arises only for types of relativity that allow a single person to occupy different points of view in succession. It cannot arise for person-relativity, where the point of view sticks to the person. But it does apply to time-relativity and to temporal-population-relativity. A single person lives at different times. Also, she lives through changes in the world's currently living population, so she belongs to a sequence of different temporal populations.

Two responses are possible. One is to reject relativity and insist that good must be nonrelative. The other is to connect ought to good through a more complex rule than relativist teleology.

The first response can be illustrated from economics. Economists are used to this problem of incoherence; they call it 'dynamic inconsistency'. Time-relative valuations will lead to dynamic inconsistency under relativist teleology. In economics, this has often been seen as an argument against time-relativity. Some economists discount future wellbeing, but in order to avoid dynamic inconsistency, they generally do so in a nonrelativist way. I explained on page 70 that nonrelative discounting is possible. It is most easily achieved by discounting at a constant annual rate – this is so-called 'exponential discounting'. Exponential discounting ensures that reversals of value, like the one I assumed above between A and B, cannot occur.[26]

The second response supports relativity rather than rejecting it. It is the response made by Partha Dasgupta, when he offers us a temporal-population-relative account of goodness.[27] In Dasgupta's theory, goodness is relative to the population of the world alive at a time, rather than to time itself. The same danger of incoherence emerges if we assume relativist teleology. Suppose the current temporal population ought to do what is best according to its own betterness relation. What is best may involve bringing some new people into the world. So if the current population does as it ought, there will then be a new temporal population, and a new betterness relation. Then perhaps the new temporal population ought to undo some of what the previous temporal population did, even though the previous one did as it ought. It is not plausible that this is correct, since the new temporal population inevitably contains many of the same people as the old.

To avoid incoherence, Dasgupta sets up a different rule linking relative good with what a temporal population ought to do. What one temporal population ought to do depends partly on good relative to other temporal populations, as well as on good relative to itself. Details appear in section 11.3 below. But this move raises a new difficulty. What does Dasgupta mean when he says something is good relative to a particular temporal population, if that population ought to pursue some other objective, including good relative to some other temporal population? Once you drop the simple link between relative good and ought, it becomes doubtful that you really have a concept of relative good at all. I shall amplify this argument in section 11.3, and in the meanwhile record it as the second reason I am cautious about relative good.

Notes

1 For example, Larry Temkin, 'Intransitivity and the mere addition paradox', and Stuart Rachels, 'A set of solutions to Parfit's problems'.
2 This example comes from Robert Sugden, 'Why be consistent?'.
3 It was given me by Johan Brännmark, and he and I had an illuminating conversation about it.
4 It is modelled on an example of George Schumm's, presented in 'Transitivity, preference and indifference'.
5 A solution is offered by Delia Graff in 'Phenomenal continua and the sorites'.
6 My way of presenting it is close to Temkin's later paper 'Health care distribution and the problem of trade-offs'. My response to that paper, 'A comment on Temkin's trade-offs', explains the technical hitch I mentioned. So do Alex Voorhoeve and Ken Binmore in 'Defending transitivity against Zeno's paradox'. In this book, I cannot do justice to the full range of Temkin's arguments against the transitivity of betterness. The argument in 'An abortion argument and the threat of intransitivity' has a different character. It works by exploiting the puzzling fact that big differences can arise from a sequence of apparently insignificant steps. Each person's car apparently makes no significant difference to pollution, but all the cars together make a smog that kills hundreds of people. The solution is to recognize that not all the differences can be as insignificant as they seem. But I cannot develop this argument properly in this book.
7 'A set of solutions to Parfit's problems', p. 216.

8 'Health care distribution and the problem of trade-offs'.

9 The term 'repugnant conclusion' is Derek Parfit's. See his *Reasons and Persons*, p. 388.

10 p. 120.

11 It is a small-scale version of the 'mere addition paradox', which stems originally from Parfit's *Reasons and Persons*, chapter 19. Temkin's own examples are large-scale.

12 'Intransitivity and the mere addition paradox', p. 159.

13 He clearly does not find this option attractive. See 'An abortion argument and the threat of intransitivity', p. 278.

14 The field of a relation is defined on page 22.

15 See Derek Parfit, 'Equality or priority?'.

16 See section 18.1.

17 For instance, Sen, 'Rights and agency', and Regan, 'Against evaluator relativity'.

18 Most authors use the term 'neutral' to contrast with 'relative', and 'neutralist' to contrast with 'relativist'. But 'neutral' has another meaning in this book, so I have to use the awkward terms 'nonrelative', 'nonrelativist', and so on.

19 A good example appears in John Rawls, *A Theory of Justice*, pp. 294–5. Rawls intends to argue against discounting, but his argument is actually aimed only against temporal relativity. He ignores the possibility of nonrelative discounting; he takes it for granted that, if we discount, we shall discount both forwards and backwards in time.

20 *Reasons and Persons*, p. 358.

21 p. 360.

22 p. 360.

23 For example, see Josh Parsons, 'Axiological actualism'.

24 Teleology is discussed in section 3.1.

25 This objection to actualism is made by Gustaf Arrhenius, *Future Generations*, p. 141. There is a thorough investigation of this type of objection – that what one ought to do cannot depend on what one does – in Krister Bykvist, 'Violations of normative invariance'.

26 All this is demonstrated in the classic source on dynamic consistency, Robert Strotz, 'Myopia and inconsistency'.

27 Dasgupta, *An Inquiry Into Well-Being and Destitution*, pp. 377–94.

5

Quantities of lifetime wellbeing

I have been taking it for granted that a person's wellbeing can be treated as an arithmetic quantity. This chapter and the next provide a basis for that assumption. They develop a quantitative notion of wellbeing.

I have to go through this argument. For one thing, we cannot presume on a quantitative notion of wellbeing without justification. For another, it will turn out there is some choice over which notion to adopt, and I shall be picking out a particular one. My choice will make a difference later in the book.

However, I am sorry to say the argument will inevitably be a bit technical. If you have no qualms about quantities of wellbeing, you can pass over it lightly. I can briefly state here the main conclusions that will emerge from these chapters. We have quantitative concepts of a person's lifetime wellbeing and of her temporal wellbeing at a particular time. Lifetime wellbeing and temporal wellbeing can be measured on cardinal scales. They are comparable between people, and temporal wellbeing is comparable between times.

These are chapters about the *meaning* of quantities of wellbeing. What does it mean, if anything, to say that my wellbeing increased more last year than the year before, or that it is only half of yours, or that yours doubled in a year? There is a formal parallel between these chapters and discussions in economics about the *measurement* of wellbeing. Economists generally hope to measure wellbeing by means of people's preferences. They assume we can in principle know what people's preferences are: we can tell whether someone prefers one thing to another. So they think preferences might provide the basis for measuring wellbeing empirically. But preferences offer a limited basis, because they constitute only an ordering of alternatives, rather than a quantitative scale. Economists have debated just how far preferences can nevertheless go in determining a quantitative scale. This debate is about empirical measurement.

In many fields, there is no doubt a close connection between the meaning of a quantitative concept and its empirical measurement. The doctrine of *operationalism* holds that the meaning of a quantitative concept is necessarily defined by the operations that are used to measure it. Since many economists have adopted operationalism,[1] they believe that an analysis of the meaning of 'wellbeing' must consist in an account of the empirical measurement of wellbeing.

Operationalism has led some economists to deny it makes sense to compare the wellbeings of different people. They could not find a way to measure the difference between one person's wellbeing and another's, and they thought that measurement was the only way to give these comparisons meaning.[2]

But wellbeing is not an empirical concept. At least, even if 'wellbeing' has one empirical meaning, I use the term differently. I use it to refer to a person's good – how well off the person is – and I do not intend this to be a purely empirical matter. Whatever the truth of operationalism, it can at best apply only to empirical concepts. I shall not found quantities of wellbeing on preferences, but on a person's betterness relation: on what is better for the person than what. Unlike preference, betterness for a person is not an empirical concept. Its meaning comes from its role within ethics, particularly in helping to determine how we ought to act.

I shall take for granted the notion of betterness for a person. I assume we understand what it means to say one thing is better for someone than another. True, we often disagree with each other about which particular things are better or worse for someone, but I assume we understand what we disagree about. So I take betterness to be a solid foundation on which to build a quantitative notion of wellbeing.

We understand what we mean by betterness, but I think we are inclined to speak of quantities of wellbeing without being very clear what we mean by them. That is why quantities of wellbeing need some analysis. More than that, they need to be made precise. For the detailed quantitative work of this book, we need more precise quantitative notions than we commonly use. We shall need to assign precise meanings where in common speech there are perhaps only vague ones. We shall need to define as well as analyse, that is to say. But our present vague meanings set limits on our definitions; we can tighten up our meanings, but we ought not to go beyond the limits. Furthermore, we must remember that our definitions delimit the significance of whatever conclusions we draw. A conclusion about wellbeing will be a conclusion about wellbeing as we define it.

This chapter deals with people's overall or lifetime wellbeing; I leave temporal wellbeing to chapter 6. In this chapter, I shall develop a quantitative notion of lifetime wellbeing in two steps. First, in section

5.2, I shall set up a cardinal scale of wellbeing for each individual. A cardinal scale is one in which differences in wellbeing – benefits, I shall call them – are comparable: one benefit to a person can meaningfully be compared with another benefit to the same person. Then in section 5.3, I shall make these cardinal scales comparable between different people. This gives us a scale for the wellbeing of everyone.

One of my main tools of analysis will be expected utility theory. I shall use it to analyse the structure of betterness, even though the theory was originally developed to analyse the structure of preferences. Section 5.1 introduces expected utility theory and describes how it works.

5.1 Expected utility theory

Expected utility theory is about how to represent relations. It was developed for representing preference relations, but I shall apply it to betterness relations. This section deals principally with some formal matters to do with representation. It explains how a person's betterness relation can be represented by a cardinal utility function. It also presents some of the assumptions that are needed to make that possible. The next section develops the formal notion of utility into a measure of wellbeing.

In this section and the next, whenever I speak of betterness or goodness without qualification, I am referring to betterness or goodness for a particular person p. For a person p, her personal betterness relation is:

... is better for p than __.

On the basis of this one, I define some more relations, following the parallel development for general betterness in section 2.1. 'A is worse for p than B' means that B is better for p than A. 'A is equally as good as B for p' means that A is neither better nor worse for p than B, and that any third thing C is better or worse for p than A if and only if it is correspondingly better or worse for p than B. There is a discussion of the parallel definition on pages 21–2.

I am interested in a person's betterness relation between *prospects*. In section 4.2 I introduced the relation as it holds between different *histories*, but I now need to generalize to prospects. I defined a prospect on page 30 as a portfolio of histories, one for each state of nature. You might doubt that one prospect can genuinely be better for a person than another. You might think that goodness must be a property of what actually occurs, rather than of an uncertain prospect. But I rejected this view in section 6.1 of *Weighing Goods*, and I do not wish to reopen the question here. I shall assume that personal betterness can apply to prospects.

I explained on page 64 that, as I mean 'better for', a person's betterness relation applied to histories can hold only between histories in which the person exists. To generalize now, it can hold only between prospects in which the person is certain to exist. That is to say, the prospects that occupy the blank places in the relation must be portfolios of histories in which the person exists.

Amongst prospects, the *field* of a person's relation is defined as the collection of prospects that are either better or worse for the person than some other prospect. Amongst prospects, then, the field of a person's betterness relation consists only of prospects in which the person is certain to exist.

Now I shall make some assumptions about the structure of p's betterness relation. I am still following the parallel development in section 2.1. First, I assume the relation is transitive and asymmetric. As I said on page 21, these are analytical features of betterness. They make betterness technically a strict partial ordering.

Next I assume that, for any two prospects A and B within the field of the betterness relation, either one is better for p than the other or they are equally good for p. This is to assume the betterness ordering is *complete* on its field.[3] It is a major assumption. You might think the comparative goodness of two prospects for a person is sometimes indeterminate, in such a way that neither prospect is better than the other and yet they are not equally good. For example, suppose two prospects tend to realize values that are very different from each other. Their relative goodness is determined by balancing these values against each other. If the values are very different, it is plausible that they cannot be balanced precisely. This possibility is often called 'incommensurability' of the values. If the values are incommensurable, the comparative goodness of the prospects may be indeterminate.

I shall ignore this possibility. This is not because I do not think it is genuine; I think it is. I think incommensurability of values is common. But I shall assume completeness for the reason that has led me to some other simplifying assumptions: so as not to have too many difficulties to deal with at once. Indeterminacy in personal betterness relations is not particularly a problem of weighing lives.

The corresponding possibility of indeterminacy in the *general* betterness relation is another matter. That is particularly germane to weighing lives, and chapter 12 examines it. The analysis developed in chapter 12 could help with indeterminacy in personal betterness relations too. But for simplicity, I am going to assume these relations have no indeterminacy: they are complete.

Next I shall assume that *p*'s betterness relation is continuous. I assumed that general betterness is continuous on page 27. I explained that the principal effect of continuity is to rule out lexical elements in the ordering. I also argued that lexical elements are implausible. I think this is an acceptable assumption for personal betterness relations too. Its chief effect is to rule out lexical elements, which are anyway implausible.

All these assumptions together are sufficient to ensure that *p*'s betterness relation amongst prospects can be represented by a function. Following the practice of economists, I shall call this function a *utility* function, and its values *utilities*. But remember it is not representing a preference ordering, as utility functions in economics typically do. It is representing a personal betterness ordering. I shall write it $U(\cdot)$. This function is so far only an ordinal representation of the ordering.[4] One prospect has a higher utility than another if and only if it is better for *p* than the other (and it follows that one prospect has the same utility as another if and only if it is equally as good for *p* as the other).

We are dealing with betterness amongst prospects. Since a prospect is a portfolio of histories, we can write it as a vector:

$$(h_1, h_2, \ldots h_S).$$

h_1 is the history that will happen if the first state of nature turns out to be the actual one, h_2 is the history that will happen if the second state is the actual one, and so on. *S* is the total number of states of nature. I am assuming it is finite, but this is only to make the presentation easy; expected utility theory does not require it. The prospect $(h_1, h_2, \ldots h_S)$ has the utility:

$$U(h_1, h_2, \ldots h_S).$$

To go further with the theory, we need a lot more assumptions about the structure of the betterness relation. We need all the *axioms* of expected utility theory, as they are called. I shall not specify what they are. Several of them are discussed in detail in *Weighing Goods*, and section 6.3 of that book argues that personal betterness relations satisfy them. The most dubious is completeness, and that one I have already adopted here. So here I shall simply take on board all these further axioms.

Granted all of them, a theorem tells us more about the form of the utility function. This theorem tells us that the betterness ordering can be represented by a utility function that has a special form. We can find nonnegative numbers π_1, π_2, and so on, one for each state of nature, and we can find a function $u(\cdot)$ that assigns numbers $u(h_1)$, $u(h_2)$, and so on to each history, in such a way that there is a utility function with the form:

(5.1.1) $U(h_1, h_2, \ldots h_S) = \pi_1 u(h_1) + \pi_2 u(h_2) + \ldots + \pi_S u(h_S).$

Furthermore, the πs add up to one:

$$\pi_1 + \pi_2 + \ldots + \pi_S = 1.$$

We can think of the πs as *probabilities* assigned to the states of nature. The function $u(\cdot)$ is called a *subutility function*. It assigns a subutility to each history.

Technically, subutilities are assigned to histories and utilities to prospects. But we do not need to worry about distinguishing utilities from subutilities, for the following reason. Consider the 'certain prospect' of a history h. This is the prospect $(h, h, \ldots h)$ that delivers h in every state of nature. Its utility is:

$$
\begin{aligned}
U(h, h, \ldots h) &= \pi_1 u(h) + \pi_2(h) + \ldots + \pi_S u(h) \\
&= (\pi_1 + \pi_2 + \ldots \pi_S)u(h) \\
&= u(h)
\end{aligned}
$$

(since the probabilities add up to one). So the utility of the certain prospect of h is the same as the subutility of h itself. We might just as well call this amount the utility of h. That is to say, we can extend the utility function $U(\cdot)$ to histories by defining the utility $U(h)$ of the history h as $u(h)$ or $U(h, h, \ldots h)$. Then we have assigned utilities to both histories and prospects. Equation (5.1.1) becomes

(5.1.2) $U(h_1, h_2, \ldots h_S) = \pi_1 U(h_1) + \pi_2 U(h_2) + \ldots + \pi_S U(h_S).$

Equation (5.1.2) shows the utility of a prospect as the mathematical expectation of utility that will result from the prospect. I call a utility function with the form of (5.1.2) *expectational*. So the conclusion of the theorem is that, provided a person's preferences amongst prospects conform to the required axioms, they can be represented by an expectational utility function. This is the fundamental theorem of expected utility theory.

I next need to go through a little algebra. Take any utility function $U(\cdot)$ that represents p's betterness amongst prospects. $U(\cdot)$ assigns a utility

$U(A)$ to each prospect A. Let us define another function $V(\cdot)$, which assigns the value

(5.1.3) $$V(A) = aU(A) + b$$

to each prospect A, where b is any number and a is any positive number. Then the function $V(\cdot)$ is said to be an *increasing linear transform* of $U(\cdot)$. The transformation is linear because (5.1.3) is a linear equation. It is increasing because $V(\cdot)$ is an increasing transform of $U(\cdot)$, as 'increasing transform' is defined on page 27. That is to say, for any pair of prospects A and B, $V(A)$ is greater than $V(B)$ if and only if $U(A)$ is greater than $U(B)$. This is because a is positive. It is easy to check that, whenever $V(\cdot)$ is an increasing linear transform of $U(\cdot)$, $U(\cdot)$ is an increasing linear transform of $V(\cdot)$.

Since $U(\cdot)$ represents p's betterness, $U(A)$ is greater than $U(B)$ if and only if A is better than B for p. Consequently, since $V(\cdot)$ is an increasing transform of $U(\cdot)$, $V(A)$ is greater than $V(B)$ if and only if A is better than B for p. This means that $V(\cdot)$ like $U(\cdot)$ is a utility function that represents p's betterness. Quite generally, if $U(\cdot)$ is a function that represents an ordering, any increasing transform of $U(\cdot)$ also represents the ordering.

Now suppose $U(\cdot)$ is an expectational utility function, and let $V(\cdot)$ be an increasing linear transform of $U(\cdot)$. Take any prospect $(h_1, h_2, \ldots h_S)$. Then

$V(h_1, h_2, \ldots h_S)$
   $= aU(h_1, h_2, \ldots h_S) + b$
                (since $V(\cdot)$ is an increasing linear transform of $U(\cdot)$)
   $= a\{\pi_1 U(h_1) + \pi_2 U(h_2) + \ldots + \pi_S U(h_S)\} + b$ (from (5.1.2))
   $= a\{\pi_1 U(h_1) + \pi_2 U(h_2) + \ldots + \pi_S U(h_S)\} + \{\pi_1 + \pi_2 + \ldots + \pi_S\}b$
                (because the probabilities add to one)
   $= \pi_1\{aU(h_1) + b\} + \pi_2\{aU(h_2) + b\} + \ldots + \pi_S\{aU(h_S) + b\}$ (rearranging)
   $= \pi_1 V(h_1) + \pi_2 V(h_2) + \ldots + \pi_S V(h_S)$.

That is to say, the function $V(\cdot)$ is expectational. We know already that $V(\cdot)$ is a utility function that represents the same ordering as $U(\cdot)$. So we have discovered that, if $U(\cdot)$ is an expectational utility function representing a person's betterness, then any increasing linear transform of $U(\cdot)$ is also an expectational utility function representing the person's betterness. The converse is also true, though I shall not prove it: any expectational utility function that represents the same betterness relation is an increasing linear transform of $U(\cdot)$.

So there is a whole family of expectational utility functions that represent p's betterness. Each is an increasing linear transform of the others. Each is an equally good representation; there is nothing to choose between them. We can arbitrarily pick one to work with; it will stand in for the whole family. A utility function that stands in for a family of functions, all of which are increasing linear transforms of each other, is called a *cardinal* utility function. We must not attach any significance to the individual properties of the function we happen to pick. Only the properties it shares with the rest of the family can be significant, since we might equally easily have picked another member of the family instead.

What properties of a cardinal utility function might be significant? What properties does it share with other members of the family? The answer is: whatever properties are preserved by an increasing linear transformation. The principal properties that are preserved are *ratios of utility differences*. Suppose we have two utility functions $U(\cdot)$ and $V(\cdot)$, each an increasing linear transform of the other. Take four prospects A, B, C and D. It is easily checked by algebra that the ratio of $\{U(A) - U(B)\}$ to $\{U(C) - U(D)\}$ is the same as the ratio of $\{V(A) - V(B)\}$ to $\{V(C) - V(D)\}$. That is to say, the ratio of utility differences according to $U(\cdot)$ is the same as their ratio according to $V(\cdot)$. When we have a cardinal utility function, then, the ratios of utility differences may be significant properties. For instance, if utility increases more between A and B than it does between C and D, that may be a significant fact. I say only that it *may* be significant, because I have not yet discussed what significance it has.

On the other hand, the zero of utility cannot be significant. If a particular prospect is assigned zero utility by the utility function we pick, that means nothing. Other utility functions in the family will assign this prospect some utility other than zero. Nor can the 'scale' of utility – the size of the unit of utility – be significant. If the difference in utility between one prospect and another is one unit according to one utility function, other utility functions in the family will make the difference something other than one. When one utility function $U(\cdot)$ in a family is transformed into another $V(\cdot) = aU(\cdot) + b$, the coefficient a (unless it is one) changes the scale, and the number b (unless it is zero) changes the zero.

The zero and the unit of a cardinal utility function are arbitrary. Within the family of utility functions that represent some given ordering, we can always find one that assigns a utility of zero to any particular prospect we choose, and a utility of one to any other prospect we choose, provided only that it is better than the first. But once we have done that, nothing else is arbitrary: the utility of every prospect is then uniquely determined. Fixing the zero and the one picks out one unique utility function from the family, which then assigns a unique utility to every prospect. To speak more generally, we are free to fix two utilities arbitrarily, but no more. It does not have to be the zero and the one. We can arbitrarily assign a utility of, say, fifteen to one prospect, and twenty-six to another. But once we have fixed two utilities, the utility of every other prospect is determined, because fixing two utilities is enough to pick one single utility function out of the family that represents the ordering. Fixing two points in a cardinal utility function is enough to fix the whole function. This is a distinguishing feature of cardinal functions.

Between objects, there is a relation 'hotter than': some objects are hotter than others. This relation is an ordering, and it can be represented by a cardinal temperature function. This function assigns a number called a 'temperature' to each object. In principle, 'hotter than' could be represented by any one of a family of functions, each an increasing linear transform of the others. The Fahrenheit and Celsius scales are the two members of the family that are commonly used. The ratio of any two temperature differences is the same, whether they are measured in Fahrenheit or Celsius. The two scales have different zeros and different units. Each is determined by fixing arbitrarily two points on the scale. Celsius (actually Linnaeus, reversing Celsius's own scale) assigned zero to the temperature of freezing water and a hundred to the temperature of boiling water; Fahrenheit assigned zero to the lowest temperature he could achieve, and ninety-six to the temperature of his body. Once each had made his two arbitrary assignments, his temperature function was fully determined.

Expectational utility functions that represent the same preferences are related together in just the way the Fahrenheit and Celsius scales are related together, and they are arbitrary to just the same extent.

5.2 A cardinal scale of individual wellbeing

The expectational utility function that represents a person's betterness relation amongst prospects is cardinal. But the way it represents betterness is still only ordinal. Better prospects have higher utilities; that is all. Nevertheless, we might suspect that a cardinal utility function could tell us more about a person's good or wellbeing than simply the order of betterness for her. Let us follow up this suspicion.

Since a utility function is only cardinal, neither the zero of utility nor the size of the unit can be significant. But the ratio of utility differences might be significant. We might suspect that the ratio of two utility differences could tell us the ratio of the corresponding amounts of a person's wellbeing. Take four histories, h_1, h_2, h_3, and h_4 where h_2 is better for a person than h_1, and h_4 better for her than h_3. Suppose the utility difference between h_2 and h_1 is, say, twice the utility difference between h_4 and h_3. We might suspect that the person's wellbeing would be increased twice as much by a change from h_1 to h_2 as it would be by a change from h_3 to h_4. If this were so, utility would measure the person's wellbeing to an extent. We could say it represents her wellbeing *cardinally*. We could call it a *cardinal scale* of wellbeing. This is what it means to say utility is a cardinal scale of wellbeing: it means that ratios of differences in utilities are equal to the corresponding ratios of differences in wellbeing.

How can we test the idea that this is so? Let us work with a simpler case where the utility difference between h_2 and h_1 is the same as the utility difference between h_4 and h_3:

(5.2.1) $$U(h_2) - U(h_1) = U(h_4) - U(h_3).$$

Now, let us construct some prospects involving these histories. Suppose there are only two states of nature, heads and tails, and they are equally probable. Compare two prospects. One, (h_2, h_3), delivers h_2 in state heads and h_3 in state tails. The other, (h_1, h_4), delivers h_1 in state heads and h_4 in state tails.

The utility of the first prospect, $U(h_2, h_3)$, is its expected utility, which is $\frac{1}{2}U(h_2) + \frac{1}{2}U(h_3)$. The utility of the second prospect, $U(h_1, h_4)$, is its expected utility. This is $\frac{1}{2}U(h_1) + \frac{1}{2}U(h_4)$. Simple algebra using (5.2.1) shows these are the same. So the two prospects have the same utility. Since utility represents the person's betterness, they are equally good for the person.

The question is whether ratios of differences in utility equal the corresponding ratios of differences in wellbeing. In this case, since the differences in utilities are the same, we need to test whether the differences in wellbeing are also the same. Have we any reason to think that the difference in the person's wellbeing between h_2 and h_1 is the same as the difference in her wellbeing between h_4 and h_3? I shall use the word '*benefit*' for a difference in wellbeing. Have we any reason to think that the benefit to the person of having h_2 rather than h_1 is the same as the benefit to her of having h_4 rather than h_3?

When the prospect (h_2, h_3) is compared with (h_1, h_4), what determines which is better? If heads comes up, the person does better under the first of these prospects; she gets the history h_2 rather than h_1, and h_2 is better for her. If tails comes up, she does better under the second; she gets h_4 rather than h_3, and h_4 is better for her. So which is the better prospect depends on weighing one possible benefit against the other. The benefit of h_2 rather than h_1 has to be weighed against the benefit of h_4 rather than h_3.

As it happens, the two prospects are equally good. So we know the two conflicting benefits must be exactly balanced. They evidently count equally in determining the relative goodness of the prospects. Now, surely, if the benefits count equally in determining which is the better prospect, it is plausible to think they are actually equal benefits. It is plausible to conclude, then, that the difference in the person's wellbeing between h_2 and h_1 is equal to the difference in her wellbeing between h_4 and h_3. So we do indeed have reason to think that the ratio of differences in utilities equals the ratio of differences in wellbeing, in this example.

Let me generalize the argument. Suppose we have to compare two prospects, where one will lead to better results in some states, and the other to better results in other states. In that case, determining which is the better prospect is a matter of weighing conflicting benefits against each other. Now, the utilities of the two prospects tells us which is actually the better prospect. In effect, their utilities tell us the result of the weighing of benefits. Indeed, differences in utility between individual histories tell us the weight of each benefit. They tell us how much each benefit counts in determining which is the better prospect. Given that, it is plausible to think they tell us the actual size of the benefits.

Here is the point in symbols. Suppose we have to compare the two prospects $(h_1, h_2, \ldots h_S)$ and $(h_1', h_2', \ldots h_S')$. The first is better than the second if and only if

$$U(h_1, h_2, \ldots h_S) > U(h_1', h_2', \ldots h_S').$$

Since utility is expectational, this is so if and only if

$$\pi_1 U(h_1) + \pi_2 U(h_2) + \ldots + \pi_S U(h_S) > \pi_1 U(h_1') + \pi_2 U(h_2') + \ldots + \pi_S U(h_S').$$

That is (rearranging): the first prospect is better than the second if and only if

$$\pi_1\{U(h_1) - U(h_1')\} + \pi_2\{U(h_2) - U(h_2')\} + \ldots + \pi_S\{U(h_S) - U(h_S')\} > 0.$$

In this formula, the utility differences $\{U(h_1) - U(h_1')\}$, $\{U(h_2) - U(h_2')\}$, and so on – some positive and some negative – are weighed against each other (adjusted by probabilities). So the utility differences tell us which is ultimately the better prospect. They tell us how the various conflicting benefits determine the relative goodness of prospects. Since utility tells us in this way how much benefits *count* in determining betterness amongst prospects, it is plausible to think it is a cardinal scale of wellbeing.

But there is also something to be said on the other side. If utility is a cardinal scale of wellbeing, that implies something I call 'Bernoulli's hypothesis' in honour of Daniel Bernoulli, who believed it.[5] By the definition of utility, one prospect is better for a person than another if and only if it gives her a greater expectation of utility than the other. If (and only if) utility is a cardinal scale of wellbeing, then one prospect has a greater expectation of utility for a person than another if and only if it gives her a greater expectation of wellbeing than the other. So, if (and only if) utility is a cardinal scale of wellbeing, this is true:

> *Bernoulli's hypothesis.* One prospect is better for a person than another if and only if it gives the person a greater expectation of wellbeing than the other.

Bernoulli's hypothesis is equivalent to the view that utility is a cardinal scale of wellbeing.

Bernoulli's hypothesis can be disputed. It implies *risk neutrality* about wellbeing. Go back to the simple example again. The prospects (h_2, h_3) and (h_1, h_4) are equally good, and according to Bernoulli's hypothesis, they offer an equal expectation of wellbeing. But let us now suppose that h_2 and h_3 are actually the same history. Then the first of these prospects is a safe option, whereas the second is risky: the first will produce the history h_2 (which is also h_3) for sure, whereas the second will produce either the better history h_4 or the worse one h_1. It seems reasonable to think there is merit in avoiding risk: that, if two prospects have the same expectation of wellbeing, the safer one is better. But Bernoulli's hypothesis denies that. It says that two prospects with the same expectation of wellbeing are equally good, regardless of their riskiness. That is what I meant when I said it implies risk neutrality. It is a reason for doubting Bernoulli's hypothesis.

A response to this objection is to suggest that Bernoulli's hypothesis is true in virtue of meaning. In determining betterness amongst prospects, conflicting benefits are weighed against each other. It is plausible that this operation of weighing is precisely where wellbeing acquires a quantitative meaning: where the notion of the size of a benefit is determined. To say the difference in wellbeing between h_2 and h_1 is the same as the difference in wellbeing between h_4 and h_3 may simply *mean* these differences count the same in determining which is the better prospect.

Suppose someone denies these differences in wellbeing are the same. We know that the prospects (h_2, h_3) and (h_1, h_4) are equally good, so this person must accept that the two differences count the same in determining the goodness of the prospects. Nevertheless, she denies they are themselves the same. They count the same, she says, but they are not the same. We might ask her what she means. What meaning does she assign to quantities of wellbeing, if not how much these quantities count in determining the goodness of prospects? We are surely entitled to expect an answer to this question. The weighing up of benefits to determine betterness amongst prospects provides a plausible source of meaning for quantities of wellbeing. So if someone denies it, she ought to produce an alternative.

She may be able to. I think the meaning of quantities of wellbeing will have to be determined in some context where benefits are weighed against each other. The context of uncertainty – comparing the values of uncertain prospects – is the one I have been considering, but weighing also takes place in other contexts. For instance, sometimes benefits that come at one time are weighed against benefits that come at another time. So there are other possible meaning-giving contexts. But our present context of comparing uncertain prospects is at least a plausible one.

I shall adopt Bernoulli's hypothesis; I shall assume that the meaning of quantities of wellbeing is determined in the context of comparing uncertain prospects. In *Weighing Goods*,[6] I gave the impression that any of several contexts where wellbeing is weighed might be the one that fixes the meaning we actually assign to quantities of wellbeing. I suggested that analysis is needed to discover which is the actual meaning-giving context. But I now think that was misleading. The natural, intuitive meaning we assign to quantities of wellbeing is vague. When we come to precise argument, we do not need to discover our actual precise meaning, because we do not have one. Instead we can make our vague meaning precise.

We may have a choice about how to do that. Adopting Bernoulli's hypothesis is one option, and I am taking that one. In fact, I am using Bernoulli's hypothesis as a *definition* of quantities of wellbeing. From now on in this book, I mean the quantitative idea of wellbeing to be fixed, not by intuition, but by this definition. Quantitative wellbeing is fixed in the context of comparing uncertain prospects. The effect is that utility is a cardinal scale for wellbeing as I have defined it. Bernoulli's hypothesis cardinalizes wellbeing by means of weighing under uncertainty. I am adopting that cardinalization.[7]

I think my definition is a reasonable way to make our vague quantitative notion of wellbeing precise. But it is important to remember I have taken this step. I have made my notion of wellbeing more precise than the intuitive one, and I have chosen one particular way of doing so. This means that all my conclusions about the aggregation of wellbeing must be interpreted through this precisification. I am no longer talking about wellbeing in our vague intuitive sense.

I have in fact identified a person's wellbeing with her utility – to be more exact, with the values of an expectational function that represents the person's betterness relation. As things stand at present, there is nothing more to wellbeing than this. Utility functions are only cardinal. This means their zero and the size of their unit have no significance. So, as things stand, we can assign no significance to the zero of wellbeing, nor to the size of the unit of wellbeing. However, these are matters I shall work on some more, beginning in the next section.

Having identified utility and wellbeing, I now no longer need to speak of utility. A person's utility function provides a cardinal scale for her wellbeing. If a person p lives in some history h, I shall use the symbol g^p for her wellbeing in h. It is simply $U^p(h)$, her utility in h. g^p is a number in any history in which a person lives. In any history where p does not live, I shall assign g^p the non-numerical value of Ω. In general, g^p is p's 'condition'. On page 25 I defined a person's condition at a time. g^p is p's overall, lifetime condition.

To summarize this section: we have established a cardinal scale of wellbeing for a person. Take prospects made up of histories in which that person exists. Apply expected utility theory to the person's betterness relation over these prospects. This will give us a cardinal utility function for the person. Granted Bernoulli's hypothesis, this function will be a cardinal scale of the person's wellbeing. So the person's betterness relation amongst prospects turns out to be enough to determine a cardinal scale of wellbeing for her.

5.3 Comparing wellbeing between people

Section 5.2 has given us a cardinal scale of wellbeing for each person. But we need to attach sense to comparisons between different people's wellbeing. We need to be able to say, for instance, that a change benefits one person more than it harms another. How can we make sense of such statements?

Correcting an error

I have changed my mind about this. I now think that in *Weighing Goods* I offered the wrong account of the meaning of interpersonal comparisons of wellbeing.[8] Suppose we compare the goodness of two alternative histories h_1 and h_2. Suppose h_1 is better for one person p, and h_2 is better for another person q, but for everyone else h_1 and h_2 are equally good. Determining the relative goodness of these histories is a matter of weighing a benefit to p (the amount by which h_1 is better for p than h_2) against a benefit to q (the amount by which h_2 is better for q than h_1). Suppose I say p's benefit is greater than q's. What does that mean? My suggestion in *Weighing Goods* was that it means h_1 is a better option than h_2. In effect, it means that p's benefit counts more than q's in determining the overall goodness of the alternatives. The size of a benefit is nothing other than the amount the benefit counts in determining general goodness. To say a benefit to one person is the same as a benefit to another means it would be equally as good if one benefit came about as it would be if the other came about. To say two benefits are equal means they count equally in overall goodness.

My idea, then, was to use the general betterness relation to give meaning to comparisons between benefits coming to different people.

In *Weighing Goods*, I only went as far as comparing benefits – differences in wellbeing – between people. But the same idea can be extended to give a meaning also to comparisons between the *levels* of wellbeing of different people. Compare two different histories h_1 and h_2. Suppose that, in h_1, a person p lives a particular life, but q does not live at all. In h_2, q lives a particular life but p does not live at all. Suppose I say p's life in h_1 is better than q's life in h_2. What does that mean? The suggestion is that it means h_1 is a better option than h_2. In effect, it means that the goodness of p's life counts more than the goodness of q's in determining the overall goodness of the alternatives.

However, I now think this whole approach to interpersonal comparisons of wellbeing is mistaken. My reason is that it makes good sense to say it is better for some given amount of wellbeing to come to one person rather than to another. Some particular benefit to one person might be equal to some particular benefit to another, but nevertheless it makes sense to say it is better for one of these benefits to come about rather than the other. So we can clearly make a distinction between an amount of wellbeing and how much that amount counts in general good.

One example of the distinction appears in the claim that the wellbeing of future people should be discounted. Wellbeing that comes to people who live in the future is sometimes thought to count for less than wellbeing that comes to people living now. Take the saving of lives, for instance. Some economists claim it is better to save the lives of ten people now rather than, say, the lives of twenty people in a hundred years' time: ten lives now count for more in general good than twenty lives in the future. These economists do not necessarily mean that life saving brings less benefit to future people than it does to present people. They may think a future person would be just as much benefited by having her life saved as a present person. They may think the benefit to the individuals is the same, but the benefit to present people counts for more in general good. If *Weighing Goods* was right that the size of a benefit is just the amount the benefit counts in general good, this view would make no sense. But it plainly does make sense, even if it is wrong. Evidently, therefore, our concept of the quantity of a person's wellbeing is not the same as our concept of how much the person's wellbeing counts in general good.

The mistake I made is to forget that wellbeing is *personal* value or goodness, which in section 4.2 of this book I contrasted with *general* goodness. When a person lives a life, her wellbeing is the goodness of the life for her. We have to separate this from the general goodness of the life, or how good it is that she lives this life. It may be generally better to save a present person rather than a future person, even though being saved is no better for the present person than it is for the future person. In *Weighing Goods* I muddled up personal and general good. I tried to build a quantitative notion of wellbeing, comparable between people, from a comparison in terms of general good. That had to fail.[9]

A person's wellbeing or personal good depends only on how things are, seen from a perspective that is personal to her in some sense or other, whereas how her wellbeing counts in general good may depend also on how things are, seen from some sort of external perspective. Certain features of the world make no difference to how the world is from the perspective of the person herself. (I mean they make no difference in themselves; they might incidentally make the world different because they are connected with other properties that make a difference in themselves.) The time in history when the person lives is one of these features. Consequently, the time when she lives makes no difference, in itself, to how well off a person is. It may be that lives in a hundred years time will be just about as good, from the personal perspective, as they are now. If so, life saving in a hundred years will be just about as good for the people who are saved as it is today. But from an external perspective, the time when a person lives may make a difference to how good it is to save her life. People who favour discounting believe that is so.

How things are for a person

What, then, *is* the basis of our concept of an interpersonally comparable quantity of wellbeing?[10] A person's wellbeing is how good things are for the person. It depends only on – supervenes on – how things are for her. If things for one person are exactly as they are for another, those two people have the same wellbeing. This is a conceptual truth, and it gives us a basis for comparing wellbeing between people.

My expression 'how things are for a person' is meant to pick out the person's personal perspective. I am not suggesting it is conceptually prior to wellbeing. I am not trying to define or analyse 'wellbeing'. I am only reminding you that a person's wellbeing depends on a limited range of features of the world: the ones that show up from her personal perspective. Your view about wellbeing will influence what you include in how things are for a person. For example, if you believe a person's wellbeing is determined only by the experiences she has, you may include only her experiences in how things are for her. For another example, if you take the view I mentioned on page 47 that posthumous events can influence a person's wellbeing, you will have to include these events in how things are for her.

I adopted the expression 'how things are for a person' to allow for the possibility that events outside a person's lifetime might influence her wellbeing. But now I have mentioned the possibility, I shall slip into a more convenient terminology. How things are for a person I shall call her *life*. So a person's life includes all the features of the world that can affect her wellbeing. If her wellbeing can really be affected by events that happen outside her lifetime, perversely I include those in her 'life' too.

Because a life includes everything that can affect a person's well-being, the person who lives a particular life has exactly the same wellbeing as any other person would have if she lived that life. We can consider this amount of wellbeing to be simply the goodness of the life. The goodness of a life is independent of who lives it.

But could the very same life be lived by more than one person? The question is not whether two people could live the same life simulta-neously. It is whether there is a life such that one person could live it, and also such that another person could live it. I assume that is possible. It is not physically possible, but conceptually or metaphysically possible. This means I assume that a person's identity is not a part of what I call her life, or of how things are for the person. I assume a person's identity does not show up from her personal perspective.

I do not assume that every possible life could be lived by every possible person. Other properties of a person besides her bare identity might prevent her from living every possible life. Perhaps I could not have lived Cleopatra's life, for example. I assume only that some lives could be lived by more than one person; the precise assumption I need is specified on page 96.

A universal scale of goodness for lives

From section 5.2, we already have a cardinal scale of wellbeing for each person separately. This scale assigns a value to each history in which the person exists, measuring how good that history is for the person. The person's wellbeing, in a particular history, depends only on what life she leads in that history. So the scale assigns a value to each life the person might lead. Now we recognize that the goodness of a life is independent of who lives it, we know our scale measures the goodness of lives. Each person's individual scale of goodness turns out to be a universal scale, measuring the goodness of lives for everyone. It follows that everyone's scale must be the same. The universal scale is cardinal. Furthermore, it provides comparisons of wellbeing between people. Each person who lives leads one of the lives on the scale, so each person's wellbeing is measured on the same scale.

A complication is that each person's scale of goodness assigns value only to lives that are possible for that person: to lives that she lives in some possible history or other. So it is not strictly true that everyone will have the same scale of wellbeing. What is true is that any two people's scales will coincide over all lives that are possible for each of those people. This turns out to be enough to ensure that every life that is possible for anyone is assigned a goodness that is fully comparable with the goodness assigned to every other life that is possible for anyone. Here is why.

Start with just one person and call her *p*. *p* has a cardinal scale that measures the goodness of all the lives that are possible for her. A cardinal scale has some arbitrary features. But I explained on page 86 that fixing two points is enough to fix the whole of it. So let us arbitrarily assign some value to one of *p*'s lives, and some higher value to another, better one. This fixes a value for each of *p*'s lives.

Now take another person, q. We have a cardinal scale of goodness for all the lives that are possible for q. Suppose two lives that are possible for q are also possible for p. We have already fixed a value for those lives in p's scale of good. Since each is equally as good for q as it is for p, we must assign each of these two lives the same value in q's scale as it has in p's scale. This is enough to fix the value of every life on q's scale, and all those values will be comparable with the values on p's scale. So long as two people's possibilities overlap to the extent of two lives, that is enough to assign comparable values to all their possible lives.

Think of all possible people together. If two of them share at least two possible lives, call them an 'overlapping pair'. I assume that everyone belongs to at least one overlapping pair, and furthermore that everyone is linked to everyone else by a chain of overlapping pairs. This is just as much as I need to assume about the extent to which lives can be lived by more than one person. Once we recognize that some lives can be lived by more than one person, the first part of this assumption is hard to doubt. Given that, I can think of only one further objection that might be raised to the second part. You might think that men's lives could not be lived by women, and vice versa. But surely there are some lives that could be lived by either a male or a female person.

For two people who form an overlapping pair, I have explained how their scales of wellbeing can be brought into line and made comparable. Now I have assumed that everyone is linked to everyone else by a chain of overlapping pairs, everyone's scales can be brought into line by repeating the process.

Zero not fixed

The zero and unit on our universal scale remain arbitrary. The unit will remain arbitrary through this book. The zero will remain arbitrary till section 18.1, where I shall specify it. Remember, then: at present the zero of wellbeing has no particular significance.

Conclusion, and an alternative approach

That is the end of the process of setting up a scale of wellbeing. The levels of individual wellbeing g^p that I set up on page 91 are now fully comparable between people.

What has all this achieved? I have been trying to specify the meaning of statements that compare one person's wellbeing with another's; what have I concluded? What does it mean, for instance, to say that p is better off than q? It means that p's life lies above q's on the universal scale of wellbeing I have defined. And where does this scale come from? First, I gave a meaning to comparisons of wellbeing for a single person by adopting Bernoulli's hypothesis. This gave me individual scales of wellbeing. Then I gave a meaning to interpersonal comparisons by merging these individual scales on the basis that two people are equally well off if they lead the same life.

In a little more detail, here is an outline of the route I took to set up a scale of wellbeing. I started with a betterness relation for each person. This relation holds between alternative prospects, and each prospect is a portfolio of histories. I took it for granted that we understand the idea of one prospect's being better or worse for a person than another, and I used that idea to build a quantitative scale of wellbeing. The first step was to produce a cardinal scale of wellbeing for each person, using Bernoulli's hypothesis. The scale assigned a value to each history. The value was particular to the person, so I then had to connect together different people's values. I made this second step by recognizing that the value of a history to a person is effectively the goodness of the life the person lives in that history, and the goodness of a life must be the same for anyone who lives that life.

I could have taken a different route to the same destination. I could have started with a betterness relation between lives. This would have been a relation of personal rather than general betterness: to say one life is better than another means it would be better to live the first than the second. It does not mean it would be generally better for the first life to be lived. Nevertheless, the relation is universal; it is the same for everyone, because living a particular life is exactly as good for one person as it is for any other. I think I could have fairly taken it for granted that we understand the idea of one life's being better or worse than another. On this understanding we could build a scale of goodness for lives. To make it a cardinal scale, we should have to start with a betterness relation between prospects that are portfolios of lives, and use Bernoulli's hypothesis as I did before. I see no difficulty with that move. We would emerge with a cardinal scale of goodness for lives that is universal from the start. No further step would be required to arrange for comparability between people.

I think this alternative route would work as well as the more round-about route I took. It would arrive at the same scale of wellbeing in the end. I chose the roundabout route because it is more familiar.

Notes

1 Daniel Ellsberg is a very clear case in 'Classic and current notions of "measurable utility"'. See also Kenneth Arrow, *Social Choice and Individual Values*, particularly p. 115.

2 On p. 9 of *Social Choice and Individual Values*, Arrow says: 'The viewpoint will be taken here that interpersonal comparison of utilities has no meaning.' But he is not firmly committed to this viewpoint. Later in the same book (p. 115) he seems willing to 'operationalize' interpersonal comparisons, in order to give them meaning.

3 See p. 22.

4 Ordinal representation is explained on p. 27.

5 Bernoulli, 'Exposition of a new theory on the measurement of risk'. Bernoulli used the Latin word '*emolumentum*' for wellbeing. Unfortunately, this word is confusingly translated as 'utility' in the *Econometrica* translation of Bernoulli's paper.

6 Section 10.3.

7 An alternative is mentioned on page 226.

8 pp. 215–20.

9 I was not alone in making this error in an account of interpersonal comparisons of wellbeing. It also appears in Peter Hammond, 'Interpersonal comparisons of utility'.

10 One economists' approach to interpersonal comparisons is through 'extended preferences' as they are called: people's preferences about living other people's lives. This approach reaches its fullest development in John Harsanyi, *Rational Behavior and Bargaining Equilibrium*, pp. 57–9. I think it cannot succeed, for reasons explained in my 'Extended preferences'. However, Harsanyi does hint at a different approach. He points out that if one person were in exactly the same causal situation as another, she would have the same 'utility' as another. By 'utility' at this point of his argument, he means 'wellbeing'. This remark offers a basis for interpersonal comparisons of wellbeing that is like mine. Unfortunately, Harsanyi confuses it with the different basis that he thinks comes from extended preferences; see my 'Extended preferences' for details. I think Arrow intends to make the same point in *Social Choice and Individual Values*, pp. 114–15, and 'Extended sympathy and the possibility of social choice', pp. 159–60 in the reprinted version. But Arrow's remarks are so brief that I cannot be sure.

6

Quantities of temporal wellbeing

Chapter 5 made sense of a quantitative scale of wellbeing for each person, and explained how different people's scales are comparable. But our distributions of wellbeing also require, for each person, a scale of her wellbeing at each time in her life. This chapter develops such a temporal scale. Its argument runs closely parallel with chapter 5's, so I can run through it quickly. Section 6.1 corresponds to section 5.2; section 6.2 to section 5.3.

6.1 A cardinal scale of temporal wellbeing

Once again, I shall take betterness relations as the basis for the scales we need. This time, I shall take people's *temporal* betterness relations. A person p's temporal betterness relation for time t is:

$$... \text{ is better for } p \text{ at } t \text{ than } \_\_.$$

I take it for granted that we understand temporal betterness. Pleasure, for instance, is good, and it comes at a particular time. Other things being equal, it is better for you at time t to have more pleasure at that time, rather than less. Eating a large cream cake is good for you now if it gives you pleasure, but it may be bad for you later on.

I do not insist that everything that is good or bad for you is good or bad for you at a particular time. Some of your goods may be pattern goods. These do not form part of your temporal wellbeing at any time; instead, they show up in the pattern of your temporal wellbeing over time. There may also be goods for you that do not show up even in the pattern of temporal wellbeing. Section 3.3 discusses goods of that sort.

Not all the influences on your temporal wellbeing at a particular time need be events that occur at that time. How well off you are at a time often depends on what happens at other times. The dependency may be through physical causation: how you feel in the morning may depend on what you did the night before. There may also be non-causal sorts of dependency. For example, completing an important and difficult task may be good for you at the time you complete it, and the goodness of completing it may depend on how much effort you put into the task at all the times you were working on it. In section 3.3 I mentioned various other ways in which wellbeing at one time might depend on events at earlier or later times.

For any person p and time t, pick out all the histories in which p exists at t. Then pick out all the prospects that are made up out of those histories. In each of these prospects it is certain that p is alive at t.

I argued in *Weighing Goods*[1] that, among prospects from this restricted class, p's temporal betterness relation, dated to t, conforms to the axioms of expected utility theory. Consequently it can be represented by a utility function. That is to say, there is a function $U_t^p(\cdot)$ such that $U_t^p(A)$ is greater than $U_t^p(B)$ if and only if A is better for p at t than B is. Furthermore, this function is expectational. It is also cardinal: any other expectational function representing the same betterness relation is an increasing linear transform of $U_t^p(\cdot)$.

On page 90, I adopted Bernoulli's hypothesis. I did so as a way of making precise our vague quantitative notion of wellbeing. Because it is intuitively vague, we have a choice about how to measure wellbeing on a precise scale. This was the way I chose. I shall now do the same for temporal wellbeing. I shall adopt this temporal version of Bernoulli's hypothesis:

> *Bernoulli's hypothesis, temporal version.* One prospect is better for a person at a time than another if and only if it gives the person a greater expectation of wellbeing at the time than the other.

Granted this hypothesis, it follows that the temporal utility function for a person at a time provides a cardinal scale of the person's wellbeing at that time. Bernoulli's hypothesis cardinalizes the scale of temporal wellbeing. In effect, it defines quantities of temporal wellbeing for us.

It is not the only possible way to cardinalize temporal wellbeing. I shall mention an alternative on page 226.

Having adopted Bernoulli's hypothesis, I no longer need to speak of utility. A person's temporal utility function provides a cardinal measure of her temporal wellbeing. If a person p lives at time t in some history h, on page 25 I assigned the symbol g_t^p to her temporal wellbeing at the time. g_t^p can now be identified with her utility $U_t^p(h)$.

6.2 Comparing wellbeing between times

That is the first step in the development of a quantitative notion of temporal wellbeing. Because it is exactly analogous to the development of a cardinal scale for the wellbeing of an individual, I have taken that step quickly. The next step is analogous too. We have to make sense of comparisons between a person's wellbeing at one time and her wellbeing at another. We might, for instance, want to say that some change improves a person's life at one time by more than it damages her life at another time. If I claim that the eventual benefits of running are greater than the unpleasantness of the running itself, what exactly does that mean?

In section 5.3, I explained the answer I gave in *Weighing Goods* to the corresponding question about interpersonal comparisons of wellbeing. I called on general betterness to give sense to comparison of wellbeing between people. Similarly, we might now call on a higher betterness relation to give sense to intertemporal comparisons of wellbeing. We might appeal to what is better for the *person*, in order to give sense to comparisons between the person's wellbeings at different times. We might interpret my claim about running like this: it is better for you to run than not. Running brings benefits in later life that count for more than the present pain it causes, in determining your overall, lifetime wellbeing.

However, I argued in section 5.3 that this approach was a mistake for interpersonal comparisons. It is a mistake for intertemporal comparisons too. It surely makes sense to think that a given amount of wellbeing counts differently at different stages in a life. David Velleman says that 'one and the same increment in one's momentary well-being may have a greater or lesser effect on the value of one's life, depending on when and how it occurs'.[2] Whether or not he is right, what he says makes sense. So the meaning of a quantity of wellbeing at a time cannot be determined by how much that wellbeing counts in a lifetime assessment.

Instead I shall take a route to intertemporal comparisons that is parallel to the one I took in section 5.3. Its basis is this: how well off a person is at a time depends only on how things are for her at that time. If things are for a person at one time exactly as they are for her at another, she is equally well off at both those times. By 'how things are for a person at a time' I mean the collection of all those features of the world that make a difference to how the world is from the perspective of the person at that time. In section 5.3, I called the way the world is from the perspective of a person a 'life'; let us now call the way the world is from the viewpoint of a person at a time a *way of life*. A way of life has to be conceived broadly enough to encompass everything that influences the wellbeing of a person at a time.

If someone were to live in exactly the same way at one time in her life as she does at another, she would be equally as well off at one time as at the other. Her wellbeing at a time depends only on her way of life at the time. We can therefore consider her wellbeing at the time to be simply the goodness of the way of life.

From here, an argument exactly parallel to the one on pages 95–6 will lead us to a scale of goodness for all of a person's ways of life. The parallel argument requires some ways of life to be possible at different times in a person's life. Could a person lead the same way of life at different times? I do not mean: could she repeat the same way of life twice in a life? I mean: is there a way of life such that she could lead it at one time and also such that she could lead it at a different time? I assume so. This means I assume that a person's precise age, or the precise date when a way of life is led, is not a part of how things are for the person at a time.

I am not assuming that any way of life could be led at any age. No doubt that is false. A teenager's way of life is presumably not possible for an octogenarian. But I do not need as much as that. The argument on pages 95–6 shows what I do need. I need that any time in a person's life overlaps with some other time to the extent that two ways of life that are possible at one of those times are also possible at the other. Furthermore, any two times in the life are linked by a chain of such overlapping pairs. Nearby times undoubtedly overlap to this extent. Some of the ways of life that are available to a thirty-year-old are certainly also available to a thirty-one-year old. By taking small steps in age, we can link all the times in a life by overlapping pairs.

This is all the argument needs. So we have a scale of goodness for all of a person's possible ways of life. Equivalently, we have an intertemporally comparable scale of temporal wellbeing for a person.

This scale also needs to be comparable between people. Here there are no extra problems. A person who is leading a way of life is exactly as well off as anyone else would be who was leading that way of life. I have already assumed on page 96 that lives can be lived by different people, to the extent that was needed for setting up an interpersonally comparable scale of lifetime wellbeing. Given that, we need have no further qualms about a parallel assumption for ways of life. That way, we can get the interpersonal comparability we need.

The symbol g_t^p, which stands for a person p's wellbeing at a time t, now has a meaning that allows comparisons both between people and between times in a life.

A zero for temporal wellbeing

A final note. I have not yet fixed a zero for temporal wellbeing, and I shall not do so precisely now. But chapter 1 contains diagrams in which a zero for temporal wellbeing is implicit, so I ought to say something about what I mean by it. In section 4.2 I mentioned the temporal sense of 'a life worth living'. I shall use that to fix a zero. I assign zero temporal wellbeing to a way of life that is just on the borderline between being worth living and being not worth living. This is done with more precision in section 17.2.

Notes

1 p. 226.
2 'Well-being and time', p. 52.

7

Separability of times

In chapter 1, I posed the general problem for this book as setting a value on a distribution of wellbeing. Wellbeing is distributed across a grid, whose dimensions are people, time and states of nature, and all this wellbeing comes together to determine the overall value of the distribution. How? Now I am ready to start work on this problem.

I said I would particularly concentrate on two-dimensional distributions of people and times. Examples are shown in figure 11 on page 12 and figure 12 on page 24. How is wellbeing aggregated across a two-dimensional grid?

To approach this problem, we might naturally hope to aggregate wellbeing across the dimensions separately, taking them one at a time. We might hope to do this in either order: first across times and then across people, or first across people and then across times. In section 7.1, I shall describe these two routes to aggregation in a bit more detail. I call them, respectively, 'the people route' and 'the snapshot route'. The rest of this chapter explains why I shall not take the snapshot route. Section 7.2 presents a *prima facie* case against it. Section 7.3 describes and rejects a counter-case. Section 7.4 describes a different sort of counter-case, which section 7.5 rejects in turn. By the end of the chapter, I hope the snapshot route will seem unattractive. At any rate, I do not think we have good grounds for taking it. Chapter 8 starts work on the people route, which I prefer.

7.1 Routes to aggregation

The idea of the people route is this. A distribution gives each person some amount of temporal wellbeing at each time in her life. We first determine a value of the distribution for each person, by aggregating across all the times in the person's life. In one of my diagrams, we first scan across the horizontal lines. We arrive at a valuation for each person by looking along the line that represents the person in the diagram. In some way we compound together all the temporal wellbeing we find spread along this line. We do this for every person – for every line in the diagram. That is the first step in the aggregation. The second step is to put together all these valuations – one for each person – that we have arrived at in the first step. This is a step of aggregation across people, and it brings us to an overall value for the distribution.

On the other hand, to take the snapshot route to aggregation, we first judge the value of the distribution at each time, by aggregating across all the people at that time. In a diagram, we scan a vertical rather than a horizontal line. We take everyone's temporal wellbeing at a single time, and put together all these amounts of wellbeing, to determine how good the distribution is at that time. This gives us what I shall call a 'snap-shot' valuation of the distribution at that time. We make a snapshot valuation for every time. Then we aggregate all these snapshot valuations across time, to determine the overall value of the distribution.

Each of these approaches involves an assumption. Take the snapshot route. It implicitly assumes that a snapshot valuation makes sense. Scanning the distribution along the vertical line that represents a particular time, and looking only at all the people's wellbeing at that time, it assumes we can arrive at a valuation for that time. That is to say, it assumes we can value the distribution of wellbeing at that time independently of the rest of the distribution – independently of people's wellbeings at other times. It assumes aggregation is possible at any time independently of other times. Moreover, the temporal aggregates we arrive at – the snapshot valuations for each time – must be enough, taken together, to determine the overall value of the distribution.

This two-part assumption is technically known as 'separability of times'.[1] It can be expressed in terms of the value function that I set up in section 2.3. This function represents the goodness of the distribution in terms of the condition of each person at each time. It has this form in general:

(7.1.1) $\quad v(g_1^1, g_2^1, \ldots g_T^1, g_1^2, g_2^2, \ldots g_T^2, g_1^3, g_2^3, \ldots g_T^3, \ldots).$

If, and only if, times are separable in the distribution, this function can be expressed in the form:

(7.1.2) $\quad \underline{v}(v_1(g_1^1, g_1^2, g_1^3 \ldots), v_2(g_2^1, g_2^2, g_2^3 \ldots), \ldots v_T(g_T^1, g_T^2, g_T^3 \ldots)),$

where v_1, v_2, and so on are all real numbers, and the function $\underline{v}(\cdot)$ is increasing in each of its arguments. To put this more precisely: if and only if times are separable, there are functions $v_1(\cdot)$, $v_2(\cdot)$, and so on, such that the goodness of distributions can be represented by a value function of the form (7.1.2), where $\underline{v}(\cdot)$ is increasing in each of its arguments. (A function is said to be *increasing* in one of its arguments if and only if the value of the function increases whenever the value of the argument increases while the other arguments remain constant.)

In (7.1.2) we can interpret $v_1(\cdot)$, $v_2(\cdot)$, and so on as themselves value functions, representing snapshot valuations at each time. But (7.1.2) does not determine these functions very tightly. Any increasing transforms of them could be fitted into the separable formula (7.1.2) just as well. On page 27, I explained that this is the mark of an ordinal value function. Each of these functions represents the snapshot value of the distribution at a time, but only in an ordinal way.

The snapshot route to aggregation requires the assumption that times are separable. The people route requires a parallel assumption that people are separable. In formal terms, to assume people are separable is to assume that the value function can be expressed in this form:

$$\bar{v}(v^1(g_1{}^1, g_2{}^1, \ldots g_T{}^1), \, v^2(g_1{}^2, g_2{}^2, \ldots g_T{}^2), \, v^3(g_1{}^3, g_2{}^3, \ldots g_T{}^3), \, \ldots)$$

where the values of $v^1(\cdot)$, $v^2(\cdot)$, and so on are all real numbers, and the function $\bar{v}(\cdot)$ is increasing in each of its arguments. This is the formal condition, but its interpretation is not straightforward. I shall leave it to chapter 8, where it will also turn out that a slightly weaker assumption will suffice. I only mention it here for the sake of comparison. The rest of this chapter concentrates on the assumption that times are separable.

7.2 The objection to separability of times

Snapshot valuations are implicit in a great deal of our thinking about the progress of wellbeing. We talk about how well off people are in a country, and this means how well off they are in that country at the present time. We talk about improvement in wellbeing over time, and how inequality in wellbeing changes. All of this implicitly involves setting a value on the distribution of wellbeing at a time, and watching how that value develops over time. So even if we are not intending to take the second step of aggregating the snapshot values across time, snapshot values commonly have a place in our thinking.

However, I shall argue that separability of times is a dubious assumption, so snapshot valuations and the snapshot route to aggregation are both dubious. At least, I shall argue that separability of times commits us to much more than most of us would be willing to accept. My principal aim in this chapter is to make this point.

Table 1

		Times					Times	
		1	2				1	2
	p	1	1			p	Ω	1
People					People			
	q	Ω	Ω			q	1	Ω

        Distribution A   Distribution C

		Times					Times	
		1	2				1	2
	p	1	Ω			p	Ω	Ω
People					People			
	q	Ω	1			q	1	1

        Distribution B   Distribution D

I shall start with the example shown in table 1. (I often find it more convenient to present examples in tables rather than in diagrams like those in chapter 1.) For simplicity, the example contains only two people and two times. The four quadrants of the table show four different possible distributions. The cells show the two people's condition at each time. That is to say, each cell shows a person's wellbeing at a time, unless it contains an 'Ω' to indicate that the person is not alive at that time. Whenever a person is alive, in this example I have always made her wellbeing just one unit. This is for simplicity again.

In A, person p lives through both times and q never lives at all. In B, p lives for one time and then dies, and q lives instead for the second time. We might say that in B, q 'replaces' p. Similarly, in D, q lives through both times and p never lives at all. In C, p replaces q.

To construct this example, I have assumed that a particular person could come into existence at one time, or alternatively at a different time. This is possible. With modern reproductive technology, indeed, it is even practicable. At several places in this book I shall take its possibility for granted.

What can we say about the relative goodness of A, B, C and D in table 1? Compare A and B first. In the first period, these two distributions are identical: in both of them, p is alive and q is not. If times are separable, we can judge between *A* and *B* on the basis of the two periods separately, and in the first period there is nothing to choose between them. Which is better therefore depends on the second period only. For the moment, let us not try and settle which is better in the second period.

Instead, let us now start to compare *C* and *D*. This pair of distributions is also identical in the first period. So if times are separable, which of the two is better depends on the second period only. Now, the difference between *C* and *D* in the second period is exactly the same as the difference between *A* and *B* in the second period. In the second period, *A* and *C* both have *p* alive and *q* not alive, and *B* and *D* both have *q* alive and *p* not alive.

It follows that *A* is better than *B* if and only if *C* is better than *D*, if times are separable. However, this is an intuitively implausible conclusion. *A* and *D* each have a particular advantage over *B* and *C*. They each contain one long life rather than two short lives. In *A*, *p* continues to live through both times, whereas in *B* she dies and is replaced by *q*. We normally think it better that a person continues to live rather than that she is replaced. So intuitively *A* may well be better than *B* and also *D* better than *C*. This is inconsistent with separability of times.

It is surely true that our intuition normally rates continued life better than replacement. For instance, we think it better to save the life of a baby if we can, rather than let her die, even if, were she to die, her parents would replace her with another baby. There may be limits to this intuition. I am not sure we would think it better to prolong a 100-year-old person's life for another 100 years, rather than have a new person live for 100 years. But we take prolonging life to be better than saving life in some cases, and that is enough to contradict separability of times.

To put it differently, we intuitively value longevity, at least within limits. Let me specify what I mean by valuing longevity. Suppose some total amount of time is lived by people, at some level of temporal wellbeing. For longevity to be valuable means that, given this fixed total of time and level of temporal wellbeing, it is better for the time to be divided up amongst fewer lives rather than amongst more lives.

In each quadrant of table 1, the total amount of life lived is the same, and the level of temporal wellbeing is constant. In *A* and *D* the time is all included in one life, whereas in *B* and *C* it is divided between two. So if longevity is valuable by my definition, *A* and *D* are better.

We normally value longevity. Yet the length of a person's life is not something that shows up when we look at times separately. It only appears when we look at several times together. So it is a value that cannot show up in a snapshot valuation. This is a strong reason to doubt separability of times.

7.3 Separatism

The objection I raised against separability is based only on the intuitive thought that longevity is valuable. One possible response to this objection is simply to deny it. This is a hard-headed, intuitively implausible response, but it is possible. I shall call it the 'separatist' view. Separatism implies that times are separable.

When we look at the wellbeing of people at a single time – surveying a vertical line in one of my diagrams – we see a lot of little pieces of wellbeing, each belonging to a different person. In the snapshot, we do not see how the pieces of wellbeing are connected with other pieces in a horizontal direction. We do not see how pieces are packaged together to make up particular lives. That is why the length of people's lives does not appear in a snapshot valuation. Yet the horizontal packaging of wellbeing seems intuitively to make a real difference to value; it is better for wellbeing to be packaged into fewer rather than more lives. The separatist denies this.

Separatism implies that horizontal connections really make no difference. All that matters is the little pieces of wellbeing that appear at each time, not their packaging in lives. Consequently, longevity is not valuable – at least, not in the sense I defined. If a person's life is prolonged, and other things remain the same, the effect is to add pieces of wellbeing to the distribution at the end of her life. A separatist values those added pieces. So in this sense she values prolonging life. But she does not value the fact that the added pieces are joined on to the end of a life that already exists. To a separatist, they might just as well be put into a new life; replacement would be just as good as prolonging an existing life. If a person dies and a new person appears in her place to enjoy the same wellbeing, that is just as good as the first person's continuing to live.

The separatist opinion that horizontal connections make no difference is an extreme version of the view that personal identity does not matter, which was propounded by Derek Parfit in part III of *Reasons and Persons*. Parfit arrives at his own less extreme view on metaphysical grounds. I shall outline a metaphysical argument for separatism in section 15.2; this argument is simply an extension of Parfit's. On page 257, I shall explain how separatism can also follow from a particular theory about the nature of wellbeing. So separatism can be given a philosophical basis, despite its implausibility.

I think separatism is a defensible view. However, it is innately implausible, and I do not think the defences are so convincing that I would rely on them. I shall not assume separatism in this book. I shall return to consider it in section 18.2.

I can mention now the simplest example of a separatist theory of value. It is a view I shall call *complete utilitarianism*. A complete utilitarian thinks the value of a distribution is simply the total of all the temporal wellbeing enjoyed at any time by anyone. To arrive at an overall value, we simply add wellbeing across the whole distribution: across people and across times. One distribution is better than another if and only if it has a greater total of wellbeing. A complete utilitarian does not care in any way about how wellbeing is distributed. For one thing, she does not care how it is packaged into individual lives. All that matters is wellbeing; who gets wellbeing is irrelevant.

7.4 Dispersing the value of longevity

In section 7.2 I suggested that times are not separable, and I am now considering responses to that suggestion. One counter-argument is the tough separatist one set out in section 7.3. But there is also a more pragmatic way to try and preserve separability in the face of the objection presented in section 7.2.

I said the value of longevity does not show up when we look at times separately, but only when we look at several times together. Consequently, it does not show up in snapshot valuations. But we can artificially make it show up. We can simply take a person's longevity – the length of her life – to be part of her temporal wellbeing at every time in her life. I shall mention a possible justification of this move on page 112–13. First I am going to compare it with other, parallel moves in the theory of value.

As a matter of terminology, I shall keep the term 'separatism' for the hard-headed view that gives no value to longevity. So I do not count this new defence of separability as a version of separatism. It is an example of a strategy within the theory of value that I call the 'dispersion' of value. I shall take a moderately doubtful stance towards the application of dispersion to longevity. Perhaps dispersion can save separability of times, but it will face difficulties in doing so. In *Weighing Goods*, I endorsed dispersion in other contexts, and used it to defend separability in those contexts. But I shall certainly not endorse dispersion for longevity. Consequently, I am not willing to assume separability of times. In this section, I shall explain the difficulties that dispersion encounters.

For the sake of comparison, let me start by mentioning a different application of this strategy. It defends separability of people, rather than separability of times. Separability of people can seem to be threatened by the value of equality. If equality is valuable, one might think its value cannot belong to any individual person, because it depends on a relation between people: it depends on the difference between some people's wellbeing and others'. It seems we first need to determine how well off each person is, before we can see how equal the distribution is. Consequently, the value of equality must be a purely social value, separate from each individual's wellbeing. So one might argue, and this argument threatens separability of people. It is developed in section 8.2 of this book.

Section 8.2 also answers this argument, using a counter-argument from *Weighing Goods*.[2] If equality is indeed a good thing, it is so because it is good for individual people. Conversely, if inequality is a bad thing, it is so because it is bad for individual people. The badness of inequality is not a separate negative value beyond people's own wellbeing. It is part of people's wellbeing itself. This argument is an example of dispersion. At first, equality seems to be a social value that cannot be captured within the wellbeing of individuals. But I took this apparently social value and dispersed it among the individuals. I argued it actually belongs to the individuals separately, despite first appearances.

It may be helpful if I compare dispersion with the assumption of distribution described in section 3.3. The assumption of distribution rules out goods that do not show up in the distribution of wellbeing. It rules out some types of good but not what I called on page 44 'pattern goods'. These are goods whose presence shows up in the pattern of the distribution, though not at any particular location in the distribution. Even if equality of wellbeing is not an individual good, it is certainly a pattern good. So it is consistent with the assumption of distribution.

However, the effect of separability is to rule out pattern goods; it requires all goods to appear at particular locations in the distribution. For example, if people are separable, we can evaluate a distribution by looking at each person separately; we do not have to look for patterns across people. The strategy of dispersion aims to support separability, so it needs to go beyond the assumption of distribution. It takes a particular good that at first seems a pattern good, and locates it at a particular place, or several particular places, in the distribution. For instance, it locates the good of equality, which at first seems a pattern good, at particular people.

An essential part of this strategy of dispersion is to justify it.[3] I ought not really to call it a 'strategy' at all. That term suggests we theorists of value are free to disperse value as we like. But truly the strategy is to make the substantive claim that value actually is dispersed. Take any value that apparently does not belong to people as individuals, so it seems to contradict separability of people. Let it be the survival of a culture, say; suppose this is indeed valuable. A theorist could always disperse this value in a formal way by arbitrarily dividing it into parts and allocating each part to a person. She could then say that each person's allocated part was a component of that person's wellbeing. But this would not be a correct move unless the theorist could demonstrate that the survival of the culture was indeed part of the person's wellbeing.

The justification needs to be made for whatever specific value is in question. In the case of the survival of a culture, it might or might not be convincing. In the case of equality, I hope I made it convincing in *Weighing Goods*[4] by producing an account of the value of equality in terms of fairness. This account made it definitely an individual value.

Unless an instance of dispersion is genuine in this way, it will be no help with aggregation. If we know the aggregate value of a distribution, we can always disperse the value arbitrarily to people. But to do that, we would have to know the aggregate value first. Since we are trying to find aggregate value, this arbitrary manoeuvre would be pointless. On the other hand, if the value is genuinely a part of each individual's wellbeing, we should be able to assess the amount of it individually for each person, and then include it in an aggregation across people.

Is it justified to disperse the value of longevity to individual times? If we knew the aggregate value of a distribution, including the value of longevity, it could be arbitrarily divided up and dispersed among the times separately. So without doubt the aggregate can be arbitrarily dispersed in such a way that the dispersed parts could be re-aggregated to reach the correct result. But as I say, arbitrary dispersion is not enough. The value of longevity must genuinely be dispersed.

I doubt it is. I suspect that the value of longevity truly belongs to a life as a whole, and not to any of the separate times within the life. But I shall not insist on that, and I recognize that dispersion can be defended. Here is one possible defence.[5] In our lives we undertake various projects that take time to complete. Leaving a project uncompleted is a bad thing; it is better for us to complete each project, rather than not.

Moreover, the goodness of completing a project is located at all the time we are engaged on the project. If a project is completed, that gives a special value to the time we spend on it. It increases our wellbeing during that time. Conversely, if a project is not completed, all that time is devalued. Death generally cuts off some of our projects. The shorter our life, the fewer completions we shall achieve. This tends to devalue the time we are alive; it reduces our wellbeing while we live. In a long life we shall complete more, and this tends to add value to the time we are alive. Here is a possible explanation of why longevity is valuable, and it locates its value at the times we are alive. It gives longevity a dispersed value.

7.5 Can dispersion be successful?

I shall not try to assess the justification for dispersion. Instead, I shall show that, in any case, it is difficult to make dispersion do the job we require from it. It may not succeed in supporting separability of times against the challenge of longevity, which is its purpose.

The idea of dispersion is to divide up the value of a person's longevity and allocate the parts to the various times in the person's life. Let us try out this idea in the example of table 2. The cells of the table show the people's conditions at different times. Anyone who is alive at any time has the same level of wellbeing, 1. I mean this to be the level of her

Table 2

		Times						Times			
		1	2	3	4			1	2	3	4
	1	1	Ω	Ω	Ω		1	1	1	Ω	Ω
	2	Ω	1	Ω	Ω		2	1	1	Ω	Ω
People	3	Ω	Ω	1	Ω	People	3	Ω	Ω	1	1
	4	Ω	Ω	Ω	1		4	Ω	Ω	1	1
	5	1	1	1	1		5	Ω	Ω	Ω	Ω

Distribution *A*   Distribution *B* wellbeing without taking account of the value of longevity. I shall add this supposed value later.

In both A and B, if we take a snapshot of the distribution at any time, we see two people alive, each having wellbeing 1. In this example, I shall assume impartiality between the people. By this I mean that the bare identity of the people cannot make a difference to value. A snapshot taken at each time will therefore have to account A and B as equally good at the time.

If times are separable it would follow that, as a whole, each of these two distributions is equally good, provided we do not accord any dispersed value to longevity. A separatist will think they are indeed equally good, but that is because she gives no special value to longevity. If we do value longevity, we shall value B above A. In either distribution, the total time lived is eight periods. In A this total is divided amongst five people. In B it is divided amongst four people. If longevity is valuable, according to the definition I gave on page 108, B is better than A.

This conclusion has nothing to do with the inequality in A. In this example, let us ignore any value equality may have.

Can we reach the same conclusion in a separable fashion, by means of dispersion? This might depend on how, specifically, we disperse the value of longevity to individual times, and there are many ways of doing that. Whichever way we choose will need to be justified, but I shall now set aside questions of justification. I shall just try out some obvious ways of doing the dispersion.

Table 3

		Times					Times		
	1	2	3	4		1	2	3	4
1	$1+a$	Ω	Ω	Ω	1	$1+2a$	$1+2a$	Ω	Ω
2	Ω	$1+a$	Ω	Ω	2	$1+2a$	$1+2a$	Ω	Ω
People 3	Ω	Ω	$1+a$	Ω	People 3	Ω	Ω	$1+2a$	$1+2a$
4	Ω	Ω	Ω	$1+a$	4	Ω	Ω	$1+2a$	$1+2a$
5	$1+4a$	$1+4a$	$1+4a$	$1+4a$	5	Ω	Ω	Ω	Ω

Distribution A	Distribution B

One way is to suppose that the length of a person's life adds to her wellbeing at all times in her life, in proportion to its length. Table 3 shows the people's wellbeing adjusted according to this principle. (The number a is the constant of proportionality.) With the dispersion done, we can now try evaluating the distribution at each time separately. At each time, people's total wellbeing in A is greater than in B. So is their average wellbeing. If we assume separability of times, these facts strongly suggest A is better than B at every time. Consequently, they strongly suggest A is the better distribution. But if longevity is valuable, we have previously concluded the opposite: that B is the better distribution.

To be sure, the conclusion that A is better than B is not inescapable. At any time, we need not aggregate across people simply by taking their total wellbeing, or their average wellbeing. But I cannot see what other procedure could be justified. True, A is an unequal distribution, whereas B is equal, and the value of equality might justify a different way of aggregating. But I have set this consideration aside because the value of longevity makes B better than A independently of the value of equality. So this way of doing the dispersion does not achieve what it aimed to achieve.

A second way is to suppose that a person's wellbeing at a time is increased by the amount of life she has in front of her. Table 4 shows this possibility. Again, with the dispersion done, let us try evaluating the distribution at each time separately. Distribution A turns out to be

Table 4

		Times						Times		
		1	2	3	4			1	2	3	4
	1	1	Ω	Ω	Ω		1	$1+a$	1	Ω	Ω
	2	Ω	1	Ω	Ω		2	$1+a$	1	Ω	Ω
People	3	Ω	Ω	1	Ω	People	3	Ω	Ω	$1+a$	1
	4	Ω	Ω	Ω	1		4	Ω	Ω	$1+a$	1
	5	$1+3a$	$1+2a$	$1+a$	1		5	Ω	Ω	Ω	Ω

Distribution A Distribution B

ahead of *B* in total and average wellbeing in two out of the four times, and behind *B* in only one. Once again, the conclusion that *A* is better is strongly suggested, if times are separable. Again, I can see no credible way of escaping this conclusion. So this way to disperse the value of longevity seems no more successful than the other in preserving separability.

I recognize that this case against dispersion is not conclusive. My arguments are not watertight, and I have not considered all the ways the dispersion might be done. Still, my example does show a fundamental difficulty in making dispersion successful. The trouble is that long-lived people live a long time. They live at many times, therefore. This means their wellbeing gets counted more often in a separable evaluation than does the wellbeing of shorter-lived people. If we disperse the value of longevity into people's wellbeing at times, the effect is that too much weight will be given to the lifetimes of the longer-lived people. For this reason, I doubt that dispersion can work.

The upshot of all this argument is that I doubt times are separable. Perhaps they are, and perhaps some argument can be found to show they are. But in this book, I shall not assume they are. I shall therefore not rely on snapshot valuations, and I shall avoid the snapshot route to aggregation.

Notes

1 Separability is explained in my *Weighing Goods*, chapter 4.
2 Section 9.4.
3 See the discussion of dispersion in *Weighing Goods*, pp. 191–2.
4 Section 9.4.
5 Rüdiger Bittner and Rolf Stoeker made this argument to me.

8

Separability of lives

In section 7.1, I described two alternative routes to aggregating wellbeing across a two-dimensional distribution of wellbeing. I then argued we should not follow the snapshot route. It relies on the assumption that times are separable, which I find dubious.

The alternative I favour is the people route. It also relies on a separability assumption. This chapter starts in section 8.1 by distinguishing two related separability assumptions: separability of people and separability of lives. Separability of lives is the weaker of the two, but it will turn out in section 8.4 to be sufficient for justifying the people route to aggregation. I shall postpone to chapter 13 a discussion of whether people are separable. But I shall argue that lives are separable in section 8.2 of this chapter.

The main basis of my argument is something I call the principle of personal good. Section 8.3 explains that this principle is inconsistent with discounting future wellbeing. If we accept discounting, that will force a modification on the principle. However, it will do no damage to the argument that lives are separable.

Section 8.5 introduces a technical assumption we shall need in due course.

8.1 Separability of people and separability of lives

To assume people are separable is to assume that the value function

$$v(g_1^{\,1}, g_2^{\,1}, \ldots g_T^{\,1}, g_1^{\,2}, g_2^{\,2}, \ldots g_T^{\,2}, g_1^{\,3}, g_2^{\,3}, \ldots g_T^{\,3}, \ldots)$$

can be expressed in this specific form:

(8.1.1) $\bar{v}(v^1(g_1^{\,1}, g_2^{\,1}, \ldots g_T^{\,1}), v^2(g_1^{\,2}, g_2^{\,2}, \ldots g_T^{\,2}), v^3(g_1^{\,3}, g_2^{\,3}, \ldots g_T^{\,3}), \ldots),$

where the values of $v^1(\cdot)$, $v^2(\cdot)$, and so on are all real numbers, and the function $\bar{v}(\cdot)$ is increasing in each of its arguments. To put the assumption differently: there are functions $v^1(\cdot)$, $v^2(\cdot)$, and so on such that the goodness of the distribution can be represented by a function of the form (8.1.1), where $\bar{v}(\cdot)$ is increasing in each of its arguments.

The formula (8.1.1) says that all the conditions g_t^p of a particular person can be grouped and valued together, independently of the conditions of anyone else. The resulting values, one for each person, together determine the goodness of the distribution.

The question of whether people are separable divides into two questions. The first is about the general value of a person's wellbeing: about the amount that a person's wellbeing contributes to the value of a distribution. Is this value independent of the conditions of other people? That is the subject of this chapter. The second question is about the general value of a person's existence: the amount her existence contributes to the value of a distribution. Is this value independent of the conditions of other people? I shall take up this second question in chapter 13.

The previous paragraph separated the two questions intuitively. I am now going to separate them formally. However, if you are not mathematically inclined you may find the formal distinction a little hard to grasp. That should not matter much, since the intuitive separation is straightforward.

First, remember the distribution we are evaluating may have gaps in the place of people who exist in some other distribution but not this one.[1] The formal mark of p's nonexistence in a distribution is that all her conditions g_t^p, at every time, are Ω.[2] In that case, the value attributed to p in (8.1.1) is $v^p(\Omega, \Omega, \ldots \Omega)$. An essential feature of separability of people, expressed in (8.1.1), is that all the values of $v^1(\cdot)$, $v^2(\cdot)$, and so on are *numbers*. In particular, $v^p(\Omega, \Omega, \ldots \Omega)$ is a number. Separability of people requires a numerical value to be assigned to a person's nonexistence. Since the value is a number, it will be comparable with the numbers that are assigned to the various possible lives the person might lead. To speak roughly, if people are separable, nonexistence has a value that can be put alongside the values of all the lives the person might lead.

Are we not interested in the value of existence rather than the value of nonexistence? Not exactly, because there is no unique value of existence. When a person exists she leads a particular life, and her living one life has a different value from her living a different life. In effect, it is the value of nonexistence that tells us the value of existence. If a particular life has a higher value than the value of nonexistence, then that life is valuable: it is better that it be lived rather than not. If another particular life has a lower value than the value of nonexistence, then that life is not valuable: it is better that it not be lived rather than lived.

But all this is a matter of the value of a person's existence or nonexistence, and I shall postpone this aspect of separability to chapter 13. In this present chapter, I shall concentrate on the implications of separability for people who do exist at some time in the distribution we are considering. If p is such a person, then for at least one time t, g_t^p is not Ω but a number.

If people are separable, each person who lives has a life that can be valued independently of other people's conditions. To concentrate on this feature of separability, setting aside the value of nonexistence, I shall define a weaker condition than separability of people. I shall call it 'separability of lives'. When I say lives are separable, I mean that any person's life, when it exists, can be evaluated independently of other people's conditions. That is to say, it can be evaluated independently of whether or not any other particular person lives, and independently of any other person's wellbeing.

To put this formally, separability of lives requires that the value function can be expressed in the form (8.1.1), but this time the v^ps are not all required to be numbers. They must be numbers if p lives. But I do not insist that $v^p(\Omega, \Omega, \ldots \Omega)$ has a numerical value. It may have some non-numerical value. It does not matter what this non-numerical value is; it simply acts as a marker in the formula (8.1.1) to indicate a person's nonexistence. Allowing a non-numerical value means that nonexistence need not be put on the same scale of value as existence. (This remark is qualified on page 143.) Separability of lives is not concerned with the value of a person's existence.

The function $\bar{v}(\cdot)$ is still required to be increasing in each of its arguments. But since some of its arguments may take a non-numerical value, this requirement needs to be interpreted with care. A function is increasing in one of its arguments if and only if its value increases whenever the value of the argument increases (and other arguments remain constant). When the argument may take a non-numerical value, the same definition still applies, but one feature of it needs special emphasis. The value of an argument increases only if it changes from one numerical value to a greater numerical value. If the argument changes from a non-numerical value to a numerical value, or vice versa, the change is not an increase. So the definition of an increasing function stipulates nothing about the behaviour of the function when the argument changes from a non-numerical value to a numerical one, or vice versa.

To say that $\bar{v}(\cdot)$ is increasing in each of its arguments means that whenever the value of $v^p(\cdot)$ for any p increases from some numerical value to a greater one, then $\bar{v}$ increases. It implies nothing about the effect on $\bar{v}$ when the value of $v^p(\cdot)$ changes from a non-numerical value to a numerical one or vice versa. That is to say, it implies nothing about the effect of someone's existence or nonexistence on the overall value of the distribution.

8.2 The argument for separability of lives

Are lives separable? I shall argue they are, on the basis of two principles, which I call respectively the principles of personal good and of temporal good. In this section, I shall first set out these principles and derive separability from them. Then I shall say something about their interpretation, and finally begin to assess their truth. Not much needs to be said about the principle of temporal good, but the principle of personal good is more complex. Section 8.3 continues the discussion of it.

> *Principle of personal good.* Take two distributions A and B that certainly have the same population. If A is equally as good as B for each member of the population, then A is equally as good as B. Also, if A is at least as good as B for each member of the population, and if A is better than B for some member of the population, then A is better than B.

> *Principle of temporal good.* Take any person p. Take two distributions A and B that are such that p certainly exists in both and is certainly alive at exactly the same times in A as she is in B. If A is equally as good for p as B at all times p is alive, then A is equally as good for p as B. Also, if A is at least as good for p as B at each time p is alive, and if A is better for p than B at some time p is alive, then A is better for p than B.

Remember that in this chapter we are concerned only with distributions that contain no uncertainty. So for the moment the word 'certainly' is redundant in these principles. I shall say more about it on page 123.

Derivation

To derive separability of lives, think first about a pair of distributions that have the same population. Suppose each member of the population has the same wellbeing in one of these distributions as she does in the other. According to the principle of personal good, these two distributions are equally good. It follows that a distribution's goodness depends only on its population, and on the wellbeing of every member of its population.

That is, a distribution's goodness depends only on each person's condition; it is a function of all the people's conditions. In symbols, it can be represented by a function of the form:

(8.2.1) $$\bar{v}(g^1, g^2, g^3, \ldots).$$

I defined g^p on page 91 as p's condition. If p exists, g^p is her lifetime wellbeing. If p does not exist, g^p has the non-numerical value Ω. The vector $(g^1, g^2, \ldots)$ shows which people constitute the population of a particular distribution, and the wellbeings of those who do.

Moreover, the principle of personal good also implies that the function $\bar{v}(\cdot)$ is increasing in each of its arguments. Compare two distributions A and B. Suppose each person apart from p has the same condition in A as she does in B. Suppose p exists in both A and B, and her wellbeing in A – call it $g_a{}^p$ – is higher than her wellbeing in B – call it $g_b{}^p$. Then the principle of personal good implies A is a better distribution than B. That is to say,

$$\bar{v}(g^1, g^2, \ldots g_a{}^p, \ldots) > \bar{v}(g^1, g^2, \ldots g_b{}^p, \ldots),$$

which is to say $\bar{v}(\cdot)$ is indeed an increasing function of g^p. The same is true for any person p. This is enough to show $\bar{v}(\cdot)$ is increasing in each of its arguments. Remember the definition of an increasing function that I gave on page 119. We need only check the effect of increasing any argument from one numerical value to another. The effect of changing an argument to or from Ω does not matter.

The principle of temporal good is parallel to the principle of personal good. In a parallel way, it determines that each person's wellbeing is a function of her condition at each time:

(8.2.2) $$g^p = g^p(g_1{}^p, g_2{}^p, \ldots g_T{}^p).$$

Again, a parallel argument establishes that this function is increasing in each of its arguments. But as it happens, I do not need to call on this fact in this chapter.

Putting (8.2.2) together with (8.2.1) gives us that the goodness of a distribution can be represented by a function of the form

(8.2.3) $$\bar{v}(g^1(g_1{}^1, g_2{}^1, \ldots g_T{}^1), g^2(g_1{}^2, g_2{}^2, \ldots g_T{}^2), g^3(g_1{}^3, g_2{}^3, \ldots g_T{}^3), \ldots).$$

This has exactly the separable form of a value function specified in (8.1.1) on page 117, and the function $\bar{v}(\cdot)$ is increasing in each of its arguments. If a person p exists, her condition g^p has a numerical value, specifically her lifetime wellbeing. If p does not exist, g^p has the non-numerical value Ω. (8.2.3) is simply a specific version of (8.1.1), in which the individual value functions $v^p(\cdot)$ are specifically individual condition functions $g^p(\cdot)$. We have met the requirements for separability of lives set out on page 119. This completes the derivation.

Points of interpretation

I introduced the idea of a person's lifetime wellbeing in chapter 5, but in that chapter left it unconnected either with general goodness or with temporal wellbeing. The principle of personal good connects it with the former, and the principle of temporal good with the latter. The principle of personal good says that the goodness of a distribution depends only on which people are alive in the distribution, and on the lifetime wellbeings of those people. The principle of temporal good says that each person's lifetime wellbeing depends only on which times the person is alive for, and on her temporal wellbeing at those times.

The principle of personal good makes a connection between the personal value of a life and its general value.[3] A life's personal value is how good the life is for the person who lives it; it is the person's lifetime wellbeing. A life's general value is how much that life contributes to general goodness. The principle of personal good connects these things. But it does so only in an ordinal way. It says that one life is generally better than another if and only if it is personally better. It does not say that the quantity by which it is generally better is the same as the quantity by which it is personally better. For instance, the formula (8.2.3) is compatible with the priority view, which makes a difference between the quantities of personal and general good, as I explained on pages 65–6.

The ordinal nature of the connection is reflected in the algebra. In the formula (8.1.1), in distributions where p lives, $v^p(\cdot)$ shows the contribution of p's life to the general goodness of the distribution. It is a measure of the general value of the life. But (8.1.1) does not determine the function $v^p(\cdot)$ uniquely. Any increasing transform of this function could be substituted into the formula in its place. (The function $\bar{v}(\cdot)$ would have to be correspondingly adjusted.) $v^p(\cdot)$ is therefore only an ordinal measure of the general value of p's life. The appearance in (8.2.3) of $g^p(\cdot)$, which measures personal value cardinally, in the place of $v^p(\cdot)$, which measures general value ordinally, makes an ordinal connection between personal and general value.

Remember, too, that the principle of personal good does not link the personal and general values of a person's existence. It says nothing at all about the value of a person's existence or nonexistence.

I have formulated the principles of personal and temporal good so that they can apply to distributions of wellbeing that contain uncertainty. That is why the word 'certainly' appears in the formulations. Uncertainty is incorporated in a distribution by means of an extra dimension of states of nature.[4] However, this chapter is concerned only with the two dimensions of people and times, not with uncertainty. The two principles are much weaker when they are applied to distributions that do not contain uncertainty than they are when applied to distributions that do. In effect, each principle has a weak version that excludes uncertainty, and a strong version that incorporates it.

In chapter 9, I shall need the strong version of the principle of personal good. In chapter 15 I shall call on the strong version of the principle of temporal good. But section 15.2 explains that, nevertheless, I do not consider it reliable. I shall use it only as a 'default' assumption.

However, in effect I have already in section 3.3 adopted the weak version of the principle of temporal good. It is an aspect of what I called 'the assumption of distribution'. It says there are no goods for a person that do not show up in the distribution of her temporal wellbeing over her life. On page 47 I recognized there might be some goods of this sort, though fewer than there may seem to be. If there are any, I excluded them from much of the argument in this book. Since I have already done that, I shall now accept the weak version of the principle of temporal good. (I shall suspend it between pages 130 and 216.)

Assessment of the principle of personal good

Weighing Goods argues for both the weak and the strong versions of the principle of personal good.[5] I shall not go over the same ground as *Weighing Goods* again. But I do need to mention some new objections to the principle that appear in our present context.

These objections are some new apparent counterexamples. I shall start with some that are also putative counterexamples to separability of lives. One is shown in table 5. In this example, two people live contemporaneously for just two times; the cells of the table show their wellbeings at each time. If lives are separable, each person's life can be evaluated independently of the other's. Compare the distributions *A* and

Table 5

		Times				Times	
		1	2			1	2
People	p	1	2	People	p	2	1
	q	1	2		q	1	2

Distribution A   Distribution C

		Times				Times	
		1	2			1	2
People	p	1	2	People	p	2	1
	q	2	1		q	2	1

Distribution B   Distribution D

B. p's life is just the same in these two distributions. So, if lives are separable, the question of whether A or B is better overall depends only on the value of q's life. For the same reason, the question of whether C or D is better overall depends only on the value of q's life. But q's life in C is exactly the same as her life in A, and her life in D is exactly the same as her life in B. So, if lives are separable, we can conclude that A is better than B if and only if C is better than D.

However, it is reasonable to think that A and D have a special merit that is not shared by B and C. In A and D, the people's wellbeings are equal at both times. If equality is valuable, this makes it plausible that A is better than B and D better than C. This contradicts the consequence of separability that I derived in the previous paragraph. So we have a putative counterexample to separability of lives. Since the principle of personal good implies lives are separable, it is also a putative counterexample to the principle of personal good.

This argument calls on the value of contemporaneous equality. In all the distributions A, B, C and D, the two people have equal wellbeing in total, taken over their lifetimes. So there is no inequality in lifetime wellbeing. One possible response to the example is to deny that contemporaneous equality is valuable: even if equality is valuable, it is lifetime equality that matters. So long as people's lives are equal as a whole, contemporaneous inequality does not matter.

Perhaps that is so, and if it is, the example is no threat to separability of lives. However, it may not be so.[6] But even if it is not, separability can be preserved nonetheless. We need to think what is wrong with inequality, if anything. The answer is unfairness. If inequality is bad, it is bad because it is unfair: people at the bottom are unfairly treated. Section 9.4 of *Weighing Goods* defends this claim, and in any case it is not particularly controversial, so I shall take it for granted here. It opens up two possible routes to preserving the separability of lives.

The first is this. For quite different reasons, I have already excluded fairness from the account of goodness in this book. It needs to be accounted for separately; I explained why in section 3.1. Separability of lives is a claim about goodness, limited in this way. So the value of equality, as a sort of fairness, should not be allowed to interfere with it.

This is a bit facile, so let me outline a second route to preserving separability. If I was to reverse my decision to exclude fairness, how would I preserve separability? I would point out that, if inequality is bad, it is bad for the people at the bottom. Those are the people who suffer unfairness. So this unfairness is an individual bad that comes to particular people. It must be included along with those people's other goods and bads, in determining their wellbeing.

More specifically, if inequality at a particular time is bad, it is a bad thing that happens to the people who are at the bottom of the distribution at that time. Table 5 specifies the wellbeing of the two people at each time. In setting up the table, I implicitly ignored any badness the people might be suffering because of inequality. Now we are allowing for this sort of bad, we need to add it into the table. This will give us a new table, which will pose no threat to separability.

Alternatively, we might suppose the quantities of wellbeing shown in table 5 already incorporate any badness of inequality that either of the people might suffer at either time. Given that, inequality provides no further reason for thinking *A* better than *B* or *D* better than *C*. The result is that either way of interpreting the table draws its sting.

This route to making the value of equality compatible with separability exemplifies the strategy of dispersion that I mentioned in section 7.4. In that section, I expressed doubts about dispersing the value of longevity. But the value of equality derives from fairness, and in *Weighing Goods* I offered an account of fairness that makes it an individual good.[7] So it is legitimate to disperse the value of equality.

What sort of harm is done by inequality to the people at the bottom? No doubt inequality often *causes* them harm. It no doubt often causes them to feel resentful at their unfair treatment, feel pangs of envy, suffer

Separability of lives

Table 6

	Times				Times	
	1	2		1	2
People p	1	Ω	People p	Ω	1
q	1	Ω	q	1	Ω

Distribution *A*   Distribution *C*

	Times				Times	
	1	2		1	2
People p	1	Ω	People p	Ω	1
q	Ω	1	q	Ω	1

Distribution *B*   Distribution *D*

distorted social relationships, and so on. All of these are bad effects of inequality. But the harm may not be entirely causal. It may simply be bad in itself for someone to suffer unfairness, even if she feels no resentment.

Another putative counterexample to separability of lives appears in table 7 on page 196. It is an unconvincing example, as I shall explain when I come to it. All the other putative counterexamples that I can think of are merely causal. Table 6 shows one of them. Separability implies that *A* in this table is better than *B* if and only if *C* is better than *D*; the argument is parallel to the one I gave for table 5. But one might think *A* is better than *B* and also *D* better than *C* because in *A* and *D* the people live simultaneously, whereas in *B* and *C* they live alone. It is plausibly better for people not to be alone. But if that is so, it can only be because it is causally better. This fact should already have been taken account of in the people's wellbeing. Given that, this sort of example gives no further reason to doubt separability of lives.

8.3 Discounting for time

That exhausts all the objections I can think of to separability of lives, and from now on I shall accept it.

However, I do know one further objection to the principle of personal good. The principle of personal good is stronger than separability of lives, and this objection to the former is no objection to the latter.

It is sometimes said that later lives should count for less than earlier ones in general goodness, even if the lives themselves are equally good. Later lives should be 'discounted' compared with earlier ones. On page 93 I said that discounting for time at least makes sense. Let us assume for the moment it is also correct. It conflicts with the principle of personal good.

To see why, compare two distributions that are the same except that a single person lives at a later time in one than in the other. (This is possible, as I said on page 107.) The person's life is the same in either distribution; both distributions are the same from what I called in section 5.3 the person's 'personal perspective'. So her life has the same personal value or wellbeing, but it occurs at a different time. This person is equally well off in both the distributions, and so is everyone else. Therefore, the principle of personal good implies these two distributions are equally good. But if later lives are discounted, the distribution where the person lives earlier is better than the one where she lives later. Discounting is therefore inconsistent with the principle of personal good.

The conflict between discounting and the principle of personal good has been used as an argument against discounting.[8] On the other hand, there are also some arguments in favour of discounting.[9] I suspect that anyone who favours discounting will not be persuaded out of it by noticing it is inconsistent with the principle of personal good. This application of the principle to changes in the time when someone lives is an arcane one. If you believe in discounting, you might reasonably reject this application whilst accepting the principle in its more mundane applications.

If we allow for discounting, thereby giving up the principle of personal good, we shall have to give up (8.2.3) on page 121 as a formula for the value of a distribution. This formula says the value depends only on the wellbeing of the people. If later lives are discounted, that is not so. The value of a distribution depends on the wellbeing of the people and also on the time when those people live. This divides the general value of a life from its personal value.

However, discounting gives us no reason to abandon separability of lives. We can fall back on the more general separable formula for value, (8.1.1) on page 117. Because this formula contains $v^P(\cdot)$ instead of $g^P(\cdot)$, it does not depend on any connection between general and personal value. The interpretation of $v^P(\cdot)$ is not specified to be wellbeing.

Are there any other potential reasons besides temporal discounting for giving up the principle of personal good? A possibility is spatial discounting. Imagine we are valuing a distribution of wellbeing from the point of view of a particular country or a particular place on earth. We might count the wellbeing of more distant people for less in our valuation than the wellbeing of nearby people. A particular person might live nearby or she might live far away. If she lives nearby, her life will count for more than if she lives far away, and this will be so even if the personal value of her life is exactly the same. This is discounting for distance, and it also conflicts with the principle of personal good.

It would not be reasonable to discount for distance unless we were making a valuation relative to some particular place. Then we might discount for distance from that place. A valuation relative to another place would discount for distance from that other place, and give a different result. But in this book, I am generally only interested in nonrelative valuations; I explained why in section 4.3. I shall therefore ignore the possibility of spatial discounting.

I also explained in section 4.3 that temporal discounting need not be relative, so I cannot ignore the possibility of temporal discounting on these grounds. But I cannot think of any other deviation from the principle of personal good that can plausibly yield a nonrelative valuation. So discounting for time is the only deviation I shall allow for.

I do not wish to enter the difficult debate about discounting in this book. I do not like discounting, but I do not feel confident about rejecting it outright. However, if I allowed for discounting throughout the rest of the book, it would add a lot of complexity to my already complex arguments. For simplicity, I shall mostly set discounting aside, and assume the principle of personal good.

At various points in this book, I shall set aside particular views that I do not find attractive but that I also cannot confidently reject. This means I shall not end up with a comprehensive theory of weighing lives, but with a 'default' theory, as I shall call it. This theory will at least be comparatively simple, so that it can conveniently serve as a starting point for more complicated theories. More than that, I think we should have good reasons before we depart from it.

I think the principle of personal good is very plausible, and for that reason I shall take it as part of my default theory. We should assume it is correct except where we have reason to think otherwise. You need good reasons if you choose to drop this principle and discount wellbeing for time.

8.4 The people route to aggregation

I have argued that lives are separable. This means the goodness of a distribution can be represented by a value function that has the form (8.1.1). I reproduce it here:

(8.4.1) $\bar{v}(v^1(g_1{}^1, g_2{}^1, \dots g_T{}^1), v^2(g_1{}^2, g_2{}^2, \dots g_T{}^2), v^3(g_1{}^3, g_2{}^3, \dots g_T{}^3), \dots).$

If the person p lives in the distribution, $v^p(\cdot)$ represents the general value of her life. If she does not live, $v^p(\cdot)$ has some non-numerical value.

Separability of lives is enough to justify the people route to aggregation. In saying this, I am correcting an overstatement I made on page 106. There, I said the people route requires people to be separable. But the truth is that it only requires the weaker condition that lives are separable. Provided lives are separable, if a person lives, we can set a general value on her life, which is independent of other people's condition. That is to say, we can aggregate across times within the life of each person who lives. This is the first step of aggregation by the people route. We can than go on to the second step, which is to aggregate across people. This second step is not just a matter of aggregating together all the values we have arrived at in the first step, because we also have to take into account people who do not exist in the distribution we are valuing. Nevertheless, it is still an aggregation across people.

On page 116, I abjured the snapshot route to aggregation, and I have now embraced the people route. In a way, this is to retreat from one purpose that I announced for this book in section 1.2. I announced I was looking for an integrated treatment of two questions about valuation: how to value prolonging people's lives, and how to value creating new people. But the people route treats these two problems separately. First it aggregates across times within each person's life. In this, it must take account of the length of the life, so the value of prolonging a person's life appears at this stage. Then it aggregates across people, taking into account their possible existence or nonexistence. This is where the value of creating people will appear.

Still, though the treatment of these two questions will not be truly integrated, we shall come across parallels and connections between them. The argument of the book benefits from treating both of them.

In the rest of this book, I shall consider the two problems in succession rather than together. I shall take them in reverse order. First, I shall examine the logically second step of aggregating across people to determine the overall value of a distribution. This will take us up to chapter 14. Second, starting in chapter 15, I shall examine the logically first step of aggregating across times within each person's life, to determine the value of her life. This means the value of creating life comes first in this book; then the value of prolonging life.

So I am about to embark on the project of aggregating across people. The project is to find the shape of the function $\bar{v}(\cdot)$ in (8.4.1). This function connects the goodness of a distribution to the individual values given by $v^1(\cdot)$, $v^2(\cdot)$, and so on. Normally, I shall assume the principle of personal good, which means that those individual values can be identified with the people's individual conditions. Then the goodness of the distribution is a function of the conditions:

$$(8.4.2) \qquad\qquad \bar{v}(g^1,\, g^2,\, g^3,\, ...).$$

The project is to find the shape of this function.

For this project, it does not matter what the people's individual conditions g^1, g^2, and so on are determined by. For a person who lives, her condition is her wellbeing, and the principle of temporal good says it is determined by the sequence of her temporal wellbeings through her life. But while we are aggregating across people, this does not matter. So we do not need to assume the principle of temporal good through the coming segment of the book. I shall have to call on it again in chapter 15. This is a worthwhile generalization because, when I adopted the principle of temporal good on page 123, I recognized there may be some exceptions to it.

8.5 The rectangular field assumption

At this point, I shall make a particular technical assumption that I shall have to call on later. This happens to be a convenient point to state it.

I shall assume that, if some person can have a particular level of lifetime wellbeing, she can have it whatever the condition of the other people might be. A person's wellbeing can run through its entire range, whatever anyone else's condition may be. In *Weighing Goods*, I called this the 'rectangular field assumption', and discussed it in section 4.4. There are some obvious objections to it. It implies, for instance, that one person can have a wonderful life even if everyone else in the world is destroyed in an appalling holocaust. It also implies that someone might exist even if her mother never exists. Neither of these things is possible.

I can offer two responses to these objections. One is that the possibility of a distribution is not really in question. The question is which distributions can be brought within the domain of the value function –

which can be judged better or worse compared with others. A distribution need not be physically possible, or perhaps even metaphysically possible, for us to evaluate it. Perhaps we can evaluate a world in which a person exists but her mother does not.

The second response is that the rectangular field assumption is sufficient for the conclusions I shall draw from it, but not actually necessary. It may be possible to prove the conclusions on the basis of a much weaker assumption, but I believe the necessary mathematics has not been done.[10]

I hope these responses are enough to justify my making the rectangular field assumption, and at any rate I shall make it.

Notes

1 See section 1.2.
2 See section 2.2.
3 I introduced the distinction between personal and general value in section 4.2.
4 See page 16.
5 *Weighing Goods*, chapters 8 and 9. In my statement of the principle on p. 165 of that book, I omitted the first sentence of the principle as it is stated here; I did not make it explicit that the principle is restricted to comparing distributions that have the same population. But this restriction was implicit. The omitted first sentence is logically redundant. If *A* and *B* had different populations, the second and third sentences would be vacuously true.
6 See Dennis McKerlie, 'Equality and time', and Larry Temkin, 'Intergenerational inequality'.
7 *Weighing Goods*, section 9.4.
8 For instance, see Tyler Cowen, 'Consequentialism implies a zero rate of intergenerational discount'.
9 For instance, see Partha Dasgupta and G. M. Heal, *Economic Theory and Exhaustible Resources*, chapter 9.
10 I used to think the mathematical task would be comparatively easy, and said so in *Weighing Goods*, section 4.4. However, a counterexample in Peter Wakker's *Additive Representation of Preferences* has convinced me it would not be easy.

9

Same-number aggregation

Chapter 8 cleared the way for the people route to aggregation by defending separability of lives. With the route cleared, we can start along it. In this chapter, I shall consider the problem of how wellbeing is aggregated across people. In formal terms, we are looking for the form of the function $\bar{v}(\cdot)$ shown in (8.4.1) on page 129. But this chapter deals principally with one special context, in which the number of people in the population is kept constant.

Section 9.1 is concerned with this special context only. On the basis of some assumptions that I shall argue are plausible, it arrives at a utilitarian conclusion. Section 9.2 begins to raise the question of how this conclusion can be extended to comparing distributions containing different numbers of people.

9.1 The same-number addition theorem

Let us set aside discounting for time, and adopt the principle of personal good. Given this principle, (8.4.1) takes the form (8.4.2), which I repeat here:

$$\bar{v}(g^1,\ g^2,\ g^3,\ ...).$$

We want to find the shape of the value function $\bar{v}(\cdot)$.

This is a problem of aggregation in one dimension. The vector $(g^1,\ g^2,\ g^3,\ ...)$ shows a one-dimensional distribution of wellbeing: a distribution across the dimension of people. We are ignoring the dimension of time, because I have postponed till chapter 15 the question of how each person's wellbeing is determined.

Next I shall simplify the aggregation problem even further. Let us pick some particular population of people, and concentrate only on distributions in which just those people live and nobody else. I shall use the symbol 'Π' to stand for the population of the distributions I am concentrating on. Π is the set of actual people, not the number of them.

The interpersonal addition theorem

What is the shape of the value function $\bar{v}(\cdot)$, confined to just the distributions that have the population Π? Which of these distributions is better than which? Since the population is fixed, this is a familiar problem of aggregation. I examined it in *Weighing Goods*, and I can extract an answer directly from that book. The value function is the weighted total of the people's wellbeing. It is

(9.1.1) $$\Sigma_{p \in \Pi} a^p g^p.$$

This formula means that, to evaluate the distribution, we take each person p's wellbeing g^p and multiply it by some constant number a^p. Then we add up the resulting products, across all the people in the population. The numbers a^p are weights given to different people's wellbeings. They are all positive. I shall say more about them on page 136. The value function (9.1.1) implies that one distribution is better than another that has the same population if and only if it has a greater weighted total of the people's wellbeing than the other.

I realize that this is a startling and spectacular claim to make just by means of an announcement. For one thing, I am rejecting the popular 'priority view', which assigns priority to worse-off people.[1] But I have devoted one entire book to this claim, and I am not going to reopen the topic here. Instead, I shall simply explain the conclusion and its basis briefly.

The argument for it is a development of one first presented as a formal theorem by John Harsanyi in his 'Cardinal welfare, individualistic ethics, and interpersonal comparisons of utility'. Harsanyi's original interpretation of his theorem was in terms of preferences. In *Weighing Goods*, I reinterpreted it in terms of betterness, and justified its assumptions as far as I could. The theorem is proved in section 10.1 of *Weighing Goods*. I called it 'the interpersonal addition theorem'.

It depends on these assumptions:

1. The axioms of expected utility theory applied to the general betterness relation.
2. The axioms of expected utility theory applied to the individual betterness relations of the people.
3. The strong version of the principle of personal good.
4. A version of the rectangular field assumption.
5. Bernoulli's hypothesis.

To explain them, I need first to describe some background to the theorem. The proof works by introducing a dimension of uncertainty into the problem. More exactly, it adds a dimension of states of nature; it works on two-dimensional distributions of wellbeing, where the dimensions are people and states of nature. The general and individual betterness relations (see (2.1.1) on page 20 and (4.2.1) on page 63) are applied to these two-dimensional distributions. The population of people is kept the same throughout; it is the same in every distribution in every state of nature. The dimension of states of nature adds a great deal of theoretical leverage, principally because the principle of personal good is a surprisingly powerful assumption when applied to these two-dimensional distributions.

Expected utility theory is described in section 5.1. Chapter 6 of *Weighing Goods* argues, with some qualifications, that the individual and general betterness relations satisfy its axioms. That chapter amounts to a defence of assumptions 1 and 2 above. I took care to state the principle of personal good on page 120 of this book in a way that allows it to apply to distributions that incorporate uncertainty. When it does, I called it on page 123 the 'strong version' of the principle. The word 'certainly' in the statement of it makes sure that it applies only to distributions that have the same population in every state of nature. In this section, we are confining our attention to distributions of this sort, so we can call on the principle.

In this context of uncertainty, the principle of personal good is defended in chapters 8 and 9 of *Weighing Goods*, so those chapters amount to a defence of assumption 3 above. On the other hand, in section 8.3 of this book, I raised discounting as a possible objection to the principle of personal good. *Weighing Goods* did not consider this objection. The consequence is to weaken the conclusions of this section; I shall come back to this weakness on page 137.

I mentioned one version of the rectangular field assumption on page 130. Assumption 4 above is a different version that I shall not spell out here. It is evaluated in sections 4.4 and 5.8 of *Weighing Goods*.

I adopted assumption 5, Bernoulli's hypothesis, on page 90 of this book. It was a way of assigning precision to our otherwise vague quantitative notion of wellbeing. I said on page 91 that, once I had adopted that precisification, all my conclusions must be interpreted through it. Together with the other assumptions, Bernoulli's hypothesis leads to the interpersonal addition theorem, that one distribution is better than another (among distributions that have the same population) if and only if it has a greater weighted total of people's wellbeing. We can now see that this conclusion arises partly because I adopted a particular cardinalization for wellbeing. Bernoulli's hypothesis cardinalizes well-being in a way that happens to support the interpersonal addition theorem.

To put it another way, I have chosen to measure wellbeing in such a way that it is appropriate to aggregate across people additively. It is not appropriate to give priority to worse-off people, for example. So the formula (9.1.1) is slightly less spectacular than it seems at first. Its degree of significance is discussed in section 10.3 of *Weighing Goods*. I shall accept it and move forwards.

Impartiality

Next I shall assume impartiality between people: that the identities of people make no difference to general goodness. Amounts of wellbeing matter, but not who has those amounts. I shall state this assumption in terms of the vector $(g^1, g^2, g^3, \ldots)$ that describes a distribution. In this vector, g^1, g^2, and so on each stand for a person's condition: they are either Ω if the person does not exist in the distribution, or her level of wellbeing if she does exist. If one vector is a permutation of another, the two vectors describe distributions that have the same number of people alive, and where the wellbeings of those people are the same. However, the actual people who are alive may differ, and the owners of the various levels of wellbeing may also differ. Impartiality may be expressed like this:

> *Impartiality between people.* If two one-dimensional distributions are described by vectors that are permutations of each other, the distributions are equally good.

I explained in section 4.3 that I am taking for granted a nonrelative notion of general good. General good is not assessed from any particular person's point of view. Given that, it is hard to think of any doubts that can plausibly be raised against impartiality. Everyone must count equally in nonrelative good.

Perhaps a doubt might come from the direction of family relationships. For example, perhaps it is better for most people to have a few children each, rather than for a few people to have a lot of children and the rest none. But I do not find ideas of this sort plausible. To be sure, people's wellbeing is causally affected by family relationships. But these causal effects are already taken into account in the amounts of wellbeing contained in the distributions, and we are comparing distributions that have identical amounts of wellbeing. Beyond the effects on wellbeing, I do not see why family relationships should make a difference to the value of a distribution. So I think we may fairly accept impartiality between people.

True, it conflicts with an idea that also seems attractive at first: the so-called 'person-affecting view'.[2] This is the view that only benefits or harms that come to people can be ethically significant. A change cannot be good or bad unless it affects someone for good or ill. It cannot be good unless it makes her better off than she otherwise would have been, and it cannot be bad unless it makes her worse off than she otherwise would have been. The original source for the person-affecting view is Jan Narveson's 'Utilitarianism and new generations'. Narveson gives it philosophical support, but in any case it is intuitively attractive.

Think about these three distributions:

$$A = (1, \Omega),$$
$$B = (\Omega, 1),$$
$$C = (\Omega, 2).$$

The principle of personal good tells us that C is better than B. Impartiality tells us that A and B are equally good. It follows from the definition of 'equally as good as' on page 21 that C is better than A. However, neither person is better off in C than she is in A. The first person is not, because she does not exist in C. The second person is not, because she does not exist in A. According to the person-affecting view, therefore, C cannot be better than A. So the person-affecting view contradicts the implication of impartiality, together with the principle of personal good, that C is better than A.

So much the worse for the person-affecting view. C is indeed better than A. To have one person living at a particular level of wellbeing is certainly better than having a different person living at a lower level. When the person-affecting view says otherwise, it is wrong. This is the objection to it that was first raised by Derek Parfit and called by him the 'nonidentity objection'.[3] The person-affecting view provides no real case against impartiality. I shall come to one of its more credible implications on page 145.

Conclusion

Impartiality immediately implies that all the weights a^p in (9.1.1) must be the same. They may as well be set equal to one. The result is that betterness is represented by the unweighted total of people's wellbeing:

(9.1.2) $$\Sigma_{p\in\Pi}g^{p}.$$

Indeed, we can go further. (9.1.1) was set up to apply to distributions that all have the same particular population. But now compare two distributions whose populations have the same size but may have different individual members. I stated the principle of impartiality in a way that makes it apply between distributions like this. If the two are identical except for the identities of the people, the principle implies they are equally good.

This allows us to determine the relative values of distributions whose populations have the same size. The formula (9.1.2) can be extended to apply to any of them. This gives us:

> *Same-number addition theorem.* Of two distributions whose populations have the same size, one is better than the other if and only if it has a greater total of people's wellbeing.

This is one part of the broad body of utilitarian doctrine.

The same-number addition theorem belongs to my default theory. To reach it, I assumed the principle of personal good, but in section 8.3 I raised a doubt about this principle. If it is correct to discount later lives, the principle is false. One consequence would be that we have to fall back on the more general form (8.4.1) of the value function, rather than the more specific form (8.4.2). We cannot rely on general good's being a function of individuals' lifetime wellbeings.

In this section, I moved from the specific form (8.4.2) to the same-number addition theorem. We might also expect to be able to move from (8.4.1) to a corresponding addition theorem in which the general values of lives replace lifetime wellbeings. But the derivation of the same-number addition theorem depends on the principle of personal good. To derive a corresponding theorem for general value would require some surrogate for this principle, and I am not sure what a suitable surrogate would be. Charles Blackorby, Walter Bossert and David Donaldson use a principle that takes account of a person's date of birth.[4] However, since people lead lives of different lengths, and since their wellbeing is differently distributed across times in their lives, I think this is not enough. Why should we be interested in a person's date of birth, particularly, rather than her date of death or some other date in her life? Finding a suitable surrogate for the principle of personal good is a task that needs to be accomplished if the conclusions of this book are to be extended to allow for discounting.

9.2 Introduction to different-number aggregation

The same-number addition theorem is remarkably specific, but it leaves open a vast range of possibilities for the comparative value of distributions that have differing sizes of population. Just to illustrate the possibilities, I shall mention two popular theories about the goodness of distributions that are each consistent with the same-number addition theorem. They represent two different attitudes a utilitarian may take when she comes to evaluate the size of the world's population.

One is the 'average principle', which says that one distribution is better than another if and only if it has a greater average of people's wellbeing. Its value function is, for any population Π:

$$\Sigma_{p\in\Pi}g^{p}/n,$$

where n is the number of people in the population.

Another possibility is the 'total principle', which says one distribution is better than another if and only if it has a greater total of people's wellbeing. Its value function is, for any population Π:

$$\Sigma_{p\in\Pi}g^{p}.$$

The total principle is not yet properly defined. Its meaning is affected by the choice of the zero on the scale of wellbeing. To see how, think about the value of adding an extra person to the world. Suppose a person is added, but no one else's wellbeing is affected. Is the distribution with the added person better or worse than the distribution without? According to the total principle, if the added person has a wellbeing above zero, it is better; if she has a wellbeing below zero, it is worse. So altering the zero on the scale of wellbeing can make a difference: it implies a different betterness ordering amongst distributions. Yet at present I have not defined a zero for wellbeing; on page 96 I declined to do so. So the total principle is as yet not properly specified. Before it even makes definite sense, we must fix a zero. I shall not give the total principle a definite meaning till chapter 14.

By contrast, the average principle is not affected by the zero. In comparing one distribution with another, all that matters is which has the higher average wellbeing. The zero does not come into this comparison. This does not mean the average principle is beyond reproach. I shall identify its faults in section 13.3.

Notes

1 See Derek Parfit, 'Equality or priority?'.
2 I believe this term was originally Derek Parfit's; see *Reasons and Persons*, pp. 370 and 394. It reflects Jan Narveson's remark in 'Utilitarianism and new generations', p. 63: 'In deciding what we are to do, the only consideration which is morally relevant ... is how others would be affected'.
3 *Reasons and Persons*, chapter 16.
4 'Birth-date dependent population ethics'.

10

The neutral level for existence

I have defended separability of lives, and drawn out its consequences. The next step in the main development of my argument is to assess the stronger condition of separability of people. I shall come to that in chapter 13. But I have a problem to deal with first, and dealing with it will take some time. I need to bring into the open one implicit consequence of the assumptions I have made so far, because it raises a difficult question that I need to consider. Section 10.1 derives this implication from the assumptions. Section 10.2 puts it in question by describing a natural and powerful intuition that conflicts with it. It is the intuition that the existence of a person is in itself ethically neutral, as a general rule. Section 10.2 also expresses this intuition as a formal principle. Section 10.3 shows this principle to be false. But that does not necessarily dispose of the intuition, because the formal principle may not be an accurate expression of it. At the end of this chapter, I shall sketch various routes the subsequent development of the intuition might follow. Chapters 11 and 12 follow up some of them.

10.1 A single neutral level of wellbeing

Given the principle of personal good, we found on page 130 a one-dimensional aggregation problem to attack. (8.4.2) expresses the problem. We start with a one-dimensional distribution of wellbeing described by the vector $(g^1, g^2, g^3, ...)$. In this vector, g^p is p's condition; it is her lifetime wellbeing if she lives and otherwise it has the non-numerical value Ω. The problem is to compare the value of different one-dimensional distributions, to determine which is better than which.

Because nonexistence is represented in this vector by a non-numerical value, it is not directly comparable in value with levels of lifetime wellbeing. The principle of personal good implies that lives are separable, but not that people are separable. I explained the difference in section 8.1. Separability of people requires nonexistence to be put on the same scale of value as lives, but separability of lives does not. Nevertheless, in a way, even separability of lives makes nonexistence comparable in value with lives.

To see how it does that, compare two one-dimensional distributions *A* and *B*. Suppose person *p* does not exist in *A*, but does in *B*. In *B* she has a particular lifetime wellbeing. Suppose everyone else's condition is the same in *A* as it is in *B*. So the only difference between *A* and *B* is *p*'s condition, which is her nonexistence in *A* and her wellbeing in *B*. On page 22, I assumed that the betterness relation is complete. Consequently, *A* is better than *B*, or else *B* is better than *A*, or else *A* and *B* are equally good. If, say, *A* is better than *B*, this means *p*'s nonexistence in *A* is better than her living a life with the wellbeing she has in *B*. If *A* and *B* are equally good, *p*'s nonexistence is equally as good as her living with this level of wellbeing. So we can already conclude that *p*'s nonexistence is in a sense comparable in value with her wellbeing in *B*. This is a matter of general value: of whether or not it is better that she exists, from the point of view of general good. This comparability at the level of general value is a direct consequence of my assuming completeness.

We can go further. Let us pick out the whole range of distributions in which *p* lives, and in which everyone's condition apart from *p*'s is the same as it is in *A*. *p*'s wellbeing is the only difference amongst the distributions throughout this whole range. The rectangular field assumption that I made in section 8.5 implies that *p*'s wellbeing in this range spans the entire gamut from the very worst she can possibly have to the very best. At the top of the range are distributions where *p* is very well off; at the bottom, ones where she is very badly off.

Compare *A*, where *p* does not exist, with the various distributions in this range. Could *A* be better than all of them? I think not; only a very great pessimist would think it is better that a person should not live at all than that she should live the very best possible life.[1] Could it be the case that no distributions in the range are worse than *A*? I think this is not possible either; there surely could be a life so terrible that it would be better if it was not lived. So at the top of the range I assume there are some distributions that are as good as *A* or better, and at the bottom some that are worse than *A*.

Given this, it follows that, somewhere in the range between the top and the bottom, there is at least one distribution that is neither better nor worse than *A*. This is a consequence of the assumption of continuity that I made on page 27; I do not need to spell out the details.

Let *C* be one of those distributions in the range that is neither better nor worse than *A*. The difference between *C* and *A* is that *p* does not live in *A*, and she lives with some particular level of wellbeing in *C*. So *p*'s living a life at this level is neither better nor worse than her not living at all. I shall say her wellbeing in *C* is *neutral*, and say she has a *neutral life*.

'Neutral' means not mattering ethically. It is a broad idea; this chapter and the next two test out various more specific interpretations of it. As I am using the term specifically at the moment, to say a life is neutral means it is neither better nor worse that this life is lived than that it is not lived. The neutrality of a life is a matter of general, not personal, good. A neutral life is such that it is generally neither better nor worse that it is lived than not lived. Whether it is better or worse for the person who lives it – whether the life is worth living – is not at issue.

I am assuming betterness is a complete relation. Therefore, because *C* is neither better nor worse than *A*, it must be equally as good as *A*. Take any other distribution in the range we are considering. This other distribution has the same population as *C*, and everyone in it apart from *p* has the same wellbeing as she has in *C*. *p* has either more or less wellbeing than she has in *C*. If she has more, the distribution as a whole is better than *C*; this is a direct consequence of the principle of personal good. It follows that this distribution is also better than *A*. Alternatively, if *p* has less wellbeing than she has in *C*, the distribution is worse than *C* and therefore worse than *A*. *C* is therefore the only distribution in the whole range that is equally as good as *A*.

The conclusion is that there is only one *neutral level* of wellbeing for *p* in these circumstances. This level forms a sharp boundary. A life for *p* that has a higher level of wellbeing is better than neutral: *p*'s living this life is better than her not living at all. A life for *p* that has a lower level of wellbeing is worse than neutral: *p*'s living this life is worse than her not living at all.[2]

That is the conclusion I have been aiming at in this section. Neutrality marks a sharp boundary between lives that are better lived than not and lives that are better not lived than lived. To appreciate its significance, bear in mind that, if one distribution is better than another, it will normally be worth some – perhaps small – sacrifice to achieve it. So if *p* would live a life that is slightly better than neutral, some sacrifice by the rest of us would be worthwhile for the sake of having her live. If *p* would live a life that is just a little less good, and slightly worse than neutral, some sacrifice by the rest of us would be worthwhile for the sake of stopping her from living.

This conclusion runs counter to strong intuitions; I shall question it in the next section. Meanwhile I have something to explain.

My conclusion makes existence fully comparable in value with nonexistence; any life is either better or worse than nonexistence, or else equally as good as nonexistence. This follows directly from the completeness of betterness. Yet on page 119, I said we might assign nonexistence a non-numerical value, and that would mean it is not comparable with the value of lives. Was that entirely wrong?

It was mostly wrong. A non-numerical value is not comparable with a numerical one, but the reason I assigned nonexistence a non-numerical value was simply that it may have no *constant* numerical value. The comparability I have established in this section may be specific to the circumstances. The distributions A and C are special in that everyone apart from *p* has the same condition: everyone else's condition is held constant. *p*'s wellbeing in C is neutral *given* everyone else's condition. But if other people's conditions were different, this same level of wellbeing might no longer be neutral.

If people were separable, other people's conditions would not influence which level of wellbeing was neutral for *p*. But so far, I have only argued that lives, not people, are separable. So at the moment I must allow that circumstances might influence which level of wellbeing is neutral. It might depend on which other people exist, and on how their lives go. The neutral level may depend on context.

In sum, nonexistence may not have a *fixed* place on the scale of value of lives but, if the betterness relation is complete, it must have a place. A person's nonexistence has a general value that is comparable in this variable way with her wellbeing. In every context, there is just a single neutral level of wellbeing. Every higher level is better than nonexistence, and every lower level worse than nonexistence.

10.2 The intuition of neutrality

That conclusion emerges from my argument so far. But it conflicts with an intuition that many people find strongly attractive. I am one of those people. We think intuitively that adding a person to the world is very often ethically neutral. We do not think that just a single level of wellbeing is neutral, and that a person's living at any other level is either better or worse than her nonexistence. But that is the conclusion I have just reached. We must examine its conflict with intuition. My argument has depended on various assumptions. Since its conclusion conflicts with intuition, we shall either have to sacrifice the intuition or reassess the assumptions.

A major problem is how, precisely, to understand the intuition. Let me first present it rough-cast, trying not to express it in the terms of any particular interpretation. We must recognize from the start that a person's existence may have either good or bad effects on other people. For example, a new person will make demands on the earth's resources, and that will probably be bad for the rest of us. On the other hand, she will bring to the world her energy, talents, strengths and abilities, and those will do us good. The intuition is that a person's existence is neutral in itself, setting aside its effects on other people. There is no consideration stemming from the wellbeing of the person herself that counts either for or against bringing her into existence.

Suppose a couple are wondering whether to have a child. Suppose they decide their own lives will be better on balance if they remain childless, and because of that they remain so. Our intuition is that they are not acting wrongly. Moreover, it is not that we think the couple might have a reason to have a child, stemming from the child's own wellbeing, but this reason can justifiably be outweighed by the couple's own good. Instead, we think there is no positive reason at all why they should have a child. If having a child would be bad for the couple themselves, even to a small degree, it is right for them not to have one.

There are limits to this intuition of neutrality. Suppose that, if this couple had a child, her life would be short and full of suffering. Then we think they should definitely not have a child. So existence at a poor level is not neutral; we are against it. Nevertheless, for a wide range of lives the child might live, having a child seems an ethically neutral matter.

Some people think this range is infinitely wide. They think that a person's existence is neutral, however good her life would be if she did exist. It is not neutral if her life would be bad, so there is a lower boundary to the neutral range. But there is no upper boundary. That is one view. A more moderate view is that the range has both an upper and a lower boundary, but there is nevertheless a range of neutral lives in between.

Here is another example of the neutrality intuition at work. Economists often concern themselves with setting a value on people's lives.[3] For example, they do cost-benefit analyses of projects that will improve safety on the roads or railways, where one of the benefits is the saving of lives. Figure 7 on page 8 is a schematic illustration of this type of problem. Economists also advise on priorities in the health service: for example on priorities between the old and the young.[4] Figure 5 on page 6 illustrates that problem. Both these problems are likely to involve the addition of people to the world. If a young person's life is saved, she is likely to have children and grandchildren who would otherwise never have existed. The diagrams illustrate this point. But when they make their judgements, economists never, or almost never,[5] take account of these added people. Why not? The explanation has to be that they think their existence is ethically neutral.

The neutrality intuition is part of the broader way of thinking known as the 'person-affecting view'. This is the view that only benefits or harms that come to people can be ethically significant; a change must be ethically neutral unless it affects a person for good or ill. A change is neutral unless it makes someone either better or worse off than she would otherwise have been; that is the view. Now, a person's coming into existence makes her neither better nor worse off than she would otherwise have been. It does not affect her for better or worse. So according to the person-affecting view, it is ethically neutral, unless it has some good or bad effects on other people. Jan Narveson says: 'We are in favour of making people happy, but neutral about making happy people.'[6]

I have already mentioned the person-affecting view on page 136, and there I rejected one of its implications. The intuition of neutrality is a different implication that is not so easily rejected. It is independently attractive in its own right.

Interpreting the intuition

This book is about goodness. If there are ethical considerations that are not to do with goodness – purely deontic rules, for example – they are beyond the book's scope. So the intuition of neutrality is relevant only in so far as it has implications for goodness. In this chapter and the next two, I shall do my best to interpret it axiologically – in terms of goodness. My aim will be to fit it into a coherent theory of goodness. This turns out to be difficult. The best interpretation I can find appears in section 12.4, and I shall explain in that section that it is not very satisfactory. Eventually in section 14.2, the consequence turns out to be that we simply have to reject the neutrality intuition, understood as an intuition about goodness.

This does not mean we have to reject the whole person-affecting style of ethics, or even the neutrality intuition specifically. It means the intuition will have to be given some interpretation other than an axiological one if it is to survive. Quite plausibly, that can be done.[7]

Interpreted axiologically, in terms of goodness, the intuition is that, if a person is added to the population of the world, her addition has no positive or negative value in itself. The only value it can have is the good or bad it brings to other people besides the person who is added. So if it brings neither good nor bad to those people, it is neutral.

In this chapter, I shall take neutrality to be equality of goodness. So I shall take the intuition to be that adding a person is equally as good as not adding her. In chapters 11 and 12, I shall return to the question of just how neutrality should be understood axiologically. This will lead us to some alternative interpretations of neutrality.

I explained that the neutrality intuition has limits. For one thing, adding a person is worse than not adding her if her life will be a bad one, and other people are not affected. But the intuition applies within some range of wellbeings that the new person might have. By calling it a 'range', I mean to imply that it has more than one member; the idea applies for several different levels of wellbeing. If we take neutrality to be equality of goodness, we can formulate the intuition of neutrality like this:

> *Principle of equal existence.* Suppose two distributions have the same population of people, except that an extra person exists in one who does not exist in the other. Suppose each person who exists in both distributions is equally as well off in one as she is in the other. Then there is some range of wellbeings (called 'the neutral range') such that, if the extra person's wellbeing is within this range, the two distributions are equally good.

10.3 Counterexamples to the principle of equal existence

This principle conflicts with the conclusion of section 10.1, because it implies there is a neutral range of wellbeings, rather than just a single neutral level. It will be useful to display the conflict in a few examples. Since the conclusion of section 10.1 is solidly founded, these will constitute counterexamples to the principle of equal existence.

My main example simply crystallizes the argument of section 10.1. Take these three distributions of lifetime wellbeing:

$$(10.3.1) \qquad \begin{aligned} A &= (1, 1, \ldots 1, \Omega), \\ B &= (1, 1, \ldots 1, 1), \\ C &= (1, 1, \ldots 1, 2). \end{aligned}$$

Each person except the last has the same wellbeing in all three of these distributions. The last person does not exist in A. She exists in both B

and C, and her wellbeing is less in B than in C. According to the principle of equal existence, there is a neutral range of wellbeings, and I mean the last person's wellbeing in both B and C to be within this range. So the neutral range includes levels 1 and 2.

I am about to compare the values of these three distributions. Comparing their values is a different matter from choosing between them. I am not assuming anyone has or could have a choice between A, B and C. I am assuming nothing about that; these options may be available as choices, or they may not.

This needs to be said, because the value of a distribution could be affected by what other distributions are available as alternatives. For example, Melinda Roberts suggests that, if anyone had a choice between B and C in this example, and chose B, she would be wronging the last person.[8] She would gratuitously be making that person less well off than she might have been, which is to do her a wrong. This is a bad feature that distribution B has if C is an available alternative, but not otherwise.

I agree that the availability of alternatives may affect the value of a distribution. But when we evaluate B in comparison to C, we must not assume B and C are actually available alternatives. Nothing says they are. So Roberts's point gives us no grounds for reducing the value of B.

Then does it mean we cannot judge the value of B, because its value may depend on what alternatives are available? It does not. The value of a distribution depends only on the condition of each person; that is a consequence of the principle of personal good. The vectors in (10.3.1) tell us the condition of each person, so they tell us all we need to know. If the presence or absence of alternatives affects the value of a distribution, it can do so only by affecting some person's condition. So its effect will show up in the vector of conditions.

For example, suppose B and C are available as choices and suppose Roberts is right. Then choosing B would wrong the last person. This is a bad thing done to that person, which must already have been taken account of in her wellbeing in B, as it is specified in (10.3.1).

After that clarification, we can get on with making the comparative valuations. According to the principle of equal existence, B in (10.3.1) is equally as good as A. According to the same principle, C is equally as good as A. By the transitivity of 'equally as good as', B is equally as good as C. Hence, by the definition of 'equally as good as' on page 21, C is not better than B. However, the principle of personal good says C is better than B, since it is better for one person and at least as good for everyone else. So we have a contradiction.

Something has to give. What? The principle of personal good can be doubted. If you discount for time, you might think C could indeed be equally as good as B, if the last person lives later in C than she does in B. If you discount, you think wellbeing is more valuable if it comes earlier rather than later. But let us add the assumption that each person's life has the same dates in B as it does in C. Under that assumption, the principle of personal good is indubitable. C is certainly better than B. The transitivity of 'equally as good as' is also indubitable, since it follows from the definition of this relation, as I explained on page 22. The conclusion therefore has to be that the principle of equal existence is false.

A better-known counterexample to this principle is Derek Parfit's 'mere addition paradox'.[9] Here is a version of it:

(10.3.2)
$$A = (4, 4, \ldots 4, 6, \Omega),$$
$$B = (4, 4, \ldots 4, 6, 1),$$
$$C = (4, 4, \ldots 4, 4, 4),$$
$$D = (4, 4, \ldots 4, 4, \Omega).$$

According to the principle of equal existence, there is a neutral range. Assume the levels of wellbeing 1 and 4 both lie within it. In order to remove any complications associated with discounting, also assume that each person's life begins and ends on the same dates in every option in which she exists.

According to the principle of personal good, A is better than D. According to the principle of equal existence, D and C are equally good. From the definition of 'equally as good as' on page 21, it follows that anything better than D is also better than C. So A is better than C.

According to the principle of equal existence, A and B are equally good. From the definition of 'equally as good as', it follows that anything A is better than, B is also better than. Therefore, B is better than C. The asymmetry of 'better than' implies that C is not better than B.

On the other hand, separate considerations imply that C is better than B. This is surely obvious, since C has more wellbeing in total than B, and has it equally distributed. Moreover, the same-number addition theorem stated on page 137 supports this conclusion. So we have reached a contradiction.

The premises that led to it are these. First, the principle of personal good. Given the assumption I made about the dates of lives, this cannot be doubted. Second, the asymmetry of 'better than', which is indubitable. Third, the separate considerations that show C is better than B; these are very hard to doubt. Fourth, the principle of equal existence.

This must be the false premise. So (10.3.2) is a counterexample to this principle.

I introduced this second example because the mere addition paradox is so well known. However, it requires the separate considerations to contradict the principle of equal existence by showing that *C* is better than *B*. Example (10.3.1) is enough to show the principle of equal existence is incorrect, and it rests on fewer assumptions. So that is the example I most rely on.

How should we respond to these counterexamples to the principle of equal existence? I can think of the following possible responses:

1. Deny the transitivity of 'equally as good as'.
2. Develop a notion of 'conditional goodness'. This is an inchoate idea that I shall explain in section 11.2. At first it promises hope of expressing the intuition of neutrality in axiological form.
3. Deny that goodness is absolute. Treat it as a purely relative notion, relative to the population. This may provide another sort of axiological formulation for the intuition, avoiding contradiction.
4. Deny that betterness is fully determinate. Again, this may allow the intuition to be formulated axiologically without contradiction.
5. Abandon the attempt to find an axiological account of the intuition of neutrality. Proceed on the basis of the conclusion established in section 10.1 that there is just a single neutral level. This response does not necessarily mean rejecting the intuition entirely, because it may still be possible to interpret it in deontic terms.

I shall pursue responses 1, 2 and 3 in chapter 11, and response 4 in chapter 12. My conclusion will not finally emerge till section 14.2, but I am ultimately inclined to response 5. Perhaps the neutrality intuition can be rescued in non-axiological terms. But if it can, that is beyond the scope of this book.

Notes

1 Christoph Fehige could possibly stand as an example of such a pessimist. See his 'A Pareto principle for possible people'.
2 The neutral level is what Charles Blackorby, Walter Bossert and David Donaldson call 'the critical level' in their various publications. In *Reasons and Persons*, pp. 412–13, Derek Parfit uses the term 'the valueless level' for a related, but different concept.
3 For a major discussion see M. W. Jones-Lee, *The Economics of Safety and Physical Risk*.
4 For example, see Alan Williams, 'Intergenerational equity'.

5 The only exception I know is W. B. Arthur in 'The economics of risks to life'.
6 'Moral problems of population', p. 73 in the reprinted version.
7 Melinda Roberts gives a persuasive non-axiological account in *Child Versus Childmaker*.
8 *Child Versus Childmaker*, section 2.5.
9 Parfit, *Reasons and Persons*, chapter 19. A different version of the same example appears on page 59 above.

11

Nonstandard betterness

In sections 10.2 and 10.3 of the last chapter, I described a powerful intuition, formulated it in terms of goodness, and argued that the formulation failed. At the end of section 10.3, I listed some of the responses that might be made to this conclusion. Most of them call into question one or other of the basic assumptions I have taken for granted so far in this book. These are assumptions about the formal structure of goodness or betterness. In this chapter I shall review three of the responses, which I think are ultimately unsuccessful. The next chapter deals with one I like more.

11.1 Intransitive betterness

Some authors have responded to examples like mine by denying that betterness is transitive.[1] By this means, one might hope to defeat the counterexamples in section 10.3, and perhaps preserve the principle of equal existence intact.

The transitivity of betterness is not directly relevant to the examples. I formulated them in such a way that I could use them to derive a contradiction from the principle of equal existence, without assuming that betterness is transitive. However, in treating example (10.3.1) I assumed that the relation 'equally as good as' is transitive, and in treating example (10.3.2) I assumed that if one distribution is better than another and the other is equally as good as a third, then the first is better than the third. These assumptions are similar to the transitivity of betterness, and questions might be raised about them.

True, in my arguments they were not strictly assumptions, since they follow from my definition of 'equally as good as' set out on page 21. In the context of the definition, they cannot be doubted. However, we have to ask whether the definition is appropriate. Does it correctly capture our ordinary notion of equality of goodness? As I explained on page 21, the definition was specifically designed to make equality of goodness an equivalence relation: transitive, symmetric and reflexive. I designed it that way to make it true to our ordinary notion of equality. But if you doubt that betterness is transitive, you may also doubt that equality of goodness is transitive. That would lead you to question my definition.

I defended the transitivity of betterness in section 4.1. I think it is incontrovertible. The transitivity of equality of goodness is even more solidly grounded. To say one thing is equally as good as another is to say the goodness of the one is equal to the goodness of the other. That is, each has the same goodness; each is good to the same degree. If we are to use the term 'equally' at all, we are committed to this implication. But now the transitivity of identity gives us the rest. It ensures that, if the goodness of A is the same as the goodness of B, and the goodness of B the same as the goodness of C, then the goodness of A is the same as the goodness of C. So if A is equally as good as B, and B equally as good as C, then A is equally as good as C. We cannot doubt this without doubting the transitivity of identity, and to doubt that is unintelligible.

The assumption I used in dealing with example (10.3.2) stems from a different feature of my definition of 'equally as good as', not from the fact that it is an equivalence relation. It stems from the condition within the definition that, if two things are equally good, then anything better than one is better than the other. This is certainly implied by our ordinary notion of 'equally as good as'. It is about as secure as the transitivity of betterness – that is to say, extremely secure. However, since I am in any case not relying on example (10.3.2), I shall not dwell on it.

So (10.3.1) remains a firm counterexample to the principle of equal existence. This first line of response to the counterexamples is unsuccessful.

11.2 Conditional betterness

The idea of conditional goodness is inspired by a response one might naturally make to example (10.3.1). This example poses a theoretical problem for the principle of equal existence, but not a practical problem for the intuition that existence is neutral. Suppose a couple were faced with a choice between the options contained in this example. They can choose whether or not to have a child, and they can influence the child's wellbeing if they have one. If the couple have the intuition of neutrality, they will think it does not matter ethically whether or not they have a child. But they will think that, if they do have a child, they should make sure her life goes as well as possible. In general, the intuition tells us it does not matter whether or not we add a new person to the population, but if we add one, we must do our best for her.

In example (10.3.1) this idea provides a comprehensive guide to action. Whatever are the couple's available options, it tells them what they should do. If they have a choice between *A* and *B* only, it says it does not matter which they choose. Likewise, it does not matter which they choose if they have a choice between *A* and *C* only. If they have a choice between *B* and *C*, they should choose *C*. If they have a choice between all three options, they should not choose *B*, but it does not matter whether they choose *A* or *C*.

The neutrality intuition provides a guide to action in this case, and on the face of it, it seems possible to express the intuition in terms of goodness. We may say that a person's existence is equally as good as her non-existence, but if she exists, it is better that her life should go well rather than less well. This formula uses an idea of conditional betterness: it is better that a person's life goes well, conditional on her existence. I shall develop this idea by applying it first to continuing an existing life rather than creating a new one.

In his paper 'The Makropulos case', Bernard Williams considers what reasons we have to continue our lives rather than die, if we have the choice. Most of us, he says, want all sorts of things and many of them are things we cannot get unless we continue to live. Death would prevent the satisfaction of these wants. That is a bad thing about death, and it constitutes a reason to live rather than die.

Williams then considers this rejoinder: 'Many of the things I want, I want only on the assumption that I am going to be alive ... It might be suggested that not just these special cases, but really all wants, were conditional on being alive.'[2] A want that is conditional on my being alive would give me no reason to avoid death. But Williams insists that many of us have wants that are *categorical*, by which he means they are not conditional on being alive. Categorical wants give us reasons for remaining alive.

What does it mean for a want to be conditional on being alive? Suppose you have a want for *X* that is conditional on *Y*. One thing this must mean is that you prefer (*Y* and *X*) to (*Y* and not *X*), whereas you are indifferent between (not *Y* and *X*) and (not *Y* and not *X*). Suppose you want the autumn this year to be warm, conditional on your being alive during the autumn. This implies you prefer living through a warm autumn to living through one that is not warm, but you do not care what the autumn will be like if you are dead by then.

Williams means more than this by the notion of a conditional want.

If you want a warm autumn, conditional on being alive then, he means this to leave you indifferent between living till the autumn and dying before then. This conditional preference is not supposed to give you any reason to continue living, even if the autumn is going to be warm. So it cannot give you any preference between living and dying, whatever the weather is going to be. In general, a want for *X* that is conditional on *Y* leaves you indifferent about the condition *Y*. You are indifferent between (*Y* and *X*) and (not *Y* and *X*), and between (*Y* and not *X*) and (not *Y* and not *X*). This is what Williams means.

Williams assumes that all reasons derive from wants, so the only reasons one could have for remaining alive are to satisfy one's wants. But I shall now try to generalize his idea to allow for the possibility that there are other good things in life apart from the satisfaction of wants. I shall introduce the more general idea of conditional *goods*.[3] To say something is a good means it is better that this thing should exist rather than not. To say something is a good conditional on *Y* means that, conditional on *Y*, it is better that this thing should exist rather than not.

I mean 'conditional' to be understood as Williams understands it. A conditional good is neutral about the condition. A good that is conditional on my remaining alive does not contribute to making it better that I remain alive rather than die. Only, if I do remain alive, it is better that I should get the good rather than not. A conditional good does not generate a reason why I should remain alive. If all my goods are conditional on remaining alive, there is no reason why I should remain alive.

Are there any goods that are conditional in this sense on remaining alive? It is not implausible that there are. If satisfying a person's want is good, then satisfying a conditional want will presumably be a conditional good. So if there are wants that are conditional on remaining alive, there will be goods that are conditional on remaining alive.

In any case, it is independently not implausible that there are such goods: that some things, though good, do not generate a reason for living in order to get them. Pleasure might be one example. The Epicureans believed that pleasure is the only good, and that it is conditional on remaining alive. They believed it is good for you to have pleasure while you are alive, but that pleasure gives you no reason to remain alive. Since they believed the only sort of good there is is conditional on living, they believed that your death does you no harm.[4] When Williams insists in 'The Makropulos case' that some wants are categorical, he is explicitly directing his argument against the Epicureans. He denies the Epicurean view that all goods are conditional, but he accepts that some are.

Are there really, as Williams thinks, any goods that are not conditional on remaining alive, so they give us a reason why we should remain alive? Plausibly, one sort of good that is not conditional in this way is furthering or completing a task we have embarked on: a career, perhaps, or bringing up children. I find it plausible that the good of finishing this book is a reason for staying alive till I finish it, so this good does not seem conditional on my staying alive.

However, the good of furthering or completing a task is perhaps conditional on starting the task. If so, the good of completing my next book, which I have not started yet, gives me no reason to live till I do. No doubt I do indeed have a reason to live till then, but the suggestion is that, if I do, it would be to get some good other than the good of completing that book. For example, it might be to get the good of furthering my philosophical development, which I have started.

This is only barefaced speculation, but I am going to carry it a bit further. Suppose that furthering or completing a task is the only sort of good that is not conditional on continuing to live, and suppose that all goods of this sort are conditional on starting the task. That is to say, suppose the reasons why we should move forward through life are always to further or complete the tasks we have embarked on. We are propelled forward by a sequence of overlapping tasks. As we go, we pick up other sorts of goods such as pleasure, but these are all conditional on living and do not themselves give us a reason for living. If this is so, it meshes with the intuition that existence is neutral.

How? According to this suggestion, the value of a person's existence is not all the good her life will contain, but all the good it will contain that is not conditional on her existence. It is only this unconditional good that generates a reason why the person should exist. My speculative suggestion is that, once a person is alive, the only goods that are not conditional on her remaining alive are completing or furthering tasks she has embarked on. Even these goods are conditional on her embarking on the task. So they are all conditional on the person's existing in the first place. If my suggestion is right, therefore, there is no value in a person's coming to exist.

To accept this conclusion, you do not have to be convinced by my speculation that all the goods in a person's life are of the specific sort I described: completing or furthering a task. So long as you agree that all the goods in a person's life are conditional on the person's existence, that is enough.

This amounts to an argument in support of the intuition that existence is neutral, but as an argument it is so speculative that I put no weight on it. Its importance for my purposes is that it offers us the idea of conditional good as a resource for trying to shape the intuition into a coherent form. When it comes to evaluating the condition itself, conditional good is neutral. If a person's wellbeing is good conditional on the person's existence, her wellbeing makes no difference to the value of her existence. Therefore, even though a life with more wellbeing is conditionally better than a life with less, both may be equally as good as no life at all.

All this sounds attractive, and seems at first to make sense. But working it out more carefully shows that in fact it does not. I think the idea of conditional good, as I have been using it, is incoherent. Suppose X is good conditional on Y. This is supposed to mean that $(Y$ and $X)$ is better than $(Y$ and not $X)$, whereas (not Y and $X)$ and (not Y and not $X)$ are equally good. As well as this, it is supposed to leave the condition Y neutral. That is, $(Y$ and $X)$ is equally as good as (not Y and $X)$, and $(Y$ and not $X)$ is equally as good as (not Y and not $X)$. But the transitivity of 'equally as good as' immediately implies that this is impossible.

The problem is this. If good is conditional on some condition, then it cannot be neutral about the condition itself. This may seem surprising at first. But remember that goods have to fit into a coherent betterness ordering. They make demands on this ordering, and the notion of conditional good, as I have conceived it, makes demands that cannot be satisfied. It implies a structure for the betterness ordering that it cannot have.

So long as we concentrate on example (10.3.1), we are able to ignore this incoherence in the structure of betterness, because it does not lead to a practical difficulty. The neutrality intuition seems able to handle this example in practice, and as I said on page 153, it seems possible to express its deliverances in terms of conditional good. That is why the idea of conditional good is attractive at first.

But other examples are not so amenable. Take the one below. It is similar to (10.3.2) on page 148; it is another version of Parfit's mere addition paradox. I have already discussed this version on page 59.

$$(11.2.1) \qquad \begin{aligned} A &= (4, 4, \ldots 4, 5, \Omega), \\ B &= (4, 4, \ldots 4, 6, 1), \\ C &= (4, 4, \ldots 4, 4, 4). \end{aligned}$$

How can we apply the idea of conditional good to this example? One application is easy: conditional on the last person's existing, C is better than B. This is because C has a greater total of wellbeing, and has it more equally distributed. Next, if we think wellbeing is only a conditional good, we shall have to think that, so far as the last person is concerned, *A* is equally as good as *B* and also equally as good as *C*. Since *B* is better than *A* for the second-last person, and *A* better than *C* for that person, we shall have to conclude that overall *B* is better than *A* and *A* better than *C*. But now we have violated the transitivity of betterness, because we previously concluded that *C* is better than *B*.

The idea of conditional good leads to this intransitivity. This failing cannot be ignored in this example, because it leaves us without practical guidance. If we had to make a choice between *A*, *B* and *C* as options, it would not tell us which we should choose.

I conclude that the pursuit of conditional good is a wild goose chase. The idea seems attractive at first, but it takes us nowhere.

11.3 Relative betterness

Example (11.2.1) may elicit thoughts of relative goodness, of the sort I discussed in section 4.3. Suppose the situation in the example is this. A couple already have one child; she is the second-last person in the vectors. They might have a second child; she would be the last person.

When we compare *A* and *B*, we may naturally do so from the point of view of the presently existing population, which includes the parents and the first child, but not the second child. From the point of view of this group of people, *B* is plausibly better than *A*. Similarly, from the point of view of this population, *A* is plausibly better than *C*. But when we compare *B* and *C*, we may naturally take up a different point of view: the point of view of the population that includes the second child as well. From that point of view, *C* is plausibly better than *B*.

These three plausible conclusions do not conflict with the transitivity of betterness, because they do not all belong to the same betterness relation. We concluded *B* is better than *A*, and *A* better than *B*, relative to the population that does not include the second child. We concluded *C* is better than *B* relative to the population that does include the second child. There is no intransitivity. So relativity might provide a way out of our problems.

Dasgupta's theory

One relativist theory has been sketched out by Partha Dasgupta.[5] Dasgupta's account is not complete, and I shall have to fill it out in some respects in order to assess it. In doing so, in this section, I shall use 'population' to mean 'temporal population': all the people who are alive at a particular time. (In the rest of the book, 'population' means all the people who are alive at any time.)

Dasgupta's account consists of two parts. The first is a formula for goodness relative to a particular population. The formula Dasgupta suggests is a weighted total of people's wellbeing, giving more weight to the members of the population. This is only meant as an illustrative suggestion; Dasgupta is not committed to this particular formula. However, the zero will certainly be significant in any formula that will serve his purposes. On page 138, I explained that the total principle, which values the total of people's wellbeing, is not properly defined until a zero has been specified. The same goes for a weighted total formula such as Dasgupta's, or for any similar formula. Dasgupta therefore needs to specify the zero to make his formula determinate. Let us assume he has done that, and in this section let us treat the zero as significant.

To illustrate the weighted total formula, let us evaluate the distributions in example (11.2.1) relative to the population consisting of all but the second child. Since the second child is not in this population, she gets a lower weight. If her weight is less than a quarter, *A* will be better than *C* from the point of view of the population that excludes her. The four units the second child gets in *C* are outweighed by the extra one unit the first child gets in *A* compared with *C*. Relative to this population that excludes the second child, *B* is better than *A*, obviously. So if the weight given to excluded people is less than a quarter, the ordering of the options relative to this population is: *B* best, *A* second and *C* worst.

On the other hand, relative to the population that includes everyone, everyone gets an equal weight. Relative to this population, the ordering is: *C* best, *B* second and *A* worst.

The weighted formula for relative betterness is the first part of Dasgupta's account. The second part is a formula determining which act is right, given the various betterness relations relative to different populations. At any time there is some population living, and it must choose what to do. Dasgupta's theory specifies what it ought to do by means of a two-stage procedure.

Stage one goes like this. First, we collect the options into groups according to their populations, so that each group contains only options that have the same population. Then from each group we pick the option that is best according to the betterness relation that is relative to that group's population. This relation gives equal weight to everyone in the population. So the best option in each group is simply the one in that group that has the greatest unweighted total of wellbeing. Dasgupta does not tell us what to do if more than one option is best in a group by this criterion – that is, if several options in a group are equally good and better than the others. So let us ignore this possibility. Then by the end of stage one, we have selected one option from each group – one for each population, that is.

In stage two, we compare all the options that we selected in stage one. We find the one that is best according to the betterness relation of the population that is actually making the choice. This means, in stage two, giving more weight to the choosing population's wellbeing compared with other people's. The option that ought to be chosen is the one that comes out best from this second stage of comparison.

Let us see how the procedure works out in examples. First take example (10.3.1) from page 146. Suppose the choice is in the hands of the population that does not include the last person. For example, suppose the last person is a potential child of an existing couple.

To apply the two-stage procedure, we first compare *B* and *C* because they form a group of options that have the same population. We compare them on the basis of their unweighted total of wellbeing. The result is that *C* is selected as the best in this group. *A* forms a group on its own, because no other option has the same population. So it is also selected at stage one, as the best in its group. In sum, stage one eliminates only *B*.

At stage two, we compare *A* and *C* on the basis of betterness relative to the choosing population. So long as this relation gives a weight of more than zero to people who do not belong to the choosing population, the best at stage two is *C*. The population should therefore choose *C*, according to Dasgupta's theory. On the other hand, if the weight is zero, *A* and *C* have the same weighted total, so it does not matter which the population chooses.

Now take example (11.2.1) from page 156. Suppose the choosing population is everyone except for the second child. At stage one we compare *B* with *C*, because these two distributions form a group with the same population. Out of these two, *C* has the greater unweighted total of wellbeing, so it is selected at stage one. *A* is also selected at stage one, because it forms a group on its own. In sum, stage one eliminates only *B*.

At stage two, we compare *A* and *C*, on the basis of betterness relative to the choosing population. If this relation gives a weight of less than a quarter to the wellbeing of the last person, who does not belong to this population, *A* comes out best. So the population should choose *A*. Otherwise, it should choose *C*.

Those are the conclusions of Dasgupta's theory for the examples. How do they square with intuition? In (10.3.1), I think most people's intuitions are clear, if they are guided by the intuition that existence is neutral. They think it would be wrong to choose *B* if *C* is available, but they think the choice between *A* and *C* does not matter ethically. Dasgupta's theory reproduces this conclusion only if a population should give a zero weight to people who do not belong to it. In any case, it is obvious that Dasgupta's theory can only hope to capture the intuition that existence is neutral if it makes this weight zero.

Given a zero weight, or any weight less than a quarter, in example (11.2.1) the theory favours the choice of *A*. I think many people's intuitions might not be clear in this example. Still, *A* is a plausible choice. So Dasgupta's theory may not only represent our intuitions adequately; in some cases it may take us beyond them, as an ethical theory should, and deliver an answer where intuition fails.

Why relative betterness?

So the theory could perhaps satisfy the intuition of neutrality in at least some cases. However, the theory still needs to be justified. The idea of relative betterness still needs to be justified, and so does the two-stage procedure. Take each in turn.

Why does Dasgupta think betterness is relative to the population, and why does he think betterness relative to a population gives more weight to the population's own wellbeing than to other people's? Good relative to a population is certainly not supposed to reflect simply the population's own interest. That would be an aggregate of the population's own wellbeing, and relative good includes more than that. It is supposed instead to be general good, but seen from the point of view of the population.

Dasgupta treats population-relativity as a sort of community-relativity. He thinks members of a community have special claims on each other that outsiders do not have. A population is a sort of community, and from its point of view people not yet born are outsiders. Dasgupta particularly has in mind the community of the family. 'Family members', he says, 'have a special claim upon one another. Potential persons don't have this claim. "They" are not members of the community.' [6]

So a person whose existence is in question is an outsider from the point of view of a population, and the population gives less weight to her wellbeing on that account. This idea assimilates the creation problems I have been discussing to adoption problems. So example (10.3.1) would get the same treatment as the problem of a childless couple wondering whether to adopt a child, if the child would have zero wellbeing were she not adopted. The adoption problem is this:

(11.3.1)
$$A = (4, 4, \dots 4, 0),$$
$$B = (4, 4, \dots 4, 1),$$
$$C = (4, 4, \dots 4, 2).$$

In general, Dasgupta's relativism treats a person whose existence is in question like an outsider whose admission to the community is in question – a sort of person-in-waiting, who might or might not be granted the privilege of existence, and who meanwhile has zero wellbeing.

Adoption problems are often difficult, like creation problems, but the two sorts of problem are undoubtedly not parallel. The intuitively correct solution to (11.3.1) is not the same as the intuitively correct solution to (10.3.1). In (10.3.1), most of us who are influenced by the neutrality intuition think it does not matter morally whether the parents choose *A* or *C*, but they should not choose *B*. But in the adoption analogue (11.3.1), most of us would think the couple ought to choose *C*: they ought to adopt the child and give her a wellbeing of 2. They are able to raise an existing person's wellbeing from 0 to 2 at no cost to themselves, so it seems they ought to do so.

Dasgupta's relativity theory is able to reproduce the conclusion of intuition in example (10.3.1) only if the child's wellbeing receives zero weight in the couple's relative betterness relation. But in (11.3.1), it would be wrong for the couple to give the child's wellbeing zero weight. Even an outsider's wellbeing should count for something.

The truth is that this type of relativism thoroughly misrepresents our intuition from the start. Our intuition is that adoption is nothing like creation; it benefits the adopted person, whereas creation does not benefit the created person. This intuition is not relativist; anyone can recognize it, including the person herself if she is created. I conclude that if we are to have a relativist theory of population, it cannot be founded on community-relativity. It needs some other basis, and I do not know what that could be.

Why the two-stage procedure?

Now to the justification of Dasgupta's two-stage procedure. For the sake of argument, let us now accept that each population has its own relative betterness relation. How should an existing population act? According to the theory, it ought not simply do the best it can according to its own betterness relation. Through the two-stage procedure, betterness relative to other populations helps to determine what a particular population ought to do. Why?

An attractive feature of the procedure appears in example (11.2.1). Suppose the population making a choice consists of everyone apart from the second child. According to this population's betterness relation, *B* is better than *C* if the weight given to the second child's wellbeing is less than a quarter. However, if this population was in a position to make an actual choice between *B* and *C*, it seems intuitively obvious that it should choose *C* rather than *B*. If a choice is to be made between *B* and *C*, it is already settled that the second child will exist. Since she will exist, her wellbeing should surely be given full weight. The two-stage procedure supports this conclusion: in a choice between *B* and *C* it favours *C*, even if the choosing population does not include the second child.

But then, what does it mean to say that *B* is better than *C* relative to this choosing population? To be sure, *B* is more in this population's interest than *C*, but its own interest is not in question. Dasgupta's relative betterness relations are not meant to express the interests of particular populations; they are meant to express general betterness from each population's point of view. Yet we have just seen they do not tell us what a population ought morally to do. So what do they tell us? The question needs answering if we are to understand Dasgupta's relativist theory, and I do not know what the answer can be.

This is an instance of a general problem about relative good. I explained in section 4.3 that if each actor – in this case a population – ought to promote its own relative good, incoherence is likely to arise. This explains why Dasgupta offers the two-stage procedure instead, for determining what a population ought to do. But then, if an actor ought to promote something other than its own relative good, it is hard to see what can be meant by saying that, nevertheless, this is the actor's relative good.

I conclude that relativism fails to deliver what we hoped for from it. We hoped it would provide a good account of the intuitions I described in section 10.2, but it does not.

Notes

1 For one, Larry Temkin in 'Intransitivity and the mere addition paradox'.
2 'The Makropulos case', p. 85.

3 I first suggested this idea in 'Some principles of population'. It was adopted by Partha Dasgupta in 'Lives and well-being'.

4 See Epicurus, 'Letter to Menoeceus', particularly pp. 30–1. Williams's 'The Makropulos case' comments particularly on the writing of another Epicurean, Lucretius, in *On the Nature of the Universe*. My own view about the Epicurean position appears in section 16.2.

5 I shall describe the version of Dasgupta's theory that appears in his *An Inquiry Into Well-Being and Destitution*, pp. 377–94. An earlier version appeared in his 'Lives and well-being'.

6 *An Inquiry into Well-Being and Destitution*, p. 386.

12

Indeterminate betterness

On page 149, I listed possible responses to the difficulties that beset the intuition of neutral existence. Chapter 11 considered the first three; I do not favour those ones. This chapter considers the fourth response, which I find more satisfactory.

Its basic idea is that betterness is not a fully determinate relation. That is surely true, but it is difficult to express the indeterminacy in a satisfactory form. Section 12.1 is a first attempt. It suggests that things are sometimes mutually incommensurate in value, and it specifies what this means. Incommensurateness can account for the neutrality intuition. But towards the end of the section, I shall raise some doubts about its account. The doubt that will in the end turn out most serious is that it makes neutrality unintuitively 'greedy', as I shall put it.

My own view is that the indeterminacy in betterness is vagueness. I think the relation 'better than' is vague. Section 12.2 argues that its vagueness is, perhaps surprisingly, incompatible with incommensurateness. It also argues that, out of these two incompatible contenders, vagueness provides a better account of the indeterminacy of betterness. Section 12.3 provides a brief outline of the supervaluationist theory of vagueness, which is the one I favour.

Section 12.4 applies my account of indeterminacy to the value of existence. It argues that the neutral level of wellbeing defined in chapter 10 is vague. (The neutral level divides lives that are better lived than not lived from those that are better not lived than lived.) It argues that this vagueness provides a moderately plausible account of the neutrality intuition. However, it too makes neutrality implausibly greedy. This problem will ultimately lead to the demise of the neutrality intuition in section 14.2.

Section 12.5 explains that supervaluation theory nevertheless provides a basis for carrying forward the theoretical development of this book. It also explains that, when we come to the formal theoretical development, it makes little difference whether we adopt incommensurateness or vagueness as our account of the neutrality intuition.

12.1 Incommensurateness

Often, when we compare the goodness of two things and ask which is better, we seem unable to give a correct answer. It seems intuitively that we cannot correctly say one is better than the other, and we also cannot correctly say the two are equally good. This most commonly happens when the two things realize very different values. It may seem impossible to weigh these different values against each other, to determine which is more weighty.

A classic example is Jean-Paul Sartre's.[1] During the Second World War, one of Sartre's students had to make a choice between staying in France to look after his mother, and leaving to join the Free French Forces in Britain. His mother very much needed him to stay, because his father had been revealed to be a traitor and his brother had been killed by the Nazis. Staying with her was a way to meet her needs. On the other hand, leaving for Britain was a way to promote the honour and freedom of France. The student was unable to weigh up determinately the values promoted by his two alternatives. The question 'Which is better: to stay or to leave?' seemed to him to have no right answer.

That is how it seemed to the student. We might give various accounts of how the situation actually was. For example, we might say the student did not know the true situation. It was actually the case that one of the two options was better than the other, or that the two were equally good, but the student did not know this. Only his ignorance prevented him from answering the question. Often questions like this seem to have no right answer, but that may always be so only because we do not know the facts well enough.

On the other hand, we may accept there is genuinely no right answer. Then we might give various accounts of why not. My own preferred account will appear in section 12.2. But for the moment, I shall assume the situation is that neither of the options facing the student is better than the other, and yet the two are not equally good.

When this happens, I shall say the two options are *incommensurate*. 'A is incommensurate with B' means that A is neither better nor worse than B, nor equally as good as B. On page 21 I defined 'A is equally as good as B' to mean that A is neither better nor worse than B, and that any third thing C that is better or worse than A is, correspondingly, better or worse than B. So when A is incommensurate with B, there is some third thing C that is better or worse than either A or B, but not correspondingly better or worse than the other. This specifies the difference between equality and incommensurateness.

One consequence of my definition is that the relation 'incommensurate with' may be intransitive. The demonstration is easy, and I shall not spell it out.

On page 22 I made the assumption that the betterness relation is complete. This ruled out incommensurateness. I mentioned at the time that it was only a holding assumption. Now I withdraw it.

Take two things *A* and *B* such that neither is better than the other. The definition of incommensurateness gives us a test for determining whether they are incommensurate or equally good. Look for some third thing *C* that is better or worse than one of them, but not correspondingly better or worse than the other. If there is such a third thing, they are incommensurate; if there is not, they are equally good.

The place to look for the third thing is amongst things that are just a little better or worse than *A* or *B*. If there is such a *C* anywhere, there will be one here. So the right test is this. Start by improving *A* a little bit, to make a new thing – call it *A+* – that is a little better than *A*. Check whether *A+* is better than *B*. If it is not, then *A* and *B* must be incommensurate. If it is, the test is not yet finished. Next make *A* a little bit worse, to give a new thing *A–* that is worse than *A*. Check whether *A–* is worse than *B*. If it is not, *A* and *B* must be incommensurate. If it is, carry out the same test on the other side: make *B* first a little better and then a little worse, and compare the results with *A*. If no part of this test shows *A* and *B* to be incommensurate, they are equally good.[2]

This is intuitively a correct test. Intuitively, when things are incommensurate, so it is not determinate which is better, a small improvement or deterioration in one of them may not settle the matter of which is better. Take Sartre's example again. Suppose one of the student's two options improves slightly. Suppose the escape route becomes slightly safer, so the option of leaving for Britain is now slightly more likely to succeed. This change need not settle for the student which is the better option; the two options may still be incommensurate. Let *A* be leaving for Britain before the improvement, and let *A+* be leaving for Britain after the improvement. Let *B* be staying at home with his mother. *A+* is better than *A*, but both *A* and *A+* are incommensurate with *B*.

The idea of incommensurateness gives us a new resource for tackling the problem raised in chapter 10. Intuition suggests that existence is neutral, at least over a range of levels of wellbeing. When a person can be added to the population, whether or not she is added is intuitively neutral, at least if her wellbeing would fall within some particular range. I expressed this intuition on page 146 in the form of the principle of equal existence. There, I interpreted neutrality as equality of goodness.

But perhaps our intuitive idea of neutrality should be understood as incommensurateness in value rather than equality of value.[3] That would give us this alternative principle:

> *Principle of incommensurate existence.* Suppose two distributions have the same population of people, except that an extra person exists in one who does not exist in the other. Suppose each person who exists in both distributions is equally as well off in one as she is in the other. Then there is some range of wellbeings (called 'the neutral range') such that, if the extra person's wellbeing is within this range, the two distributions are incommensurate in value.

No contradictions arise from this principle as they did from the principle of equal existence, because incommensurateness need not be transitive. For instance, in example (10.3.1), *C* is better than *B* by the principle of personal good. Both *B* and *C* are incommensurate with *A* by the principle of incommensurate existence. There is no contradiction there, and none arises in the other examples either.

The completeness assumption was vital to the argument of section 10.1. On its basis, I demonstrated that there is only one neutral level of wellbeing. Now I have dropped the assumption, the conclusion no longer follows. There may be a whole range of neutral levels. This is just the intuition of neutrality that I described in section 10.2. Our formal theory is no longer in conflict with this intuition.

Comparing distributions

To store up for later, I need to make a technical remark that I hope is obvious, though tedious. Take two distributions *A* and *B* that meet the conditions of the principle of incommensurate existence: they share the same population except that *B* has an extra person who does not exist in *A*, and each person who exists in both *A* and *B* is equally as well off in *A* as she is in *B*. Let the extra person's wellbeing in *B* be *g*. Here is a tedious way to determine the relative values of *A* and *B*.

Suppose there is a neutral range. Start by taking any level of wellbeing *v* within the range, and for a moment treat that as the single neutral level. Supposing it is the neutral level, ask whether either *A* or *B* is better than the other. The answer will be that *A* is better if *g*, the new person's wellbeing in *B*, is below this level *v*, and *B* is better if *g* is above *v*. Then pick another value for *v* in the neutral range, and ask the same question, supposing now that this is the single neutral level. Run through every level in the range, asking the same question for each. If the answer for every value of v in the neutral range is that *A* is better than *B*, then *A* is indeed better than *B*. This is because the extra person's wellbeing *g* must lie below the whole neutral range. If the answer for every level is that *B* is better than *A*, then indeed *B* is better than *A*, because *g* must lie above the whole neutral range. If neither *A* nor *B* turns out better than the other by this test, the two are incommensurate. In this case the extra person's wellbeing lies within the neutral range.

So this tedious test determines correctly whether *A* is better than *B*, or *B* is better than *A*, or *A* and *B* are incommensurate.

Doubts

The principle of incommensurate existence seems to solve the problems raised in section 10.3. It may be the right way to accommodate the intuition of neutrality into an account of the value of lives. However, I have some doubts about it.

The first is that it seems arbitrary to call on the idea of incommensurateness to deal with the problems raised in section 10.3, without some justification. Why should two options be incommensurate in value just because they have different populations? That needs to be explained.

I introduced incommensurateness through Sartre's example, and in that example there is a plausible explanation of why the options might be incommensurate. They achieve, or aim to achieve, very different values. The student's option of leaving for Britain aims to achieve the values of honour, patriotism and national freedom. His option of staying with his mother aims to achieve the values of kindness and filial love. It is not surprising if such very different values cannot be precisely weighed against each other. One would not expect precise commensurability among them.

But our case is not at all like Sartre's. We are not dealing with differing values. One option has a different number of people from the other. Whatever the value of people might be, each option realizes that value; one simply realizes a greater quantity of it than the other. So if our options are really incommensurate in value, we need some explanation of why.

Without one, the appeal to incommensurateness of value seems a fudge. Our intuition is that existence is neutral. Neutrality is most naturally understood as equality of value; that is to say, a person's existing is equally as good as her not existing. But under this interpretation, we find ourselves in trouble caused by the transitivity of 'equally as good as'. So we say: why not treat neutrality as incommensurateness instead of equality? Incommensurateness of goodness is like equality of goodness with the transitivity deleted. By this move, we shrug off the inconvenience caused by transitivity. But it looks like a fudge unless we can offer some reason why the neutrality of existence really amounts to incommensurateness rather than equality. This account requires some more explaining; that is my first doubt about it.[4]

My second doubt emerges only after some analysis. The relation 'better than' is surely not absolutely precise; it must be vague to some extent. That is to say, there must be borderline cases of betterness: cases where the question 'Is this thing better than that?' does not have a definite answer. We cannot say it is better, and we cannot say it is not better. There must be cases like this, just because betterness must be vague to some extent. However, it turns out on analysis that incommensurateness of value is incompatible with vagueness. Since betterness must be vague to some extent, there cannot be incommensurateness of value.

Do not be confused: incommensurateness is not itself vagueness. When two options A and B are incommensurate, A is not better than B and B is not better than A. There are definite answers to the questions 'Is B better than A?' and 'Is A better than B?'; both have the answer no. So incommensurateness could exist without vagueness in betterness. But it turns out that it cannot exist with it.

I am not suggesting this incompatibility is obvious; indeed it is surprising. It emerges on page 175 from an argument in the next section. I must also admit that not everyone finds the argument as convincing as I do. So not everyone will be troubled by this second doubt.

My third doubt is the most serious. It is that incommensurateness simply does not capture accurately the intuitive idea of neutrality. Here is a feature of the intuitive idea. Suppose two things happen together. One is bad, and the other neutral. Intuitively, the net effect of the two things should be bad. A bad thing combined with a neutral thing should be bad. Intuitively, neutrality cannot act against badness to cancel it out, so the net effect should not be neutral. This was how the neutrality intuition first surfaced in section 10.2. Adding a person to the world seems intuitively not to have a value that can be set against the value of other things.

Now look again at example (10.3.2) on page 148, the mere addition paradox. I reproduce it here:

(12.1.1) $A = (4, 4, \ldots 4, 6, \Omega)$,
                           $B = (4, 4, \ldots 4, 6, 1)$,
                           $C = (4, 4, \ldots 4, 4, 4)$,
                           $D = (4, 4, \ldots 4, 4, \Omega)$.

The example is based on the assumption that 1 and 4 are both within the neutral range. Interpreting neutrality as incommensurateness, we conclude that A is incommensurate with B, and C with D. No contradiction can be derived, which is why this is not a counterexample to the principle of incommensurate existence.

But compare the relative value of A and C. Could C be worse than A? It could not, because for the sake of this example we are taking it for granted that B is worse than C. It has less wellbeing in total, and has it unequally distributed. So if C were worse than A, B would be worse than A. But B is not worse than A; it is incommensurate with A. C is therefore not worse than A.

However, the intuitive implication of neutrality I have described is that C is indeed worse than A. Moving from A to C involves two things. First, the second-last person's wellbeing is reduced from 6 to 4. This is a bad thing. Second, an extra person is added at level 4. This is a neutral thing. The net effect of one bad thing and one neutral thing should be bad. But according to our theory, it is not bad; it is neutral.

Incommensurateness is not neutrality as it intuitively should be. It is a sort of greedy neutrality, which is capable of swallowing up badness or goodness and neutralizing it. This is implausible, but the full extent of its implausibility will not emerge till section 14.2, when we have some more theory worked out. Greedy neutrality will turn out to have some practical implications that are very implausible indeed.

I have a way to avoid the first two doubts about the principle of incommensurate existence. I started this chapter with the idea that betterness is in some way indeterminate. I shall next suggest that this indeterminacy is not incommensurateness as I defined it on page 165, but nothing other than vagueness itself. This suggestion provides a way of supporting the intuition that existence is neutral, and of responding to the problems of section 10.3. It does not encounter my first two doubts about incommensurateness. It is perfectly comprehensible why the betterness relation should be vague when it comes to enlarging the population: we can expect it to be vague in all contexts. And of course, vagueness is not incompatible with vagueness. For this reason, I find vagueness preferable to incommensurateness as an account of indeterminacy in betterness. This account is set out in sections 12.2 to 12.4.

The vagueness account overcomes my first two doubts about incommensurateness, but I have no remedy for the third. The vagueness account will turn out to be equally subject to it. We shall not be able to assess it properly until section 14.2.

12.2 Vague betterness versus incommensurateness

Many terms in our language are vague. 'Friendly' is one of them. Their vagueness leads to a particular sort of indeterminacy; because of vagueness there may be no determinate answer to the question 'Is Tony friendly?'. 'Yes' may not be a correct answer, and nor may 'No'. There is a hazy zone between people who are friendly and people who are not, and Tony may be in this boundary zone. There is also indeterminacy in betterness. For two options *A* and *B*, there may be no determinate answer to the question 'Which is better: *A* or *B*?' My suggestion is that this, too, is the result of vagueness. It results from the vagueness of 'better than'.

At first, this suggestion may seem plainly wrong. It seems the latter question may have no answer for a reason that has nothing to do with vagueness. Like 'Have you stopped beating your wife?', the question 'Which is better: *A* or *B*?' makes a presumption. It presumes that one or the other of *A* or *B* is the better of the two. If this presumption is not satisfied, the question has no answer just for that reason.

For instance, the question has no correct answer when *A* and *B* are equally good. 'Neither' would be a correct answer if it was permissible, but strictly the grammar of the question does not permit it. Still, although the question has no answer when *A* and *B* are equally good, there is no vagueness here and indeed no real indeterminacy. Vagueness puts a question mark over the truth of certain statements. Because 'friendly' is vague, there can be a question over the truth of the statement 'Tony is friendly'. We may be unhappy to assert this statement and also unhappy to deny it. But when two things are equally good, no question mark hangs over the truth of any statement. All relevant statements are straightforwardly true or straightforwardly false. The statement '*A* is better than *B*' is straightforwardly false. So is the statement '*B* is better than *A*'. 'Which is better?' has no answer only because it does not directly ask about the truth of any statement. It is not a yes-or-no question; it does not specify a statement and ask whether it is true.

Like equality, incommensurateness as I defined it also raises no question about the truth of any statement. When two things are incommensurate, the statement 'A is better than B' is false, and so is the statement 'B is better than A'. The only difference between incommensurateness and equality is that, when A and B are incommensurate, the statement 'A and B are equally good' is also false, whereas when A and B are equally good, this statement is true. So incommensurateness has nothing to do with vagueness.

Vague betterness

However, that is not the end of the story. To begin with, notice that some comparative relations are vague, just like some monadic predicates such as 'friendly'. 'More friendly than' is vague, for example. Compare people one by one with Tony, to see whether or not they are more friendly than him. Of some people we can say firmly that they are more friendly than Tony, and of others we can say firmly that they are not. But we shall not be able to divide all people into two classes: those that are more friendly than Tony and those that are not. There will be a zone of borderline cases. These are people of whom we would not willingly assert that they are more friendly than Tony, nor willingly deny it. For people in the borderline zone, there is a question mark over the truth of the statement 'This person is more friendly than Tony'.

Which people are *less* friendly than Tony is another matter. I have not raised that question at all.

The comparative 'better than' is also vague. Take Sartre's example again. Take the student's option of leaving for Britain, and imagine varying the circumstances of it. In different circumstances, it would have very different values. For each set of circumstances, compare this option of leaving for Britain with the student's option of staying at home to look after his mother. If the circumstances are that the student can easily reach Britain, and can contribute so greatly to the liberation of France that he would soon be back home victorious, then leaving for Britain is better than staying at home. On the other hand, if the student can contribute nothing to the war effort, the option of leaving for Britain is not better than staying at home. Those are extreme circumstances; what happens in intermediate cases?

It is incredible that there should be a sharp boundary between cases that are better than staying at home and cases that are not better, leaving no borderline cases in between. There must be cases of which we would not willingly assert that they are better than staying at home, and also not willingly deny it. For these cases, there is a question mark over the truth of 'Leaving for Britain is better than staying at home'.

Whether leaving for Britain is worse than staying at home is another matter. I have not so far raised that question.

So betterness is undoubtedly vague, but this need have nothing to do with incommensurateness. Cases that are incommensurate with staying at home are ones that are not better than staying at home and also not worse than staying at home. But the borderline cases I have just mentioned are ones where we cannot say they are not better than staying at home. So we cannot say those borderline cases are incommensurate with staying at home.

Imagine looking down a list of cases, starting with very good ones, where the student would greatly contribute to a quick victory for France, and running right down to bad ones, where he would achieve nothing. At the top of the list are cases that are better than staying at home. Further down are borderline cases, of which we cannot say they are better than staying at home, but cannot deny it either. Further down still are incommensurate cases. These are not better than staying at home. However, they are also not worse. Further down the list still, we shall no doubt encounter cases that are on a different borderline: the borderline between cases that are worse than staying at home and those that are not worse. Of cases on this borderline, we cannot say they are worse than staying at home, but cannot deny it either. At the bottom of the list, we shall finally come to cases that are worse than staying at home.

That is the picture I have built up so far. It recognizes the vagueness of 'better than', but distinguishes it from incommensurateness. Vagueness creates borderline cases, but incommensurateness is not a borderline of that sort.

Vagueness and incommensurateness are incompatible

But I do not think this picture can be correct. Take one of the borderline cases I have been considering: leaving for Britain under such circumstances that we cannot say this case is better than staying at home, and cannot deny it either. Is this case worse than staying at home? In the present picture, definitely not. There are incommensurate cases that are worse than this, and even those are not worse than staying at home. So our case is definitely not worse than staying at home.

To say the same thing another way, staying at home is definitely not better than leaving for Britain in these conditions. We can firmly deny that staying at home is better than leaving for Britain. On the other hand, we cannot deny that leaving for Britain is better than staying at home. That is what we have concluded about this case.

However, this conclusion constitutes an unsustainable position. Suppose Sartre's student aims to do what is best. What should he do in this case? Obviously, he should leave for Britain. The case is not like the one I described at the beginning of this chapter. There, the student faced the choice between staying at home and leaving for Britain, when neither option was better than the other. It was therefore not the case that he should choose one option, and not the case that he should choose the other. He was in a genuinely difficult predicament. But in the case we are now dealing with, we cannot say that neither option is better than the other. True, staying at home is not better than leaving for Britain. But we cannot say that leaving for Britain is not better than staying at home. There is this clear asymmetry between the two options. That is enough to give the student a clear reason to leave for Britain. He need not hesitate.

But then, he could not have such a clear reason unless leaving for Britain was actually the better thing to do. There is an asymmetry between the two options in respect of their goodness. When we compare the options with each other, one scores higher than the other for its goodness. An asymmetry like this is enough to determine that one option is better than the other.

In sum, it is an unsustainable position to deny that staying at home is better than leaving for Britain, refuse to deny that leaving for Britain is better than staying at home, and yet also refuse to assert that leaving for Britain is better than staying at home.

The point about asymmetry is expressed in this general principle:

Collapsing principle. For any predicate F and any things A and B, if we can deny that B is Fer than A, but we cannot deny that A is Fer than B, then A is Fer than B.

The collapsing principle is defended in my paper 'Is incommensurability vagueness?'.[5] It seems obvious to me, and scarcely in need of defence. However, I have to confess that I have not been able to convince everyone of it, so perhaps it would be proper for me to take a cautious attitude towards it.[6] If the collapsing principle is incorrect, the argument I am making fails. Vagueness and incommensurateness will be compatible after all. I think they are incompatible but I may be wrong. If I am, it will not make a great difference to the theory developed in the rest of this book. I shall explain why not on page 185.

In passing, I need to mention one further consequence of the collapsing principle. The principle also implies that borderline cases of the statement '*A* is better than *B*' coincide with borderline cases of the statement '*B* is better than *A*'. The argument for this point appears in 'Is incommensurability vagueness?', and here I shall take it for granted.

We got into an unsustainable position because we separated the vagueness of 'better than' from incommensurateness. Vagueness creates cases where we cannot say *A* is better than *B*, but cannot deny it either. On the other hand, incommensurate cases are ones where *A* is not better than *B*, and *B* is not better than *A*. We have found that cases of these two types cannot coexist. If there is vagueness, there cannot be incommensurateness, and if there is incommensurateness there cannot be vagueness. Which is there, then?

I do not think there can be any doubt that 'better than' is vague. I cannot imagine there being a sharp boundary between cases that are better than the student's staying at home and cases that are not better than this. On the other hand, I aim to show in the rest of this chapter that we can do without incommensurateness as I defined it. Our intuitions can be satisfied equally well with vagueness. So I suggest we should abandon the idea of incommensurateness in favour of vagueness.

The upshot will be this. Suppose we have to compare two options *A* and *B*. Four possible conclusions might emerge from the comparison. One possibility is that *A* is better than *B*. Another is that *B* is better than *A*. The third is that *A* and *B* are equally good. The fourth is the case of vagueness: we cannot say *A* is better than *B*, nor deny it, and we cannot say *B* is better than *A*, nor deny that. In this fourth case, we also cannot say *A* is equally as good as *B*. There is no fifth possibility, where *A* is not better than *B*, and *B* is not better than *A*, but *A* and *B* are not equally good.

12.3 Supervaluation

Up to now, I have been talking about vagueness in a way that is in itself vague and perhaps obscure. For example, I have talked about a question mark hanging over the truth of particular statements. I have constantly used the locution 'We cannot say ...'. I had to talk in such a loose way because theories of vagueness abound, and each has a different account of what vagueness really is.[7] Before I can speak more clearly, I need to adopt a particular theory. I shall do that next.

I shall adopt supervaluation theory, and I shall start by explaining it.[8] Since vagueness is not the subject of this book, I shall keep my explanation as short and informal as I can. Unfortunately, I cannot avoid mentioning one difficult issue within the theory. That will come on page 177.

As logicians do, let us talk about 'interpretations' for our language. An interpretation assigns a meaning to each term. For example, some interpretations assign Notre Dame to be the meaning of 'the Eiffel tower'. Others assign Montmartre to be the meaning of 'the Eiffel tower'. The 'standard interpretation' is the interpretation that assigns every term the meaning it actually has. For one thing, it assigns the Eiffel Tower to 'the Eiffel Tower'.

The standard interpretation assigns vague meanings to those of our terms that actually have vague meanings. It assigns a vague meaning to 'tall', for instance. But there are other interpretations that assign sharp meanings to all the terms in the language, including 'tall'. Call these 'sharp interpretations'. Some sharp interpretations assign 'tall' the meaning of pregnant. Others assign it the meaning of more than two metres in height; others, more than one metre eighty in height; and so on.

Some of these sharp interpretations count as *sharpenings* of the standard interpretation – of the actual meaning of our language. The actual meaning of 'tall' determines which sharp interpretations are sharpenings of 'tall', and which not. More than one metre eighty in height is a sharpening of 'tall'. Pregnant, and more than two metres in height are not.

I have not been quite accurate in speaking of sharpenings of 'tall' on its own. To be accurate, the notion of a sharpening has to be fixed holistically. A sharpening is an interpretation of the whole language, and the whole language determines which interpretations are sharpenings of it. Sharpenings of individual terms cannot be determined separately, because the meanings of different terms are linked together. For example, we could not fix the sharpenings of 'better painter than' independently of sharpenings of 'equally as good a painter as'. It might be that in some sharpenings of our language, Turner is a better painter than Gauguin, and in other sharpenings Turner is equally as good a painter as Gauguin. But in no sharpening is Turner a better painter than Gauguin and also equally as good a painter as Gauguin.

Do not misunderstand the idea of sharpening. I cannot define it, because it is a primitive notion in supervaluation theory. It would be misleading to describe it as a way in which the language might be sharpened. In some sharpenings, Turner is equally as good a painter as Gauguin. But this does not mean we might come to say that Turner is equally as good a painter as Gauguin. Betterness amongst painters has to be a vague concept. We need it to be vague, or we could not use it. The idea of a sharpening is a device with which we can specify the meaning of vague terms. That is all.

Supervaluation theory next specifies how to evaluate a statement that contains vague terms. We first evaluate it under all sharpenings of the language, one by one. We may assert a statement if and only if it is true under every sharpening. This is the core of supervaluationism.

(12.3.1)   *Supervaluation.* We may assert 'S' if and only if 'S'
                is true under every sharpening.

For example, to evaluate 'Richard is tall', we might start by assigning to 'tall' the interpretation of more than one metre eighty in height, and check whether Richard is tall under that assignment. That is to say, we check if he is more than one metre eighty in height. Then we assign to 'tall' the interpretation of more than one metre eighty-five in height, and check whether Richard is tall under that assignment. We do the same for every sharpening of 'tall'. We can say Richard is tall if and only if Richard is tall under every sharpening. Similarly, we can say Richard is not tall if and only if he is not tall under every sharpening. To put it another way, in those circumstances, and only in those, we can deny he is tall.

If Richard is tall under some sharpenings but not under others, he is a borderline case of tallness. We cannot assert that he is tall, and we also cannot deny it.

Although I shall use the term 'borderline case', it can be misleading. One might expect a borderline to be rather narrow, whereas vagueness can be very extensive. The borderline between the Pacific Ocean and the Southern Ocean is vague to the extent of hundreds of miles.

There is a delicate issue in supervaluation theory. In the schema (12.3.1) for supervaluation, 'S' cannot stand for just any statement at all. For example, it could not be ' "Tall" is not a vague term'. This statement is true in every sharpening, because every sharpening assigns a sharp meaning to every term. So if supervaluation applied to it, we could assert ' "Tall" is not a vague term'. But clearly we cannot assert that. Evidently, supervaluation does not apply to every statement, and statements containing 'vague' are amongst those it does not apply to.

The consequence is that we have to recognize a distinction between the object language, to which the theory applies, and the metalanguage in which we present the theory. Supervaluation will not apply to the metalanguage. The delicate issue is where to draw the line: which terms to include in the object language and which to keep in the metalanguage. 'Vague', 'sharpening' and other terms belonging to supervaluation theory itself must be in the metalanguage. But what about 'true'?

The original presentations of supervaluation theory kept the predicate 'true' in the metalanguage and excluded it from the object language.[9] Supervaluation was presented in this form:

(12.3.2)   'S' is true if and only if 'S' is true under every sharpening.

But this causes a difficulty. Suppose 'S' is a borderline case, which means it is true under some sharpenings and not under others. Then according to (12.3.2),

(12.3.3)   'S' is not true.

The negation of 'S', 'not S', is also true under some sharpenings and not under others. So according to (12.3.2),

(12.3.4)   'Not S' is not true.

However, now let us take account of the so-called disquotation principle for truth, which is:

'S' is true if and only if S.

Disquotation and (12.3.3) together imply not S. Disquotation and (12.3.4) together imply not not S. So we have reached a contradiction. There are good reasons for sticking to the disquotation principle.[10] So we need to give up (12.3.2). This is one of the powerful objections to supervaluation theory presented by Timothy Williamson in *Vagueness*.

To avoid this difficulty, I have expressed supervaluation differently in (12.3.1). This makes it possible for me to put the truth predicate into the object language.[11] Since there are good reasons for sticking to the disquotation principle, we should presumably take it to be true under every sharpening. Therefore, according to the supervaluation principle, we may assert the disquotation principle.

On the other hand, in my formulation, the expression 'we may assert' must be excluded from the object language; it belongs to the metalanguage only. Supervaluation does not apply to statements containing this expression. The same argument as before shows we cannot have this disquotation principle for assertibility:

We may assert 'S' if and only if S.

This is a hardship, but I think we should be able to live with it.

A bigger hardship is that my version of supervaluation theory leads to more awkward modes of expression. Throughout this chapter, when talking about borderline cases, I have had to make such remarks as 'We cannot say that leaving for Britain is better than staying at home'. It would have been nicer to say 'It is not true that leaving for Britain is better than staying at home'. But I am not entitled to say that of borderline cases. By the disquotation principle, it is equivalent to 'Leaving for Britain is not better than staying at home', and this cannot be asserted of borderline cases.

12.4 The vague value of existence

To repeat my conclusion: the indeterminacy of value in examples like Sartre's comes from the vagueness of the betterness relation. We cannot say it would be better for the student to leave for Britain, rather than stay at home, but nor can we deny it. We also cannot say it would be better for him to stay at home rather than leave for Britain, but nor can we deny that either. This is the student's predicament.

To say the predicament is one of vagueness does not make it trivial. It does not make it a mere matter of language, as though the problem would go away if only we organized our language better. It is in the nature of betterness that it is vague. This remark is independent of its metaphysical nature. Betterness is a concept of ours that has its role in our ethical thinking. Whether or not betterness belongs to the fabric of the world, it is an essential feature of our ethics that betterness is vague. It could not become precise without our ethics becoming something quite different from what it is.

The predicament of Sartre's student is caused by the fact that different values cannot be weighed against each other in a precise way. The vagueness of the process of weighing causes betterness to be vague in this context. When we turn to the value of a person's existence, the source of vagueness is different. It is the vagueness of the 'neutral level' of wellbeing.

I defined the neutral level on page 142. Remember the context. We were comparing a distribution A in which a person p does not live, with a range of other distributions in which p does live, but in which each other person's condition is the same as it is in A. In each distribution from the range, p has some level of wellbeing. The neutral level is the boundary between distributions that are worse than A and those that are better than A. If, in some distribution B, p's wellbeing is above the neutral level, then *B* is better than *A*. If *p*'s wellbeing is below the neutral level, *A* is better than *B*. To put it in terms of the value of lives, the neutral level is the boundary between lives that are better lived than not lived, and lives that are better not lived than lived. I am now saying this boundary is vague; the neutral level is a vague concept.

Some levels of wellbeing are definitely below neutral. If a person would live a short life, full of pain, it is definitely better that she not live than that she live. But for some levels of wellbeing higher than this, we cannot say a life is better not lived than lived, and nor can we deny it. These are borderline lives. Some even higher levels may be so good that they are definitely above the borderline: it is better that these lives are lived than not.

I do not insist there are lives so good that they are better lived than not. It may be that the vague borderline extends all the way up to infinity, so that, however good a life is, we cannot say it is better lived than not. If this is so, it will not be the only instance of vagueness that extends infinitely. Take the concept of a perfect day. We might never be able to say definitively that a day was perfect, however good it was. True, the term 'borderline' is inappropriate for infinitely extended vagueness. But for convenience I shall continue to use it; it should do no harm.

Let me put all this more formally in terms of supervaluation. For simplicity, let us assume the vagueness of the neutral level is the only source of vagueness we have to worry about. There is a range of levels of wellbeing that are sharpenings of the term 'neutral level'. They occupy a band or interval, extending from some lower limit to some upper limit. Any sharpening lies somewhere between the limits. I shall assume the limits are sharp, even though that seems implausible. The two limits mark the boundaries of the vagueness of the neutral level, and it seems implausible that the boundaries of vagueness are themselves sharp. We would expect 'second-order vagueness', as it is called. However, I shall ignore this complication. On the other hand, I shall not mind if the upper limit is infinite. I shall not mind if the vagueness of the neutral level of wellbeing extends from some lower limit all the way up to infinity.

Within each sharpening, the betterness relation is complete. Since this is true in each sharpening, it follows by supervaluation that the betterness relation is indeed complete. On page 166, when dealing with incommensurateness, I withdrew my original assumption that the betterness relation is complete. But if the indeterminacy of betterness consists in vagueness, I can maintain this completeness assumption.

Each sharpening is sharp. Each consists of a single level of wellbeing v, which constitutes the sharp boundary between lives that are better lived than not lived, and those that are better not lived than lived. This boundary constitutes a single neutral level. So in each sharpening there is only one neutral level. By supervaluation, there is indeed only one neutral level.

However, it is vague – we could say indeterminate – what that single level is. This is a remark within the metalanguage, where the term 'vague' resides. So it is not itself subject to supervaluation.

The terms 'better than' and 'worse than' will inherit vagueness from the vagueness of the neutral level. We are interested in betterness between distributions, and in particular in the value of adding a person to the population. So, as before, take two distributions A and B that share the same population except that B has an extra person who does not exist in A. Suppose that each person who exists in both A and B is equally as well off in A as she is in B. Let the extra person's wellbeing in B be g. Let us evaluate the statement 'A is better than B'.

We first evaluate it within each sharpening, which is to say for each value of v in the borderline zone. When the neutral level is v, the statement is true if and only if g is above v. We can say that A is better than B if and only if A is better than B in every sharpening. This will be so if and only if g is clear above the borderline zone. If and only if g is within the borderline zone, we cannot say that A is better than B, and nor can we deny it. If and only if g is clear below the borderline zone, we can deny it.

Conversely, let us evaluate 'A is worse than B'. We can assert this statement if and only if g is below the borderline zone, and deny it if and only if g is above the borderline zone. If and only if g is in the borderline zone, we can neither assert nor deny it.

We emerge with this principle:

Vagueness principle. Suppose two distributions have the same population of people, except that an extra person exists in one who does not exist in the other. Suppose each person who exists in both distributions is equally as well off in one as she is in the other. Then there is some range of wellbeings (called 'the neutral range') such that, if the extra person's wellbeing is within this range, we cannot say that either distribution is better or worse than the other.

All of this chapter has been a response to the problem we encountered in chapter 10. In section 10.2, I described the intuition that there is a neutral range of wellbeings: for some range of wellbeings, it is neutral whether or not a life at a level of wellbeing within that range is lived. The problem is how to interpret this intuitive idea of neutrality. In section 10.3, I interpreted it as equality of goodness. Under that interpretation, the intuition becomes the principle of equal existence stated on page 146. But this principle turned out to contradict itself. In section 12.1 I interpreted neutrality as incommensurateness, which gives us the principle of incommensurate existence on page 167. This avoids contradiction, but in section 12.1 I raised doubts of a different sort about it. Now I am interpreting neutrality as vagueness; more precisely, when a person's existence is neutral, we cannot say it is better and nor can we say it is worse.

Is this at last a satisfactory way of interpreting the intuition? It does not satisfy my own intuition perfectly. My own intuition of neutrality is stronger than this. It tells me that adding a person to the population is definitely not better than not adding her, and definitely not worse either, at least within some range of wellbeing. Yet according to the vagueness account, we cannot say that. Take high levels of wellbeing, for example. My intuition tells me that adding a person at a high level is definitely not worse than not adding her, but on the other hand, I am not happy to say it is definitely better. Yet according to the vagueness account, these high levels are either within the zone of vagueness or they are not. If they are not, then adding a person at these levels is definitely better than not adding her. If they are, then we cannot say that adding a person at these levels is not worse than not adding her. I find neither of these options attractive.

Nor does the vagueness account satisfy the neutrality intuition in the mere addition paradox, example (12.1.1) on page 170. I explained on page 170 that C in that example is worse than A according to the intuition of neutrality. But according to the vagueness account of neutrality, we cannot say C is worse than A. If we could, we could conclude that B is worse than A, since in this example B is worse than C. But B is just the same as A except that it has a person added within the neutral range. So we cannot say B is worse than A.

This is the very same problem as I raised against the account of neutrality as incommensurateness. It makes neutrality implausibly greedy: able to swallow up badness. It was my most serious doubt about the incommensurateness account, and it is equally serious against the vagueness account. In the end, I think it will vitiate the whole attempt to fit the neutrality intuition into an axiological formulation. But that will have to wait till section 14.2.

For the moment, the vagueness account gives us a way to move forward in the project of weighing lives. The next section explains how.

12.5 The way forward

According to the vagueness account, whatever statement we are interested in must first be evaluated in each sharpening. In each sharpening, we can accept the implication of my theory that I developed in section 10.1: the implication that there is just one sharp neutral level. Within a sharpening, that is indeed true. Within a sharpening, betterness is complete relation. This means a value function exists within a sharpening. Indeed all the formal theory in this book is correct, within a sharpening. So we can continue to develop this theory.

Each sharpening consists of a particular value for the neutral level. Actually, it is more complicated than that. On page 143 I explained that the neutral level for adding a person to the population might depend on the context. It might depend on which other people exist and how well off they are. This context dependence is a quite separate matter from the vagueness of the neutral level. In chapter 13 I shall argue that actually the neutral level is the same in all contexts, but for the moment we are not entitled to assume that. So for the moment a sharpening has to consist of not just one neutral level, but a neutral level for each context.

The assertions we can eventually make will be those that are true in every sharpening. Most claims of the formal theory are unaffected by which particular level of wellbeing is neutral. The claim in chapter 8 that lives are separable is not affected, for example. If these theoretical claims are true at all, they are true in every sharpening, so they can be asserted unconditionally.

On the other hand, claims about the comparative value of particular distributions may well be affected by the neutral level, if the distributions contain different numbers of people. The truth of these claims will depend on the specific limits of the neutral range. So to evaluate such particular claims as 'A carbon tax at 20% is beneficial as a means of controlling global warming' or 'It would be better not to have more than two children', we may need to know the neutral range. This is no doubt very difficult.

Some theories may be able to specify an actual neutral level; section 14.3 considers theories that do. They specify a single neutral level, or at least constrain the neutral range. If you are able to believe any of these theories, they may help you evaluate some particular claims.

However, I think the best approach to evaluating a claim in practice will most often be a sort of 'sensitivity analysis'. Work out all the neutral levels of wellbeing that make it true and all those that make it false. It may turn out that the ones that make it true obviously include all sharpenings. If so, we can confidently assert the statement. Alternatively, if the neutral levels that make it false obviously include all sharpenings, we can confidently deny it. If such a satisfactory result does not emerge, we shall still have information that may be useful.[12]

If we eventually conclude we can neither assert nor deny a statement, that may create a difficult practical problem. Suppose the question is whether a particular policy to control global warming will be beneficial. Suppose it turns out that we can neither assert nor deny that it will be. If teleology is correct, whether or not we ought to adopt the policy is determined by whether or not it is beneficial. So we shall not be able either to assert or deny that the policy ought to be adopted. But the policy makers still need to decide whether to adopt it. It is difficult to know how one should make a choice when we cannot say that one or the other of the options ought to be chosen. I am sorry to say this difficult problem lies beyond the scope of this book.[13] This book is about evaluating options in terms of goodness. If practical problems result from the correct evaluation, that is another matter.

Incommensurateness again

I have said how the vagueness account of the neutrality intuition tells us to move forward. The incommensurateness account tells us to move forward in exactly the same way.[14]

On pages 167–8 I described how to compare distributions formally on the basis of the incommensurateness account. On page 181 I did the same for the vagueness account. The two procedures are identical. When we compare two distributions, in both cases we start by making the comparison for each level of wellbeing within the neutral range, treating each level in turn as if it is the neutral level. If all these separate comparisons agree that one distribution is better than the other, we can conclude it is indeed better.

The only difference appears if the separate comparisons do not agree – if one distribution is better than the other for some values of the neutral level, and not better for other values. Then on the vagueness account, we cannot say one is better than the other; nor can we say it is worse; nor can we say it is not better; nor can we say it is not worse.

But on the incommensurateness account we can indeed say it is not better, and we can also say it is not worse.

This is a real difference. To deny that one distribution is better than another is different from refusing to deny it. However, it does not make much difference in practice. Suppose you have a choice between two options. If they are incommensurate, then neither is better than the other. Let us assume teleology, so that which you ought to choose is determined by the goodness of the options. Then it is not the case that you ought to choose one, and not the case that you ought to choose the other. In those circumstances, it is difficult to know how you should choose. Under the vagueness account, we cannot say you ought to choose one, or the other. We also cannot say it is not the case that you ought to choose one, or the other. But the practical problem of knowing how to choose is just as difficult.

In the future, when I treat particular single levels of wellbeing as if they are the neutral level, I shall take them to be sharpenings of 'the neutral level'. This is because I believe we are dealing with a vague neutral level. For the time being, if you prefer the incommensurateness account, you may still accept the same formal theory. However, I shall in the end reject the incommensurateness account on page 206.

Either account requires us to continue to develop our theory of the value of lives on the basis of the conclusion reached in section 10.1 that there is a single neutral level. This will allow us to make comparisons correctly for single levels. Afterwards we shall need to put together the conclusions for all the single levels, to see whether they agree or disagree.

So the next chapter takes up again the train of argument from the point where I broke off from it at the end of chapter 9.

Notes

1 In 'The humanism of existentialism'.
2 A similar test is described by Joseph Raz in 'Value incommensurability'.
3 This suggestion appears in Derek Parfit's *Reasons and Persons*, pp. 430–2, and it is worked out in detail by Charles Blackorby, Walter Bossert, and David Donaldson in 'Quasi-orderings and population ethics'. Another account appears in Mozaffar Qizilbash, 'The mere addition paradox'.
4 This doubt is raised by Tyler Cowen in 'What do we learn from the repugnant conclusion?'.
5 In that paper I use the term 'incommensurability' more broadly than I use 'incommensurateness' in this chapter.
6 Just as this book went to press, I received Erik Carlson's paper, 'Broome's

argument against value incomparability', which contains a strong objection to the collapsing principle. Crispin Wright has also shown me a good objection.

7 See Timothy Williamson, *Vagueness*.
8 My version of supervaluation theory resembles Van McGee and Brian McLaughlin's in 'Distinctions without a difference'.
9 See Kit Fine, 'Vagueness, truth and logic'.
10 See Williamson, *Vagueness*, pp. 162, 188–9.
11 Saul Kripke explains how to do so in 'Outline of a theory of truth'.
12 Charles Blackorby and David Donaldson's 'Pigs and guinea pigs' contains several example of this method.
13 I have begun to approach it in my 'Are intentions reasons? And how should we cope with incommensurable values?'.
14 I believe it was David Donaldson who first impressed this point on me.

13

Separability of people

We may now at last return to our main line of argument. I suggested in chapter 12 that the neutral level may be vague. If it is, we must treat our developing theory of value as a theory for each individual sharpening of the neutral level. We can continue developing it in that spirit.

I broke away from the line of argument after arguing in chapter 8 that lives are separable and deriving the same-number addition theorem in chapter 9. Now we are back on track, the first question must be whether people, as well as lives, are separable. What separability of people amounts to is explained in sections 8.1 and 10.1. Section 13.1 is a brief review. It explains that people are separable if and only if the neutral level is constant: independent of context.

If the neutral level is not constant, there are only two features of the context it can depend on: the number of people who exist, and their average wellbeing. This follows from conclusions I reached earlier in this book. Section 13.2 shows how.

It means that, to decide whether people are separable, we only need to check whether the neutral level depends on either of those two features. Section 13.3 argues that it does not depend on average wellbeing, and section 13.4 that it does not depend on the number of people. I conclude that people are separable.

13.1 The argument to this point

This section summarizes where we got to in chapters 8 and 9.

I started chapter 8 by making a distinction between the two separability conditions: separability of lives and separability of people. I hope I successfully argued for separability of lives in that chapter. It is a claim about the value of the lives a person might lead. I mean their general value – how good it is that the life is lived – rather than how good they are for the person. Separability of lives says that, if a person exists, the value of her life is not affected by the conditions of other people. It is independent of which other people live, and of how well off are the ones who do live.

Separability of lives implies that for each person there is an individual value function, which assigns a numerical value to each life the person might lead. There is an individual value function for each person, and general value is a function of these individual values.

When a person does not exist in a particular distribution, her value function assigns a value to her nonexistence. However, this value need not be numerical. The only significance of this technical fact is that a non-numerical value is not directly comparable to the numerical values of the various lives the person might lead. So it does not imply that her nonexistence is better or worse than any of these lives.

If we assume in addition the principle of personal good, we can be more specific about the general value function. It takes the form:

$$\bar{v}(g^1,\ g^2,\ g^3,\ ...),$$

where g^1, g^2, and so on stand for the individuals' conditions. If a person p lives, g^p is her wellbeing, and if p does not live, g^p has the non-numerical value Ω. So the value of a distribution depends only on who exists in it, and on the levels of wellbeing of those who do.

Although a person's value function need not assign a numerical value to her nonexistence, nevertheless her nonexistence is in a way comparable to any life the person might lead. Each life she might lead is better, worse, or equally as good as the person's nonexistence. Moreover, the person has just one neutral level of wellbeing: one level such that her living at that level is equally as good as her nonexistence. All this follows from separability of lives and some more fundamental assumptions. Its most particular source is the assumption I made on page 22 that betterness is a complete relation.

A person's neutral level is the level of wellbeing such that the person's living at this level is equally as good as her not living. If she lives, she will join a population of other people, each possessing a particular level of wellbeing. This population constitutes a context, which may affect the person's neutral level; this level may depend on the conditions of other people. That is why the person's value function may not assign a numerical value to her nonexistence. If her nonexistence had a numerical value, then any life with a wellbeing equal to that value would be equally as good as her nonexistence. That is to say, this value would be the neutral level for her. Since it would be just a number, the neutral level would not vary with the context; it would be constant. But separability of lives is not enough to ensure that it is constant.

Constancy is added by the stronger condition of separability of people. To separability of lives, separability of people adds the condition that the general value of a person's nonexistence is unaffected by the conditions of other people. This means that the neutral level for each person is constant if and only if people are separable. In this chapter I shall argue for separability of people or equivalently for the constancy of the neutral level.

13.2 What the neutral level may depend on

The question at issue in this chapter is whether the neutral level for a person is constant, independent of context. There is a way to simplify the work of the chapter. Conclusions we have already reached ensure that there are only two features of the context that the neutral level *could* depend on: the number of people who exist and their average wellbeing. More precisely, if two distributions contain the same number of people and have the same average wellbeing, they must have the same neutral level. There is a single level of wellbeing such that adding a person to either population at this level is neutral.

This follows from the same-number addition theorem on page 137, but unfortunately, I know no way to demonstrate it except by some algebra. Here goes.

Start with distributions that all contain a particular number of people, say n. The same-number addition theorem tells us that one of these distributions is better than another if and only if it has a greater total of wellbeing. That is to say, the total of wellbeing represents the goodness of these distributions ordinally.[1] To put it another way, the total of wellbeing is a value function for these distributions. Any other value function for them, which represents their goodness, must be an increasing transform of total wellbeing.[2]

Suppose we had a value function that represents the goodness of every distribution, not just of distributions containing n people. When this function was applied to an n-person distribution, it would have to be an increasing transform of total wellbeing in this distribution. Otherwise it would not correctly represent the goodness of n-person distributions. Therefore, applied to n-person distributions, the value function would have to take the form:

$$f_n(G_n),$$

where G_n is the total wellbeing of all the people and $f_n(\cdot)$ is an increasing transform. The subscript n in $f_n(\cdot)$ shows that this is the particular transform that applies to n-person distributions, whatever that transform might be.

In the same way, applied to distributions containing $n{+}1$ people, the value function has the form:

$$f_{n+1}(G_{n+1}).$$

Now take a particular n-person distribution, with total wellbeing G_n. Add a single person to make an $(n{+}1)$-person distribution, leaving everyone else's wellbeing unchanged. Suppose the new person's wellbeing is her neutral level in the context, v. Before the addition, the value of the distribution is $f_n(G_n)$. After, total wellbeing is $(v{+}G_n)$, so the value of the distribution is:

$$f_{n+1}(v + G_n).$$

Since the new person is added to the population at her neutral level, the distribution after her addition is equally as good as the distribution before. That is to say:

$$f_n(G_n) = f_{n+1}(v + G_n).$$

The total wellbeing G_n is n times the n-person distribution's average wellbeing, which I shall write A_n. So this equation can be written:

$$f_n(nA_n) = f_{n+1}(v + nA_n).$$

This is a general equation, which applies to any distribution. Given a distribution, it could in principle be solved for v, to find the neutral level in the context of that distribution.

Take two distributions that contain the same number of people n and have the same average wellbeing A_n. The function $f_n(\cdot)$ is the same for both, and so is the function $f_{n+1}(\cdot)$. So the very same equation applies to both of them. For both, therefore, it has the same solution for v.

That is to say, distributions that have the same number of people and the same average wellbeing have the same neutral level. If the neutral level depends on context at all, it depends on either the number of people or the average wellbeing. To show the neutral level does not depend on context, I therefore only need to show it does not depend on either average wellbeing or the number of people.

I need to mention another conclusion in passing. Till now, I have left open the possibility that the neutral level for one person is different from the neutral level for another, in the same context. Adding one person to a distribution might have a different value from adding a different person to the same distribution. The argument of this section closes that possibility. Given a context, everyone has the same neutral level. In any case, this follows directly from the condition of impartiality between people, set out on page 135.

13.3 Average wellbeing

The leading nonseparable theory of value is the average principle, which I introduced on page 138. Its value function is

$$\Sigma_{p \in \Pi} g^p / n,$$

for any population Π, of size n. The average principle values a distribution by the average wellbeing of the people who live.

Adding a person increases this function if and only if the person's wellbeing is above the average wellbeing of the people who already exist. Adding a person with wellbeing equal to the average is neutral. This means that a person's neutral level of wellbeing is equal to the average of existing people's wellbeing. It is not constant; it depends on the conditions of other people. So the average principle implies people are not separable.

The average principle is commonly taken for granted amongst those who determine policy, at least implicitly. For example, many economists assume the objective of economic policy is to maximize income per head of population. They evidently think of income as the source of wellbeing, and value average wellbeing. Many people find it natural to think in per capita terms when judging the state of the world, and this again leads them to the average principle.

Since I support separability of people, and since the average principle is so popular, it forms my main target in this section. The first part of the section is particularly aimed at the average principle. I shall first offer one explanation of why people are attracted to it, and explain that the attraction is spurious. I shall then comment on an important argument that has been offered in favour of the average principle.

However, this section's main purpose is to argue against any theory in which the neutral level depends on average wellbeing. The average principle, in which the neutral level is equal to average wellbeing, is just one of those theories. This main argument starts on page 194.

The average principle and the intuition of neutrality

What is attractive about the average principle? Since utilitarians first thought about the size of population, they have generally set themselves the question of deciding between the total principle and the average principle, as though those were the only two contenders.[3] I suspect many people take up the average principle by default; they reject the total principle, and the average principle is the only alternative they think of.

They might have good reasons for rejecting the total principle. One reason (which may not be a good one) is calculated to throw people into the arms of the average principle if they are a little careless. This is the intuition of neutral existence.

A utilitarian aims to improve the wellbeing of the people around her. She may see her goal as increasing the total of people's wellbeing, if she forgets about the possibility of adding people to the population. But once she recognizes this possibility, she will see there are two different ways to increase the total of wellbeing. One is to improve people's wellbeing; the other is to create new people with positive levels of wellbeing. A utilitarian values the first, but she may not value the second. She will not value it if she is influenced by the neutrality intuition, which is the intuition that adding new people to the population is ethically neutral. She will therefore reject the total principle.

On the other hand, maximizing people's average wellbeing may appear to achieve her aim of improving the wellbeing of the people around her. It ensures that the people who exist are, on average, as well off as they can be, and that seems to be what our utilitarian aims at. The average principle may seem to capture the neutrality intuition. I think this goes a long way to explain its popularity.

But if so, its popularity is misplaced. The average principle does not really capture the neutrality intuition at all. Our utilitarian's aim is to improve the wellbeing of people who exist. That is to say, she aims to take the people who exist and make them as well off as possible. The objective of the average principle is to make the people who exist as well off as possible, but that is not the same thing. Just as there are two ways of increasing the total of people's wellbeing, there are two ways of increasing the average of people's wellbeing. One is to make existing people better off; the other is to create new people whose wellbeing is above the average wellbeing of the people who already exist. Our utilitarian is only interested in the first of these ways, but the average principle equally favours the second. It favours adding people to the population if their wellbeing will pull up the average, even if adding these people brings no benefit to the people who exist. This flies in the face of the neutrality intuition, rather than supporting it.

An argument for the average principle

Though many adherents of the average principle accept it simply by default, there is at least one well-known genuine argument in its support. It comes from John Harsanyi via John Rawls.[4] Rawls rejects utilitarianism, but if he was to be a utilitarian, this is the sort he would be.

Here is the argument. Imagine a person sitting behind a veil of ignorance, who is offered a choice of possible worlds to live in, and asked to choose amongst them. A condition of her choice is that she will find herself occupying a random position in the population of her chosen world; this randomness is one feature of the veil of ignorance. She might be any one of the people in the world, and she has an equal chance of being any one of them. Assume her aim is to maximize the expectation of her wellbeing. Then, out of all the worlds available, she will choose the one that has the greatest average wellbeing. This is therefore the best world.

The last step of the argument, from 'This is the world a person would choose behind a veil of ignorance' to 'This is the best world' is difficult to justify. There is a general problem and a specific one. The general problem is to explain why the choice that someone would make behind an imaginary veil of ignorance should tell us the value of a real world. The specific problem is to justify the particular conditions of the veil of ignorance: to explain why a choice made in these particular imaginary conditions is the one that tells us the value of a real world.

We do not have to worry about the general problem, because whatever solution we may find to it, the special problem is acute in our context. Because we are concerned with the value of population, our subject behind the veil of ignorance must be choosing among worlds that have different populations. Yet the conditions of the veil of ignorance guarantee her that she will live in whichever world she chooses. Whether she chooses a large or a small population, she is guaranteed a place in it. It is very hard to see how these could be appropriate conditions, if her choice is to determine the value of population. I do not need to dwell on this objection to the original position argument. It was so convincingly developed by Brian Barry in 'Rawls on average and total utility' that we can fairly consider this argument for the average principle defeated.

The objection from separability

According to the average principle, the neutral level depends on average wellbeing. But a simple argument shows this cannot be so. It shows the average principle cannot be correct, and nor can any other principle that makes the neutral level depend in any way on average wellbeing.

The simple argument is this. The average in question is a global average: the average wellbeing of everyone who ever lives. It includes the wellbeing of people who live at very remote times from now, for example in the stone age and in the very distant future. The wellbeing of such remote people affects the average. So if the neutral level depends on the average, their wellbeing affects the neutral level. For one thing, it affects the value of adding a person to the population now. But this is not credible. The goodness of adding a person now cannot depend on how well off people were in the stone age. It cannot be correct that the neutral level depends on the global average of wellbeing, because it has this incredible implication.[5]

I say the goodness of adding a person now cannot depend on how life was or will be at times in the remote past or the remote future. This is only an intuition, and Erik Carlson has challenged it in his 'Mere addition and two trilemmas of population ethics'.[6] He points out that our primary intuition is normative rather than evaluative. We think intuitively that the standards of life in the stone age cannot influence whether or not one ought to have a child now. Carlson accepts this intuition, but points out that it is not an intuition about the goodness of distributions.

That is true. Still, the normative intuition does immediately *imply* that the standard of life in the stone age cannot affect the goodness of now adding a person to the population. Carlson suggests the opposite: that the standard of life in the stone age might affect the goodness of now adding a person, even though it cannot possibly influence whether or not one ought to add one. This makes no sense to me. I understand that the goodness of adding a child may not fully determine whether or not one ought to add one. It does according to teleology, but teleology may be wrong. But I do not understand how something that affects the goodness of what one does *could not* influence whether or not one ought to do it. Goodness cannot be so radically detached from rightness.[7]

The simple argument I gave is based on separability. Its basis is that the value of a person's existence must be separable from the wellbeing of temporally remote people. This is one part of separability of people, and it seems obviously true.

Local averaging and separability of lives

However, separability of people implies that the value of a person's existence is separable from the wellbeing of nearby people, as well as remote ones. That seems less obvious. It is more plausible that the value of adding a new person to the world now depends on the wellbeing of people alive now. In practice, no one who adopts the average principle includes the stone age in the average.[8] Instead they use a local average of some sort: for instance, the average wellbeing of the people who are alive at the time in question. So they make the neutral level depend on a local average and not a global average.

But the neutral level cannot depend on a local average; that has already been ruled out by the same-number addition theorem. Section 13.2 showed on the basis of this theorem that the neutral level can depend only on the global average and the number of people. More specifically, local averaging is ruled out by separability of lives, which is one of the inputs into the same-number addition theorem.

I think it is worth explaining just how local averaging is ruled out. The example of table 7 shows its conflict with separability of lives. For simplicity in the table, I am assuming each person lives for one time only. The cells in the table show the people's temporal wellbeing at the time they are alive. The example assumes it is possible for a particular individual p to live at one time or alternatively at another. This is indeed possible, as I said on page 107.

Compare the distributions A and B. Both q's life and r's are equally as good in A as they are in B. So if lives are separable, the relative value of A and B depends only on how p's life goes. For the same reason, the relative value of C and D depends only on how p's life goes. p's life in A is equally as good as it is in C, and p's life in B is equally as good as it is in D. So separability of lives implies that A is better than B if and only if C is better than D.

Yet if you believe in a local average principle, you may think differently. In A, p lives at a time when average wellbeing is low, and her wellbeing of two units pulls up the local average at the time she lives. On the other hand, in B she lives at a time when the average is high,

Table 7

		Times					Times	
		1	2				1	2
	p	2	Ω			p	2	Ω
People	q	1	Ω		People	q	3	Ω
	r	Ω	3			r	Ω	1

Distribution *A*   Distribution *C*

		Times					Times	
		1	2				1	2
	p	Ω	2			p	Ω	2
People	q	1	Ω		People	q	3	Ω
	r	Ω	3			r	Ω	1

Distribution *B*   Distribution *D*

and her wellbeing of two units at that time pulls down the local average. If you care about local averages, you may think *A* better than *B* on those grounds. For the same reason, you may think *D* better than *C*. This conflicts with separability of lives. Not every local averager will think this a good example, but for every local averager we shall be able to find some example of the sort, where her view conflicts with separability of lives.

Suppose life on average will be worse a thousand years from now than it is now. If you believe in a local average principle, you should prefer a person to live a thousand years from now, rather than now, provided her life will be equally good in either case. Her life can do more for the average a thousand years from now than it can for the average now. Table 7 is a stylized illustration of this point.

So local averaging conflicts with separability of lives. In this example, separability of lives seems clearly on the right side. It is surely absurd that a person should be more valuable living at one time rather than another, just because of her effect on the local statistics of the time. We are right to rule out local averaging on the basis of separability of lives.

I conclude from this section that the neutral level does not depend on average wellbeing.

13.4 Numbers of people

The next question is whether the neutral level might depend on the number of people in the population.

Humanity may have a value that is separate from the value of the people who make up humanity. It might have an ecological value just as other species are often thought to. Alternatively, it might derive a special sort of value from humanity's special features such as rationality. If humanity has a separate value, the first few people will be especially valuable, since without them there will be no humanity. This means the neutral level will depend on how many other people there are. The fewer there are, the lower the neutral level. I do not find it easy to dismiss this view.[9]

However, I shall not concern myself with it. I shall ignore it on the grounds that there are already enough people to satisfy fully the value of humanity. If numbers are small, they may affect the neutral level. But by the time we have reached a few thousand million, we must be sufficiently beyond the first few to ignore this source of value. When the numbers are this big, the value of humanity gives us no reason to think that increasing or decreasing those numbers will affect the neutral level. I shall ignore distributions with just a few people, by excluding them from the domain of the value function. For the distributions that remain, we can assume the numbers of people do not affect the neutral level.

Yew-Kwang Ng suggests that a similar sort of value might be much more extensive in its importance.[10] He thinks extra people might have diminishing marginal value, however many there already are. I am not sure why this should be, and it seems implausible to me. Suppose we discovered another planet full of people, so that our numbers are twice what we thought them to be. Ng's theory would imply that all the new people being born on Earth day by day are less valuable than we thought. That is implausible.

Provided we exclude small numbers, I think it is safe to assume the number of people has no effect on the neutral level. In section 13.3 I argued that people's average wellbeing also has no effect. These were the only possibilities left open by section 13.2. So we can conclude that the neutral level is constant. The neutral level for a person is independent of which other people exist, and of the wellbeing of those who do exist. People are separable, that is.

I explained on page 191 that, also, everyone has the same neutral level. So there is a single, universal neutral level. This conclusion invites the question 'What is it, then?'. But I shall not face up to that question till section 14.3. It will be useful to develop some more theory first. In any case, the likelihood remains that the neutral level is vague.

Notes

1 See page 27.
2 See page 27.
3 See the discussion in Henry Sidgwick's *Methods of Ethics*, pp. 414–16.
4 John Harsanyi, 'Cardinal utility in welfare economics and in the theory of risk-taking'; John Rawls, *A Theory of Justice*, pp. 161–7.
5 This objection to the average principle appears in Jeff McMahan, 'Problems of population theory', and in Derek Parfit, *Reasons and Persons*, p. 420.
6 p. 290.
7 Carlson offers an explanation that depends on separating the causal consequences of having a child from its other consequences. But I am sorry to say that, despite his patient help, I have not been able to understand the distinction.
8 Versions of the average principle that are adopted in practice are often confused, but none that I know includes the stone age. See the survey in my *Counting the Cost of Global Warming*, pp. 117–21.
9 Thomas Hurka presents this view in 'Value and population size'. On p. 212 of their 'Critical level utilitarianism and the population-ethics dilemma', Charles Blackorby, Walter Bossert and David Donaldson introduce a principle they call 'independence of the utilities of the dead'. This principle implies that the number of people does not affect the neutral level. On pp. 290–1 of his 'Mere addition and two trilemmas of population ethics', Erik Carlson plausibly criticizes it for this reason. Carlson implies that his criticism also supports the view that the neutral level may depend on people's average wellbeing. But it does not.
10 'Social criteria for evaluating population change'.

14

The standardized total principle

Now we know that people are separable. Taken together with the same-number addition theorem that I derived on page 137, separability of people implies a specific principle for aggregating across people. I call it the 'standardized total principle'. It is derived in section 14.1. It is simply the total principle, when the zero of people's wellbeing is set at the neutral level. However, I do not myself set the zero this way.

Once this principle is in place, we need to return to a problem that came up in chapter 12. In that chapter, I suggested the neutral level is vague, and used its vagueness to give an account of the intuition of neutrality. But if neutrality is accounted for that way, it turns out to be 'greedy', as I put it. We are now able to assess just how serious this problem is. Section 14.2 gives examples of the effect of greedy neutrality. It argues the problem is so serious as to be fatal to the intuition of neutrality. That intuition has to be rejected. The neutral level is likely to be vague nonetheless.

Section 14.3 takes up the question of what the neutral level, whether vague or not, actually is. Section 14.4 responds to some well-known objections to the standardized total principle.

14.1 Derivation of the principle

Chapter 13 concluded that there is a single, universal neutral level. There is one level of wellbeing such that, if a person lives at that level, her living is equally as good as her not living at all. This will allow me to produce a comprehensive value function, specifying the value of any distribution, whatever its population.

We already know from the same-number addition theorem stated on page 137 that, amongst distributions that have the same size of population, their value can be represented simply by their total wellbeing. So we now need only to find the comparative values of distributions that have populations of different sizes. Take two distributions A

and A' where A has a smaller population than A' has. Let the populations of A and A' – the sets of all their people – be Π and Π', and let the numbers of people in the two populations be n and n'. So n is less than n'. Let the conditions of people in A be g^1, g^2, g^3, and so on, and let the conditions of people in A' be g'^1, g'^2, g'^3, and so on.

Take the distribution A and enlarge it by adding a person at the neutral level v. Because the extra person lives at the neutral level, the enlarged distribution is equally as good as A. Then enlarge the distribution further by adding a second person at the neutral level. The further enlarged distribution is still equally as good as A. Then add a third person at the neutral level, and so on. At each stage of enlargement, we have a new distribution that is equally as good as A. Continue the process till $(n' - n)$ people have been added. Then we have a distribution that contains n' people, the same number as A'. It is equally as good as A.

The total wellbeing in this enlarged distribution is the total wellbeing in A, which is $\Sigma_{p\in\Pi}g^p$, plus the wellbeing of the added people, which is $(n' - n)v$. That is:

$$\Sigma_{p\in\Pi}g^p + (n' - n)v.$$

Since the enlarged distribution contains the same number of people as A' does, we know it is better than A' if and only if it has a greater total of wellbeing. That is to say (since the total wellbeing in A' is $\Sigma_{p\in\Pi'}g'^p$) if and only if:

$$\Sigma_{p\in\Pi}g^p + (n' - n)v > \Sigma_{p\in\Pi'}g'^p.$$

The size of population Π is n and the size of population Π' is n'. I can therefore rewrite the condition:

$$\Sigma_{p\in\Pi}(g^p - v) > \Sigma_{p\in\Pi'}(g'^p - v).$$

This is a necessary and sufficient condition for the enlarged distribution to be better than A'. But the enlarged distribution is equally as good as A, so it is also a necessary and sufficient condition for A to be better than A'. The left hand side is a function of the distribution A and the right hand side is the same function of the distribution A'. So this function is actually a value function that represents (ordinally) the goodness of the distributions.

The same calculation will work for any pair of distributions. So we have discovered a value function that represents the value of all distributions, however many people they contain. It is:

(14.1.1) $$\Sigma_{p\in\Pi}(g^p - v).$$

It says that the value of a distribution can be found as follows. For each person, take the amount by which her wellbeing exceeds the neutral level. (This amount will be negative if her wellbeing falls below the neutral level.) Add up all these amounts across the population.

This is the value function that Charles Blackorby and David Donaldson derived and recommended, originally in their 'Social criteria for evaluating population change'. I recommend it too. The way I have derived it follows roughly the method Blackorby and Donaldson used, with Walter Bossert, in their 'Intertemporal population ethics'. These authors call the formula 'critical-level utilitarianism'.

If we use (14.1.1) to compare two distributions that have the same size of population, the neutral level v drops out of the calculation. Only the total of people's wellbeing matters. The formula conforms to the same-number addition theorem, therefore. The neutral level only makes a difference when differences in population are in question.

I shall call the principle of value expressed in (14.1.1) the *standardized total principle*. Let us call the difference between a person's wellbeing and the neutral level her 'standardized wellbeing'. The standardized total principle says that the value of a distribution is the total of people's standardized wellbeings.

Remember I have not set a zero for the scale of wellbeing; on page 96 I declined to do so. So there would be nothing to stop me setting v equal to zero if I chose; this would be one possible normalization for the scale of wellbeing. If I did that, (14.1.1) would simplify to the ordinary formula for the total principle:

(14.1.2) $$\Sigma_{p\in\Pi}g^p.$$

The standardized total principle is truly a version of the total principle. The total principle is not properly specified until we set a zero of wellbeing, and the neutral level would be an appropriate one to set.

Indeed, the standardized version is the only version of the total principle that could possibly be correct. The value function (14.1.2) implies that adding a person at level zero is equally as good as not adding her. That is to say, it implies that the zero of wellbeing is the neutral level. Therefore it cannot be a correct value function unless the zero is set at what actually is the neutral level. So far as the total principle is concerned, there is no alternative to the standardized version. Do not think the standardized version is one option among others.

Very unfortunately, I cannot normalize the scale of wellbeing to make the neutral level zero. To do so would be more transparent now, but it would lead to greater confusion later on. I shall adopt a different and ultimately more convenient normalization on page 254. I therefore express the standardized total principle, not as (14.1.2), but in the more general form (14.1.1). But remember that a normalization is only a matter of notation. The standardized total principle, expressed in (14.1.1), is genuinely a version of the total principle. Indeed, since no other version can possibly be correct, it is really *the* total principle.

14.2 Vagueness and the intuition of neutrality, again

Now we have an actual formula for the goodness of a distribution, this is the time to return to the topic of indeterminate betterness.

In chapter 12 I argued that the neutral level of wellbeing is vague, and consequently that betterness is a vague relation. Supervaluation gives us a way to evaluate statements that contain vague terms. To check whether one distribution is better than another, we first have to check whether it is better under each sharpening of the neutral level. It is better if, under every sharpening, it is better. It is not better if, under every sharpening, it is not better. Otherwise we cannot say that it is better, nor that it is not.

Suppose we wish to compare the value of two distributions on the basis of the value function (14.1.1). We need to check the distribution's relative value for each sharpening of the neutral level v. The fact that we need to use different values for v is one reason why I declined to normalize v to zero. That would have implied a sharp neutral level.

Take an example. Let us suppose that all levels of wellbeing between 0 and 10 constitute sharpenings of 'the neutral level'; this is the zone of vagueness. Given that, let us compare these two distributions:

(14.2.1) $A = (4, 4, \ldots 4, 4, \Omega)$,
                  $B = (4, 4, \ldots 4, 2, 4)$.

We need to make the comparison for each sharpening of the neutral level. So we need to consider values of v between 0 and 10. According to (14.1.1), for any value of v, the value of A is:

$$(4 - v) + (4 - v) + \ldots + (4 - v) + (4 - v).$$

The value of B is, correspondingly:

$$(4 - v) + (4 - v) + \ldots + (4 - v) + (2 - v) + (4 - v).$$

So *A* is better than *B* if and only if:

$$(4 - v) > (2 - v) + (4 - v),$$

which is so if and only if v is more than 2. Some sharpenings of the neutral level are more than 2 and some less than 2. So we cannot say that *A* is better than *B*, nor that it is not.

I chose this example because it is problematic. In chapter 12 I offered vagueness as a way to accommodate the intuition of neutrality. The idea is that adding a person to the population is neutral if the person's wellbeing is within the zone of vagueness. Moving from *A* to *B* involves two things. First, one person's wellbeing is reduced from 4 to 2. This is a bad thing. Second, an extra person is added with a wellbeing of 4. This is supposed to be a neutral thing. The net effect of one bad thing and one neutral thing should intuitively be bad. *B* should therefore be worse than *A*. But according to the vagueness account, we cannot say it is worse.

This example is a variant of (12.1.1) on page 170, which I later considered in the context of vagueness on page 182. It shows that, if we try to interpret neutrality as vagueness, it turns out not neutral enough. This sort of neutrality is greedy: able to swallow up badness and neutralize it. But neutrality is intuitively not like that. The original attraction of the neutrality intuition in section 10.2 is that adding a person to the world seems not to have a value that counts against other values. However, neutrality that is greedy does count against other values.

To emphasize just how implausible greedy neutrality is, I shall add some life to the example. I shall make it a stylized version of the problem of global warming that I mentioned on page 10. Global warming will kill lots of people; let us suppose a hundred million. In shortening their lives, let us suppose it reduces these people's lifetime wellbeing from 4 to 2. Simultaneously it will have an effect on the world's population. Let us suppose it will make the population bigger than it would have been; let us say a hundred million bigger. Our intuition is that this change in population is neutral in value. So let us assume the wellbeing of the added people falls within the zone of neutrality. Let us assume it is 4, and this is within the neutral zone.

These figures reproduce example (14.2.1), scaled up a hundred-million-fold. *A* is the world's distribution of wellbeing as it would have been without global warming. *B* is the distribution global warming will bring about. I have already done the calculations; we know the net effect is neutral. According to our theory, therefore, we cannot say that the

net effect of global warming will be a bad thing. It will do the tremendous harm of killing a hundred million people. But it will also do the
neutral thing of bringing a hundred million new people into existence.
This neutral thing swallows up and neutralizes the tremendous harm.

You might think this neutralization happens because I assumed that
global warming will specifically add people to the population. It will
certainly affect the population, but it is not clear in what direction. So
let us suppose instead that it will subtract people. Let us suppose it will
reduce a hundred million people's wellbeing from 4 to 2 by killing them,
and that it will also remove a hundred million people from the population. (These are not the people who are killed. They are people who are
never born but would have been born had global warming not occurred.)
Assume the wellbeing of these subtracted people would have been 4,
within the neutral zone. The example is now:

$$C = (4, 4, \ldots 4, 4, 4),$$
$$D = (4, 4, \ldots 4, 2, \Omega).$$

scaled up a hundred million times.

For a particular value of the neutral level v, C is better than D if and
only if:

$$(4 - v) + (4 - v) > (2 - v),$$

which is so if and only if v is less than 6. We are assuming any value of
v between 0 and 10 is a sharpening of 'the neutral level'. So C is better
than D in some sharpenings, and worse than D in others. We cannot
say C is better than D.

If it subtracts people from the population, the net effect of global
warming is once more neutral. The tremendous harm of killing people
is neutralized by the reduction in the population, which is neutral.
Notice that the people who are subtracted in this latest example would
have (were they not subtracted) exactly the same wellbeing as the people
who are added in the previous example. Both subtracting people and
adding people at the very same level of wellbeing can neutralize the
badness of killing.

Global warming will kill lots of people. However, so long as it also
alters the population sufficiently, upwards or downwards, and we take
these changes in population to be neutral, then we cannot say it is a bad
thing. This is a consequence of our present theory, and it is incredible.

Our theory is likely to give us this sort of incredible conclusion rather
often. Very many events affect the world's population. When they do, the
effect is likely to be large, because it is likely to continue for a very long

time. If, say, some extra people are added in the next few years, they will add their children later, and in due course a chain of descendants will be added through the generations. So in practice very many events will have a large effect on the population. Intuitively, we take this effect to be ethically neutral. But in our theory, neutrality is greedy. Since the effect is large, it is likely to swallow up and neutralize any other good or harm the event may do. According to our theory, very many events will turn out neutral, whatever good or harm they do.

The wider the neutral range, the greedier the neutrality will be. Erik Carlson gave me a poignant example. On page 144 I mentioned some people's intuition that the neutral range extends upwards to infinity: no level of wellbeing is so good that a person's living at this level is better than her not living at all. Suppose that is so, and think about the following example.

Take first a distribution in which many people live, all of them dreadfully badly off. Suppose their lives are full of suffering. Compare this with another distribution, in which all the same people live, but this time all tremendously well off, and there is one extra person, also tremendously well off. To go from the first of these distributions to the second, we do two things. First, we enormously improve the wellbeing of all the existing people; this is an extremely good thing. Second, we add a person at a tremendously high level of wellbeing, which is supposed to be a neutral thing. Intuitively, the combined effect obviously should be good. But if the neutral range really extends up to infinity, the combined effect is neutral according to our formula. We cannot say the second distribution is better than the first. Because the neutral range is infinite, the huge benefit to all the existing people is swallowed up by the neutral value of adding one person.[1]

The end of the intuition of neutrality

Carlson's example can be dealt with by keeping the neutral range finite. But the incredible practical conclusions I have mentioned can only be avoided by giving up the neutrality intuition altogether. It has reached its last gasp. Nothing would be gained by moving back from the vagueness account of this intuition to the incommensurateness account. I explained on page 170 that the incommensurateness account is subject to exactly the same objection. The source of the trouble is the whole idea that there is a neutral range of wellbeings: a range such that adding a person at some level of wellbeing within the range is neutral. If there is a neutral range, then neutrality will be greedy, and greedy neutrality is not intuitively true neutrality. Attractive though it is, the neutrality intuition has to go.

At least, we have to give up the hope of interpreting it in terms of goodness. No interpretation in those terms adequately captures the intuition. If it has an interpretation in, say, deontic terms, well and good. That is beyond the scope of this book.

We have to give up the neutrality intuition, but we do not have to give up the view that the neutral level is vague. It would be extraordinary if it was not: if there was a crisp boundary between lives that are better lived than not and lives that are better not lived than lived. I would not expect betterness to be as precise as that; I would expect there to be a vague borderline. We can continue to allow for vagueness.

But we cannot interpret the vague borderline as a zone of neutrality, so that adding a person at a level of wellbeing within the borderline is neutral. If we interpret the borderline that way, we shall fail to meet an essential intuitive condition on neutrality, that it is not greedy.

Indeed, I can now reveal something I dishonestly concealed in section 12.4. Despite what I said in that section, strictly we should never have treated the vague borderline as a zone of neutrality. Treating it that way is inconsistent with supervaluationism. Adding a person at a level of wellbeing within the borderline is neutral according to one sharpening of 'the neutral level': the level of the added person's wellbeing. But it not neutral according to other sharpenings. So according to supervaluationism, we cannot say it is neutral.

At the end of chapter 12, incommensurateness remained an acceptable alternative to vagueness as a way of capturing the neutrality intuition. Now the intuition has had to go, but I have said that vagueness is still to be expected. Could incommensurateness still be an alternative to vagueness?

No, because we no longer have any reason to believe in incommensurateness in our context. Technically, it could still exist. Technically, there could still be an incommensurate zone between lives that are better lived than not lived and lives that are better not lived than lived. Lives in this zone would be neither better nor worse lived than not lived. They could not be neutral, however, because if they were, their neutrality would be greedy. But it was originally only the neutrality intuition that gave any grounds for thinking there might be a zone of incommensurateness. Now those grounds have gone.

On the other hand, we still have a good reason to believe in a vague borderline; the neutral level is surely vague. So incommensurateness is no longer an acceptable alternative to vagueness.

Continuing problems

What about my examples of global warming? What should we think about them? Hard though it may be, we must give up the idea that changes to the population are neutral. Adding to the population, or subtracting from it, may be either good or bad. Given that, we must expect that adding to the population, or subtracting from it, could cancel out the badness of all the killing done by global warming. The most implausible thing was that changes to the population could cancel out badness even though they are themselves neutral. We no longer have to accept that, since they are not neutral. But we do have to accept that they could cancel out badness.

I cannot pretend all the implausible consequences will disappear. Changes in the population, either increases or decreases, may turn out to cancel out the badness of the killing. It depends on the quantitative details. If the people who are added or subtracted would live on average at about the neutral level, then the badness of killing will not be cancelled out. But in other cases it will, and that in itself seems implausible. It is implausible that changes in the population can be good enough to compensate for a hundred million deaths. However, this implausibility is nothing other than the intuition of neutrality. The intuition is false, and we have to accept the implausible consequences of recognizing that.

In my examples, *both* subtracting people *and* adding people at the same level of wellbeing could cancel out badness. This is particularly hard to believe. It happened because I assumed a vague borderline that was wide on the scale of the example. Now we do not interpret the borderline as a zone of neutrality. Nevertheless, if we maintain the assumption that the borderline is wide, we shall reach the same conclusion that both adding and subtracting can cancel out badness. That is still very implausible.

There is a way to escape this particular conclusion. I assumed the borderline is wide in order to accommodate the intuition of neutrality. The intuition is that adding a person is neutral for a wide range of levels of wellbeing, so it needed a wide borderline to accommodate it. Once we give up the intuition, we do not have this reason to assume the vagueness of the neutral level is so extensive. If the vague borderline is not very wide, we can avoid the conclusion that both adding and subtracting people can cancel out badness. Unfortunately, however, that is not the end of the matter. Section 14.4 will create some renewed pressure for a wide borderline. Once again, we shall be exposed to the same implausible conclusion. It seems impossible to be rid of it.

At this point I bid farewell to the intuition of neutrality. But I shall continue to accept that the neutral level may be vague.

14.3 What is the neutral level?

The position we have reached is this. For some neutral level v, (14.1.1) is the correct value function. Alternatively, the neutral level may be vague, and if v is a sharpening of it, (14.1.1) is the correct value function within the sharpening. But so far we have nothing to tell us what the neutral level is, or what the range of its vagueness is. What is it, then?

I am sorry to say I have no real answer. My conclusion in this section will be mainly negative: I shall reject one theory that implies a particular neutral level. It is a sort of hedonism. Section 14.4 mentions some other considerations that may contribute to fixing the level.

Ordinary ethical hedonism is a theory of personal value; I shall call it 'personal hedonism'. It says what is good for a person – what a person's wellbeing consists in. It says that wellbeing consists in the preponderance of good experiences over bad ones. Some sorts of experience are good, others bad, and one life is better than another if and only if it has a greater preponderance of good experiences over bad ones.

Any theory of personal value has implications for general value if we assume the principle of personal good. This principle tells us that increasing the personal value of a life increases its general value. But even if we add the principle of personal good to personal hedonism, we can draw no conclusion about the neutral level. The neutral level is a matter of which lives are equally as good as nonexistence from the point of view of general value. Personal hedonism tells us nothing about that.

However, we might add another element to hedonism. Personal hedonists think that the goodness of a person's life depends on the amounts of pleasure and pain it contains. We might add that the goodness of a distribution as a whole depends on the amount of pleasure and pain that are contained in the lives of all the people together. I shall call personal hedonism with this added element 'general hedonism'. The ground for it must be that good or bad experiences are in themselves good or bad things to have in the world, quite apart from the personal benefit or harm they contribute to the life of the person who has them.

Take a life that contains no good experiences and no bad ones; call it a 'blank life'. A life lived in a coma throughout would be blank.

General hedonism implies that a blank life is neutral; it is equally as good that it is lived as not lived. Adding a blank life to the world adds no experiences, so it does not affect the balance of good experiences and bad ones. Therefore it is neutral.

Should we accept general hedonism? I find it harder to believe than ordinary personal hedonism. No doubt good experiences benefit the people whose experiences they are. But I do not see why we should think that, independently of this benefit to people, good experiences are in themselves good to have in the world.

A second doubt is this. General hedonism implies it does not matter whose life a particular experience occurs in, because it is the experience itself that is valuable. The packaging of experiences into lives does not matter. This is a form of the view I called 'separatism' in section 7.3: that the packaging of bits of wellbeing into lives does not matter. I expressed a doubt about separatism in section 7.3 because it has the implausible consequence that longevity has no value. This doubt applies to general hedonism too.

Third, I think it is intuitively implausible that a blank life is neutral. Suppose a person might come into the world and live a blank life. Suppose she would never be conscious. Would her living be equally as good as her not living? I would say not; I think it would be better if she did not live. Her life as a whole would be meaningless, and the occurrence of a meaningless human life is intuitively a bad thing.

So I doubt general hedonism and its implication that the neutral level of wellbeing is the level of a blank life. Indeed, I have gone a little further. I said a blank life is worse than not living at all. This means a blank life is definitely below the neutral level. If the neutral level is vague, a blank life is below the lower limit of its vagueness.

General hedonism is an instance of a broader theory.[2] The broader theory says, first of all, that a person's life has various good and bad features – not necessarily just pleasure and pain – and the goodness of the life depends on the quantities of these features that it possesses. It says, second, that the general goodness of a distribution depends on the quantities of these same features that there are in the world. For example, you might think virtue is one of these features; you might think it is good for a person to be virtuous and it is generally good for there to be virtue in the world. Christoph Fehige supplies another example.[3] He thinks it is bad for a person to have an unsatisfied desire, and it is generally bad for there to be unsatisfied desires.

If you accept this broader theory, you will think a life that has none of these good and bad features is neutral. Adding a person whose life contains none of these features does not change the quantities of the features in the world, so it does not change the goodness of the distribution. Since Fehige believes there are no good or bad features apart from unsatisfied desires, he thinks a life is neutral if and only if it has no unsatisfied desires. He thinks that in practice all lives fall below this level.

I have the same doubts about the broader theory as I have about general hedonism.

Summary

We have now arrived at my final conclusion about aggregating wellbeing across people. The correct formula for doing so is the standardized total principle (14.1.1) on page 201. One distribution is better than another if and only if it has a greater total of standardized wellbeing. The standardization is given by the neutral level. But the neutral level may be vague. Therefore, to determine whether one distribution is better than another, we need to check whether it is better under every sharpening of the neutral level. If it is, we can say it is better; otherwise we cannot.

14.4 Objections

As I said on page 202, the standardized total principle is really the total principle. It is the only version of the total principle that can possibly be correct. So if an objection to the total principle has a real target, it must be an objection to the standardized version.

The best known objection is that the total principle implies what Derek Parfit calls the 'repugnant conclusion'.[4] Take a distribution in which everyone lives very good lives. Call it 'the quality distribution'. Compare it with a distribution in which everyone lives only just above the neutral level of wellbeing, but in which there are lots more people. Call this 'the quantity distribution'. Provided the quantity distribution contains enough people, it will have a greater total of standardized wellbeing than the quality distribution; that is inevitable. Therefore, according to the total principle, it is the better distribution of the two. I shall call this 'the repugnant conclusion' in honour of Parfit, but I do not mean to prejudge the question of whether it is really repugnant. That is the question I am about to ask.

The neutral level is likely to be vague. If it is, concentrate for the moment on a single sharpening of 'the neutral level'. I shall come to its vagueness on page 213.

The repugnant conclusion follows from the assumptions we have made. The assumptions eventually led to the value function (14.1.1), and this value function implies the repugnant conclusion. But to an extent, we can cut through the detailed argument that led to this conclusion. Here is an argument that purports to reach the repugnant conclusion more directly. Start with the quality distribution. Add one person just above the neutral level. Since this person is above the neutral level, it is good to add her, and adding her will be worth a small sacrifice of the wellbeing of the original people. So at the same time as adding her, slightly reduce the wellbeing of these people. The result will be a distribution that is better than the original. It contains all the original people, with a wellbeing slightly below their original level, and one extra person just above the neutral level.

Now add another person just above the neutral level, again slightly reducing the wellbeing of the original people. Again, the result is a better distribution. Add people one by one, just above the neutral level, each time slightly reducing the wellbeing of the original people. In the end the original people's wellbeing too will be reduced to just above the neutral level. We shall arrive step by step at the quantity distribution. Each step is an improvement. Our conclusion is that the quantity distribution is better than the quality one. Does this way of reaching the conclusion suggest it is repugnant?

It is certainly unintuitive. The intuition of neutrality suggests that adding people to the world is not in itself a good thing, at least if their lives are not very good. It is certainly not worth a sacrifice on the part of existing people. It is not worth a sacrifice to add a single person, nor to add lots of people.

But we have had to abandon the intuition of neutrality. It simply cannot be made to fit into a coherent theory of value. As an intuition about goodness, it cannot be correct. There is a single neutral level, and against intuition we have to accept that adding a person to the population above the neutral level is valuable. It is valuable even if the person's wellbeing is only just above the neutral level.

So does giving up the intuition of neutrality force us to accept the repugnant conclusion, by forcing us through the steps of the argument I gave? It does not. Look again at the stepwise sequence I described, starting from the quality distribution. We have to accept that adding a person above the neutral level is a good thing. It does not immediately follow that it is worth some sacrifice of the original people's wellbeing.

Its goodness could be lexically dominated by the goodness of wellbeing. If so, the sequence of steps would not get under way.

Even if the sequence does get under way, because the goodness of adding a person is worth some sacrifice of wellbeing, it might not reach the end I predicted; it might not eventually reach the quantity distribution.[5] At each step we add a person and reduce the original people's wellbeing a little. However, this process need not eventually reduce the original people's wellbeing to just above the neutral level. A sequence of wellbeings can reduce at every step, yet never get down to near the neutral level. This is a mathematical fact. The sequence of numbers 1.5, 1.05, 1.005, 1.0005, ... reduces at every step, but it never gets near zero.

The theory developed earlier in this book rules out both these possibilities. I assumed away lexical domination in section 2.2. Other assumptions ensure that adding a person with a particular degree of wellbeing is always worth the *same* sacrifice of the original people's wellbeing, however many people have already been added. This follows from a complex conjunction of the assumptions I made in defining a scale of wellbeing, and in deriving the same-number addition theorem. All these assumptions eventually led us to the standardized total principle expressed in formula (14.1.1), which implies the repugnant conclusion.

Because these assumptions have brought us to this conclusion, should we now go back to re-evaluate them? I think not. I agree the repugnant conclusion is unintuitive, because of the intuition of neutrality. But that intuition, understood in terms of goodness, must be wrong. Apart from that, I see nothing repugnant about the repugnant conclusion. Everyone's wellbeing is above the neutral level. If that was the level of a mediocre life, the repugnant conclusion might be unattractive. But it need not be that level. All I said in section 14.3 about the neutral level is that it is better than a blank life. It might be a lot better. It might be a reasonably good level of life.

In any case, the idea that the repugnant conclusion is repugnant relies on an intuition about large numbers. Roughly, it is the intuition that large numbers of people cannot outweigh a loss in quality of life. On page 57 I argued that we should not rely on intuitions like this. If we are to apply our intuition to the quantity distribution, we need to grasp intuitively a world containing vast numbers of people, each living life at a particular level. I do not think we can grasp numbers like that.

Our homely intuitions about a few people are best, and we should rely on theory to derive conclusions about large numbers. I therefore prefer to concentrate on the intuition of neutrality. In rejecting that, I am happy to accept the consequence that the repugnant conclusion is not repugnant.

If the neutral level is vague, the standardized total principle implies a consequence only if it implies it for every sharpening of 'the neutral level'. It only implies the repugnant conclusion if the quantity distribution is understood in a particular way. All the people must live at a level just above the upper edge of the vague borderline between lives that are better lived than not and lives that are better not lived than lived. This diminishes its intuitive repugnance.

The repugnant conclusion has a mirror-image. Once again compare two distributions. In one, everyone lives a life of terrible suffering. Call this 'the negative quality distribution'. In the other, everyone lives a life that is only just below the neutral level, but there are lots more people. Call this 'the negative quantity distribution'. The standardized total principle implies the negative quantity distribution is worse than the negative quality distribution, provided it contains enough people. (The derivation is simple.) Call this 'the negative repugnant conclusion'. It too may seem repugnant.[6]

To ease the discomfort of the positive repugnant conclusion, I suggested that the neutral level might be a reasonably good level of life. If this is so, the negative repugnant conclusion is more poignant. A life just below the neutral level will also be reasonably good. It may contain no suffering, so the negative quantity distribution may contain no suffering. Yet according to the negative repugnant conclusion, this distribution is supposed to be worse than a distribution that contains a very great deal of suffering. Gustaf Arrhenius calls this 'the sadistic conclusion',[7] and evidently finds it very implausible.

The implausibility arises principally from the interaction of the positive and negative repugnant conclusions. To make ourselves comfortable with the positive one, we need a high neutral level, but this makes us uncomfortable with the negative one. We find it hard to believe there is a level of wellbeing such that it is good to add people to the population at any higher level, and bad to add people at any lower level. But this is just the neutrality intuition again: it is implausible that there is just a single neutral level. It is hard to reject this intuition, but we have to. Once we have rejected it, we have to recognize there is a single neutral level. Adding people below this level is a bad thing, and its badness must weigh against other bad things such as suffering.

The vagueness of the neutral level can make the pair of repugnant conclusions more acceptable together. The standardized total principle implies the positive repugnant conclusion only if we understand the positive quantity distribution in a particular way: everyone's wellbeing must be just above the upper edge of the vague borderline. It implies the negative repugnant conclusion only if we understand the negative quantity distribution in a corresponding way: everyone's wellbeing must be just below the lower edge of the vague borderline. If the borderline is wide, that can make both conclusions more acceptable.

However, if the borderline is wide, that brings us up against the problem I mentioned at the end of section 14.2. We may find that, if many people die, and many people are subtracted from the population, we cannot say the net effect is bad. And we may also find that, if many people die, and many people are added to the population, even at the same level of wellbeing, we cannot say the net effect is bad. Adding and subtracting can both cancel out badness. This seems incredible, and argues in favour of a narrow borderline.

There is a conflict between our intuitions about the two repugnant conclusions and our intuitions about this last conclusion. A wide borderline satisfies one better; a narrow borderline the other. The best we can hope for is a compromise that reduces the strain on our intuitions to a tolerable level. I see no guarantee that this is possible. The neutrality intuition may not be the only one we have to sacrifice. Some of our intuitions about large numbers may also have to go.[8]

Notes

1 Gustaf Arrhenius mentions a further incredible conclusion on p. 80 of *Future Generations*.
2 Gustaf Arrhenius and Krister Bykvist impressed this point on me.
3 'A Pareto principle for possible people'.
4 *Reasons and Persons*, p. 388.
5 If I understand him correctly, this is the point made by James Griffin in *Well-Being*, p. 87.
6 Compare the 'reversed repugnant conclusion' in Erik Carlson's 'Mere addition and two trilemmas of population ethics', p. 297.
7 'An impossibility theorem for welfarist axiologies'.
8 In 'An impossibility theorem for welfarist axiologies', Gustaf Arrhenius proves that a number of very plausible intuitions, including intuitions about large numbers, are incompatible.

15

Same-lifetime aggregation

In section 8.4, I adopted the people approach to aggregating wellbeing. I divided the task of aggregation into two steps: aggregating across times within a person's life to determine her lifetime wellbeing, and then aggregating across people to determine the overall value of a distribution. I am taking these steps in reverse order. I have now finished with the second. In this chapter I start on the first.

Section 15.1 sets up the problem of aggregating across times within a life. It draws an imperfect analogy between intertemporal aggregation and the interpersonal aggregation we have already investigated. This analogy can guide our path through the various steps of aggregation; we can follow the steps I took previously for interpersonal aggregation. Previously, I started by comparing distributions of wellbeing that all have the same population. Now I shall start by comparing distributions of a person's wellbeing where the person lives for the same period of time in each. That is the subject of this chapter.

Section 15.2 launches into it by asking whether the analogous conclusion about it can be drawn from analogous principles. This section examines the analogue of the principle of personal good. I call it 'the principle of temporal good'. In this section, I conclude that the principle of temporal good is not as securely founded as the principle of personal good, so we should not rely on it in developing our theory.

The result is that we need to consider various alternative views. Section 15.3 does so. Unfortunately, this is a messy operation, because it has to be done without the help of general organizing principles. The conclusion I draw in section 15.3 is that the principle of temporal good is at least a reasonable default.

It implies an additive value function for lives: one life is better than another life of the same length if and only if it has a greater total of wellbeing. Section 15.4 sets out this conclusion, recommending it as an appropriate default theory for aggregating within lives of a constant length. It is a default theory only; it might need to be modified or even radically altered if one of my default assumptions proves false.

15.1 Intertemporal aggregation

During her life, a person experiences a sequence of levels of temporal wellbeing. How do the components of this sequence come together to determine how well the person's life goes as a whole? This chapter starts to answer this question.

Even to ask the question, we must assume this sequence of well-beings does indeed determine how well the person's life goes. It is possible that the goodness of her life is partly determined by goods and bads that do not appear in the sequence of her temporal wellbeings. On page 47 I recognized there might be some goods of this sort. If there are, I have to set them aside.

They are ruled out by the principle of temporal good, which I stated on page 120 and repeat here:

> *Principle of temporal good.* Take any person p. Take two distribu-
> tions A and B that are such that p certainly exists in both and is
> certainly alive at exactly the same times in A as she is in B. If A is
> equally as good for p as B at all times p is alive, then A is equally
> as good for p as B. Also, if A is at least as good for p as B at each
> time p is alive, and if A is better for p than B at some time p is
> alive, then A is better for p than B.

This principle is formulated in a way that can take the dimension of uncertainty into account. I explained on page 123 that it has a weak and a strong version; the weak version excludes uncertainty and the strong one incorporates it. I adopted the weak version as an assumption on page 123, but for the sake of generality suspended it again on page 130. Now I have to reinstate it for the rest of the book. I shall examine the strong version in section 15.2.

The weak version implies that nothing can affect a person's lifetime wellbeing unless it affects her temporal wellbeing at some time. It implies that a person's lifetime wellbeing depends only on which times she is alive at, and her temporal wellbeing at all times she is alive. That is to say, for a person p:

$$g^P = g^P(g_1{}^P, g_2{}^P, \, \dots \, g_T{}^P).$$

This is equation (8.2.2) on page 121. From here till section 18.1, I shall only be talking about the wellbeing of a single person. I shall continue to call her 'p', but I may as well drop the superscript 'p' in formulae. Then the equation is:

(15.1.1) $$g = g(g_1, g_2, \ldots g_T).$$

g_t is p's condition at the time t. If p is alive at that time, g_t is her well-being at that time. If she is not alive, g_t is Ω. g, without the subscript, is p's overall condition. If p never lives at all, g is Ω; otherwise it is p's overall or lifetime wellbeing. Our task now is to find the form of the function $g(\cdot)$.

We already know one thing about its form from page 121: the function is increasing in each of its arguments. ('Increasing' has the meaning I described on pages 119–20.) This is extremely plausible. It means that, if a person's life improves at a particular time, and other things are equal, her life as a whole improves.

We also know a second thing. On page 91, I assigned the value Ω to a person's overall condition when the person never lives at all, just as on page 25 I assigned the same value Ω to a person's condition at any time she does not exist. These are only matters of notation, but they imply that:

$$g(\Omega, \Omega, \ldots \Omega) = \Omega.$$

The vector

$$(g_1, g_2, \ldots g_T)$$

is a one-dimensional distribution of wellbeing. It is the distribution of p's wellbeing across time. Equation (15.1.1) specifies p's lifetime wellbeing g as an aggregate of her individual temporal wellbeings. The task of finding the form of $g(\cdot)$ is the task of aggregating wellbeing across the single dimension of time. It is therefore analogous to the task of aggregating wellbeing across the single dimension of people. I set up this analogous task at the beginning of chapter 9, and pursued it from there to the end of chapter 14. All that previous work will speed us a little through the new task of aggregating across time. We can exploit the analogy between interpersonal aggregation and intertemporal aggregation.

Unfortunately, the analogy is not perfect, so it will speed us less than we might have hoped. The degree of analogy is itself a subject for debate. 'A person is like a nation', says Derek Parfit.[1] We shall have to consider how much like. Still, we can at least follow a parallel route through the analysis.

I shall start to follow it immediately. In chapter 8, I used the principle of personal good to derive the separability of lives. It eventually gave us the value function (8.2.2) on page 121. In our new task of intertemporal aggregation, we have a head start, because we begin from (15.1.1), which is the analogue of (8.2.2). So we do not need any analogue of separability of lives.

15.2 The principle of temporal good

In our parallel progress through intertemporal aggregation, we are now level with the start of chapter 9 on interpersonal aggregation. That chapter started by concentrating on the special case of distributions that share the same population. Analogously, let us start our investigation of intertemporal aggregation by considering only distributions where our subject p's life occupies the same stretch of time. This is to exclude changes in the length of p's life, and even changes in the date of her birth. Let Λ be the fixed set of times that constitute p's life.

For the special case of interpersonal aggregation, I obtained the formula (9.1.1) on page 133 for the value function. I derived it from the 'interpersonal addition theorem'. The analogous 'intertemporal addition theorem', if we could believe it, would give us

(15.2.1) $\sum_{t \in \Lambda} a_t g_t$

as a value function representing the goodness of p's life.[2] According to this formula, when we compare lives that persist over the same period, the better one is the one that has the greater weighted sum of wellbeing, weighted according to date. For each t, the number a_t in (15.2.1) is the weight attached to the wellbeing p enjoys at the time t. Remember the formula only applies to lives that persist over the same stretch of time; it says nothing about the value of extending or shortening a life. I shall call (15.2.1) an 'additive' value function.

The interpersonal addition theorem rests on the assumptions listed on page 133. The analogous assumptions that would be required by the intertemporal addition theorem are:

1. The axioms of expected utility theory applied to a person's individual betterness relation.
2. The axioms of expected utility theory applied to each of a person's temporal betterness relations.
3. The strong version of the principle of temporal good.
4. A version of the rectangular field assumption.

5. The temporal version of Bernoulli's hypothesis, which is stated on page 100.

If we could justify these assumptions, the value function (15.2.1) would follow.

If we add the lifetime version of Bernoulli's hypothesis from page 89 we get more. We get that (15.2.1) is a cardinal representation of the person's lifetime wellbeing. That is to say, this function is an increasing linear transform of her lifetime wellbeing g.

I have already adopted assumption 1 on page 82 and assumption 2 on page 100. The grounds for them come from chapter 6 of *Weighing Goods*. I shall adopt assumption 4 without more ado; I described the rectangular field assumption on page 130, and it is evaluated in sections 4.4 and 5.8 of *Weighing Goods*. I adopted assumption 5 on page 100, and the lifetime version of Bernoulli's hypothesis on page 90. Assumption 3, the principle of temporal good, is the only one of the five assumptions I shall question. It is crucial because it is actually necessary for the theorem's conclusion: unless the principle of temporal good is true, (15.2.1) cannot be a cardinal representation of the person p's wellbeing.

The principle of temporal good is set out on page 216. The intertemporal addition theorem requires the strong version of it. This is the version that applies to distributions with the dimension of uncertainty. Bringing uncertainty into the picture gives the principle of temporal good enough theoretical leverage to produce the additive value function (15.2.1).

Table 8 illustrates an implication of the principle of temporal good when applied to an uncertain situation. It shows the wellbeing of a single person who lives for two times. Uncertainty is modelled with states of nature. There are two states, and let us assume they each have

Table 8

	Times				Times	
	1	2			1	2
States of nature 1	1	1	States of nature 1	2	1
2	2	2	2	1	2

Distribution *A*   Distribution *B*

50% probability. Each of the two distributions *A* and *B* gives the person a different pattern of wellbeing across her life. *A* gives her a constant level: either the lower level 1 or the higher level 2, depending on the state of nature. *B* gives her an uneven life, with the worse time coming at either the beginning or the end, depending on the state of nature.

Distributions *A* and *B* are equally good for the person at the second time, because at that time they give her the same wellbeing in either state of nature. At the first time, *A* gives her more wellbeing in state 2, and *B* gives her more in state 1. But the states are equally likely, so it makes no difference which state brings the person the higher level of wellbeing. Consequently, the two distributions are equally good for her at the first time too. They are equally good for her at the first time and at the second.

As a result, the principle of temporal good implies the two distributions *A* and *B* are equally good. It says in effect that a distribution can be evaluated entirely on the basis of how good it is for the person at the two times separately. We might fairly say the principle of temporal good implies times are separable. However, since I used the term 'separability of times' differently in chapter 7, I shall avoid it here. In chapter 7 I was dealing with two-dimensional distributions where the dimensions were people and times. Now the dimensions are states of nature and times, I shall not use the same terminology.

Still, the principle of temporal good does imply that a distribution over states of nature and times can be evaluated by looking at it time by time. Each time can be evaluated independently of other times. The indirect effect, which is transmitted through the intertemporal addition theorem, is to rule out some sorts of pattern goods. I mentioned pattern goods in section 3.3. They are goods that consist in the distribution's having some particular shape or configuration when we regard it as a whole. The shapes of lives appear in my diagrams such as figure 11 on page 12. These shapes may reveal pattern goods, but shapes show up only when we compare wellbeing at one time with wellbeing at another. They do not show up if we try to evaluate distributions time by time, taking each time separately.

One example of a putative pattern good is evenness in a life; it may be good, or perhaps bad, for a life to pass at an even level of wellbeing, rather than oscillate up and down.[3] The example of table 8 shows how the principle of temporal good rules out the value of evenness. If evenness is good, then distribution *A*, which leads to evenness for sure, is better than *B*, which leads to unevenness for sure. But the principle of temporal good implies these distributions are equally good. If evenness really has a value, or if there are any other pattern goods within a life, the principle of temporal good is false.

The metaphysical defence

Is the principle of temporal good true or false? To assess it, I shall start by outlining one argument in its favour. It is a metaphysical defence of the principle.

The metaphysical defence rests on two premises. The first is a claim about the metaphysical nature of people: that people are in some way made up of a sequence of temporal parts. Each part is a distinct entity, and the person is in some way an aggregate of these entities. I call this a *disuniting* metaphysics of personhood. Different versions of it take different positions over what the temporal parts are like and how they are aggregated together to make up a person. But these details do not matter for the argument. It does matter that all the properties a person has at a time are seen as properties of the entity that constitutes the person at that time. They are properties of a temporal part of the person. For example, the wellbeing a person has at a time is a property of the person-at-the-time.

If people do indeed have temporal parts, some collections of temporal parts make up a person and some do not. The collection that consists of all the parts of me up to 1 January 2000 and all the parts of you after that date does not make up a person. But the collection that consists of all the parts of me at every date I am alive does make up a person. The difference is that particular relations hold between members of the latter collection that do not hold between members of the former collection. I call these the *unifying* relations. The unifying relations are the relations that hold between the temporal parts of a person in virtue of which those parts together constitute a person.

The second premise of the metaphysical argument is that the unifying relations are not axiologically significant: they are not significant in respect of good. If we take some collection of temporal parts, it makes no difference to goodness whether or not the unifying relations hold between them. Compare two possibilities. One is that a person lives out her full lifetime. The other is that this person dies early, and another person comes into existence and lives out the rest of her life in her place. This could not happen in reality, but imagine it happening magically. In the second case, there is a sequence of temporal parts, each of which is qualitatively identical to a corresponding part in the first case. But in the second case, the sequence is not unified by unifying relations as it is in the first case. According to the second premise, the unifying relations are not axiologically significant, so these two cases do not differ in respect of good. They are equally good.

The two premises together imply the principle of temporal good. The full argument for this point is in *Weighing Goods*,[4] and I shall not repeat it here. I hope it will seem obvious that the principle of temporal goods does indeed follow from these premises. If people have temporal parts, and if it makes no difference to goodness whether or not the temporal parts of a person belong to a single person, then I hope it will seem obvious that a person's life will have to be evaluated time by time separately. Pattern goods in her life will be ruled out.

Moreover, the premises themselves can be defended. Many authors defend some variety of the disuniting metaphysics.[5] A defence of the second premise can be drawn out of Derek Parfit's writings.[6] So this metaphysical argument gives some significant support to the principle of temporal good. It strengthens the analogy between interpersonal and intertemporal aggregation. It makes the relations between times within a person's life closely analogous to the relations between different people. It likens the principle of temporal good to the principle of personal good, which is reliable.

However, neither of the argument's premises is indubitable. Furthermore, their consequences go far beyond the principle of temporal good, and that itself makes them questionable. In the context of this book, these assumptions imply what I called 'separatism' in section 7.3. They imply that the packaging of wellbeing into lives does not matter. If people have temporal parts, and if the unifying relations between the parts are not axiologically significant, then it does not matter which person a particular part belongs to. It does not matter which life a particular piece of wellbeing belongs in. For instance, one long life is no better than two short ones; longevity is not valuable. This metaphysical argument is indeed a defence of separatism.

If you are suspicious of separatism because you value longevity, you should therefore be suspicious of the two metaphysical premises. On the other hand, the principle of temporal good does not imply separatism. It is only a claim about the relative values of lives that have the same length, so it implies nothing about the value of longevity. You may therefore reject the metaphysical defence without rejecting the principle of temporal good.

However, apart from the metaphysical defence, I know no other clean, straightforward argument either for or against the principle of temporal good. Unfortunately, my argument at this point will become messy. I have reached an awkward juncture in developing the theory of value. Up to now, I have been able to move forward on the basis of fairly high-level theory. General principles have taken us a long way in finding specific formulae for value. These helpful principles have mostly been principles of separability. The principle of temporal good would have moved us forward in our present context at the same high theoretical level. But we do not have solid grounds for this principle. I do not think we should rely on it.

15.3 Other values

We therefore have no solid basis for the additive value function (15.2.1). My aim is to find a value function for the purpose of aggregating across times within a person's life. (15.2.1) was the first attempt. The trouble now is that a great many value functions seem possible. If we cannot rely on the principle of temporal good, there are scarcely any limits on the form the value function might take. I said on page 217 that it is increasing in each of its arguments, but that is about the only formal constraint it is subject to.

Nevertheless, I am going to adopt the principle of temporal good as a default position, and with it the additive value function (15.2.1). I do this because I need a way to move forward in the development of the theory in this book. I do not pretend the formula is well grounded, though the metaphysical argument may give it some support. However, it yields a simple theory, which can serve if necessary as a starting point for more complicated ones. If you do not like the additive function, you will need to amend my future conclusions in whatever way you think is necessary. Indeed, I shall help you. Some amendments are very easy, and in this section I shall explain how to make them.

All I can do now is consider in turn various objections to the principle of temporal good. Each will call on some putative value that is inconsistent with the principle. Each will have its own implications for the form of the value function. Each will be a rather low-level specific theory, rather than a general principle. With each, I shall have to try and judge whether it is indeed a genuine value. I find this difficult. These judgements generally have to be based on nothing more than a specific intuition. I find my own intuitions on such specific matters can easily dissolve under pressure. I do not trust them.

Many possible values conflict with the principle of temporal good. I shall not be able to cover them all.

Risk to total wellbeing

I shall start with a putative value that reveals itself in table 8 on page 219. Because the principle of temporal good requires us to evaluate distributions time by time separately, it precludes our taking the perspective of the person's life as a whole. Regarding the life as a whole may give us reasons for favouring one distribution over another. I have already mentioned evenness as one possible reason; now I come to another. A difference between A and B is that A is risky for the person's total wellbeing over her life, whereas B is not. In A the person might have a total wellbeing of two or four. In B she has a total of three, for sure. Risk to a person's lifetime total may be a bad thing, because risk in general may be bad. If so, B is better for the person than A. But as I explained on page 220, the principle of temporal good implies A and B are equally good. So it denies the putative value of avoiding risk to the total of wellbeing. This value only appears from the perspective of the life as a whole, which the principle of temporal good ignores.

The value of avoiding risk to total wellbeing could be incorporated into the value function by modifying (15.2.1). We could adopt the value function:

(15.3.1) $h(\Sigma_{t\in\Lambda} a_t g_t),$

where $h(\cdot)$ is some increasing function. (15.3.1) is an increasing transform of (15.2.1). Since (15.2.1) is supposed to be a cardinal representation of p's wellbeing, this transformation is a genuinely different representation, unless it is linear. If $h(\cdot)$ is strictly concave, it will make the value function 'risk averse'.[7] (A strictly concave function is one whose graph curves downwards, like the one in figure 13.)

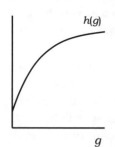

Figure 13

$h(g)$

g

The value I was considering was the value of avoiding risk to unweighted total wellbeing, rather than to the weighted total contained in (15.3.1). But the weights will drop out on page 231, so it is safe to ignore them here.

I am doubtful about the value of avoiding risk to total wellbeing. Remember I have already adopted Bernoulli's hypothesis, and its temporal version. Adopting the temporal version was a way to make precise the scale of temporal wellbeing. Intuitively, the notion of temporal wellbeing is quantitatively vague. It leaves us some choice of ways to make it precise, and the one I chose was Bernoulli's hypothesis. I explained on page 89 that

Bernoulli's hypothesis amounts to risk neutrality about wellbeing. So I made precise the scale of temporal wellbeing in such a way that there is no value in avoiding risk to temporal wellbeing at any individual time. Given that, I do not see why it should be valuable to avoid risk to the total of temporal wellbeing across time.

Nevertheless, it happens to be easy to amend my default theory to incorporate the transformation $h(\cdot)$. The transformation can be carried through into my final formula for value. Although I shall work with default theory through the rest of this book, I have shown in formula (18.1.3) on page 256 how this transformation can be incorporated into the final formula.

Priority to bad times

A different modification of (15.2.1) is this:

(15.3.2) $$\Sigma_{t \in \Lambda} a_t f(g_t),$$

where $f(\cdot)$ is some increasing function. This function puts the person's wellbeing at each time through a transformation given by $f(\cdot)$, before taking a weighted sum across time. It applies a transformation inside the aggregation, whereas (15.3.1) applies one outside the aggregation.

At first sight, the transformation in (15.3.2) might seem to be most plausible if $f(\cdot)$ was strictly concave. Figure 13 illustrates a strictly concave transformation. The effect of this sort of transformation is to make an increase in wellbeing count for more if it comes at a time when wellbeing is lower than if it comes at a time when wellbeing is higher. It gives temporal wellbeing diminishing marginal value, we may say. This function gives priority to times in a person's life when things are not going well for her. It is the analogue of giving priority to worse-off people in interpersonal aggregation.

It is an attractive idea on the face of it. However, things are not as straightforward as they seem. We are up against an issue in the measurement of wellbeing. (15.3.2) says that, when we aggregate across time, we should add together the amounts $f(g_t)$ for each time t (weighted by a_t), rather than the amounts g_t. Then why should we not treat $f(g_t)$ as a measure of the person's temporal wellbeing at t? It is what is added across time, rather than g_t, to determine lifetime wellbeing, so why should we not consider it to be temporal wellbeing itself?

I defined my quantitative scale of temporal wellbeing in section 6.1. There was a choice, because of the vagueness of our intuitive quantitative notion of wellbeing. I chose a scale that makes the temporal version of Bernoulli's hypothesis true.[8] This hypothesis says that the goodness of a prospect for a person at a time is the expectation of the person's temporal wellbeing at that time. This expectation is found by adding up the amounts of wellbeing the person will receive at the time in each state of nature, weighted by the probability of the state. So according to Bernoulli's hypothesis, temporal wellbeing is added (with probability weights) across states of nature. In effect, then, I scaled temporal wellbeing so that it can be added across states of nature. But I could instead have scaled it so that it could be added across times. That would have been to choose $f(g_t)$ rather than g_t as my measure of wellbeing.

We have found ourselves two alternative ways to *cardinalize* the scale of wellbeing: to make it additive across states of nature, or to make it additive across times. Briefly, it can be cardinalized by uncertainty or by time. Either cardinalization will yield a genuine, sensible scale for temporal wellbeing.[9] The scales will coincide only if the principle of temporal good is true (in its strong version involving uncertainty). But we have no strong reason to believe it is true. If it is false, the choice between the cardinalizations is arbitrary. I made my choice in chapter 6. I plumped for cardinalization by uncertainty.

The transformation $f(\cdot)$ converts one cardinalization to the other. The difference between (15.2.1) and (15.3.2) is as much a matter of how wellbeing is measured as a matter of how it is aggregated. One conclusion to draw is that we should not assume automatically that $f(\cdot)$ is strictly concave. Its shape reflects the complex relationship between aggregating across times within a life and aggregating across states of nature. If $f(\cdot)$ is strictly concave, that means in effect that we should give more priority to low levels of wellbeing when we aggregate across times than when we aggregate across states of nature. I see no particular reason why we should do that.

A second conclusion I draw is that we have no solid grounds for ruling out a value function such as (15.3.2). I take (15.2.1) as my default, but (15.3.2) is also very plausible. Fortunately, when the conclusions of this book eventually emerge in chapter 18, it will be extremely easy to modify them to incorporate the transformation $f(\cdot)$. Formula (18.1.3) on page 256 does so.

Evenness

If we adopt the transformation $f(\cdot)$ in (15.3.2), we may well also want an external transformation like $h(\cdot)$ in (15.3.1). On pages 224–5 I cast some doubt on the external transformation, but if there is also an internal transformation $f(\cdot)$, the grounds for my doubt do not apply. An external and internal transformation together may give us a sensible value function.

For instance, they can give us a reasonable way to capture the putative value of evenness, which I mentioned on page 220. A value function that gives positive value to evenness is the product function:

(15.3.3) $\Pi_{t\in\Lambda}g_t.$

This function takes the product of all the person's wellbeings at different times, rather than their weighted sum. ('Π' is the symbol for a product.) It is easy to check this function values A above B in table 8, as it should do if it is to give value to evenness.

(15.3.3) may alternatively be written:

$$\text{antilog}(\Sigma_{t\in\Lambda}\log(g_t)).$$

(Remember that any product can be written this way; the product ab can be written antilog(log(a) + log(b)).) That is:

$$h(\Sigma_{t\in\Lambda}f(g_t)),$$

where $h(\cdot)$ is the antilogarithm function and $f(\cdot)$ is the logarithm function. So here we have an internal and an external transformation together.

Formulae of this sort seem plausible. Once again, fortunately the transformations may be carried forward together through to my final value function in chapter 18. Formula (18.1.3) on page 256 incorporates both.

Improvement

The value of evenness, if it exists, is a pattern good. Another putative pattern good is improvement: it is plausibly better to have a life that improves over time, rather than one that deteriorates.

We must be careful to separate two distinct putative values. One is the value of a good ending; it seems plausible that a good end to life is more valuable than, say, a good middle life. If so, this value can be captured within the default additive formula (15.2.1) by using the weighting factors a_t to attach more weight to wellbeing at the end of life. It is therefore no reason to reject the default formula.

On the other hand, improvement itself may also have a distinct value.[10] To identify improvement, we have to compare one period of life with another: there is an improvement if a period is better than the previous one. (15.2.1) does not allow for comparisons between periods, so the value of improvement definitely conflicts with this default formula.

A value function that incorporated this value would be difficult to construct, and I shall not try to do so. I am not entirely convinced that improvement is valuable. A number of things might make it seem so when it is not. One is the possible value of a good ending, which I have mentioned. Another is the role of expectations. In the modern world, people often expect to become progressively better off as time goes by. Consequently, they are depressed if they do not. So lack of improvement may have the indirect bad effect of causing depression. This does not mean it is valuable in itself. Because of my doubts, I shall ignore the value of improvement.

Peak and end

Another putative pattern good is having a high peak. It may be part-icularly valuable to have one very good time in one's life. At the extreme, one might think the peak is the only thing that counts; the only point of life is to live very well once. It that were correct, it would give us the value function:

$$(15.3.4) \qquad \max\{g_1, g_2, \ldots g_T\}.$$

Another view about the value of a life is the 'peak-and-end' rule, whose value function is:

$$(15.3.5) \qquad g_T + \max\{g_1, g_2, \ldots g_T\}.$$

This says the value of a life depends only on how good it is at the end, and how good it is at its best, but not on anything else about it. (I have put the peak and the end together by simple addition, but that is only for the sake of a simple illustration of the rule. I would be just as happy with some other combination.)

The formulae (15.3.4) and (15.3.5) conflict more radically with the principle of temporal good than the others I have mentioned in this section. As functions of a person's temporal wellbeings, these ones are not increasing in all their arguments. As I said on page 217, this makes them inconsistent with even the weak version of the principle of tempor-al good.

The peak-and-end rule gets some remote support from a feature of our psychology. When we evaluate episodes within our lives, it seems we apply the peak-and-end rule. We take account of how good the episodes were at their best, and how good they were at the end, and ignore almost anything else about them.[11] When we evaluate the lives of people who have died, the peak and the end also seem intuitively important, though perhaps not in this extreme way. We give a lot of weight to a person's main achievements, and to how things went for her at the end. The length of a person's life is also intuitively very important, but that is not actually ruled out by (15.3.5). Remember that at this stage in the argument we are only dealing with lives of a constant length.

So (15.3.5) is perhaps not entirely absurd. Still, I am sure neither (15.3.4) nor (15.3.5) represents the truth about the value of a person's life. I mention these functions only to show the very wide range of possible value functions that is opened up once we abandon the principle of temporal good.

Conclusion

That brings me to the end of my review of putative values that conflict with the principle of temporal good and with the default theory represented in the additive value function (15.2.1). It happens that the most plausible of these values require simple amendments to the default theory, and I have explained how to make these amendments. I have expressed more scepticism about the other values, but I do not flatly deny them. If they really exist, they will demand more radical amendments to the default.

15.4 Temporal impartiality

I shall now continue with developing the default theory. Its value function (15.2.1) values a life as the weighted total of the temporal wellbeing within it. What should the weights be? In the analogous problem of interpersonal aggregation, the analogous question was quickly answered on page 135 with the principle of impartiality between people. It made all the weights equal. Can we now adopt an analogous principle of impartiality between the times in a person's life?

A person lives equally through every time in her life, so in evaluating her life it seems natural to count every time in it equally. We should not depart from impartiality without good reason.

I can only think of two reasons why we might consider departing from it. I have mentioned the first one already. It seems intuitively plausible that the end of a life should have more weight than the rest of it. But I have no argument why it should, and I am by no means convinced it should. I do not think this constitutes good reason to depart from impartiality.

The second reason is discounting. Some empirical evidence suggests that, in planning their lives, people typically give more weight to benefits that will come to them in the nearer future than to benefits that will come in the further future.[12] That is to say, people typically discount their own future wellbeing in their planning. This fact has sometimes encouraged value theorists – most often economists – to give less weight to people's future wellbeing in their own evaluations. Are they right to do so?

One confusion needs to be got out of the way first. My question is about the goodness of people's lives. It is not about the processes of decision making in a democracy. If people discount their own future wellbeing in their own planning, perhaps a democratic government should do the same.[13] Perhaps it should aim to do on behalf of people what the people would have done on their own behalf, if they had had the opportunity. Alternatively, perhaps it should aim to do what people want. We certainly cannot assume it should aim to achieve the best result. This would be to assume teleology, and in the context of a democratic government teleology is particularly contentious.[14] Suppose, say, the people want something that is not the best. Then perhaps the government should aim to achieve it for them, even though it is not the best. So even if it is right for the government to discount later times in its decision making, it does not follow that we should discount later times in assessing the goodness of the results.

A second clarifying remark is that I am still pursuing a nonrelative idea of goodness. To be sure, in this chapter I am interested in a person's lifetime wellbeing, which means I am interested in her personal value. I am interested in what is good for her, rather than in what is simply good. Personal value is relative to the person in a sense. But I mean it to be temporally nonrelative. I am not valuing a person's life from the point of view of any particular time. I rejected relativism in section 4.3, and the reasons I gave there apply particularly to temporal relativism.

We are asking whether people's future good should be discounted because people themselves discount it in their own decision making. For example, when making a decision in 2010, a person might count her wellbeing in 2011 for more than her wellbeing in 2015. These grounds could at most support discounting from a relativist point of view. They might make it credible that, from the perspective of 2010, the person's wellbeing in 2011 counts for more than her wellbeing in 2015. But they do not make it credible that it should count more from a nonrelative perspective.

It seems to me entirely incredible that, if we stand back from a life to judge its value from a nonrelative perspective, we should give more weight to earlier times in the life than to later times. We would never think of doing so when we judge the life of a historical figure, for example.

I explained in section 4.3 that, technically, discounting is not necessarily temporally relativist. I was there referring to discounting general good, which economists sometimes call 'social' discounting. Even in that context, I said nonrelative discounting strains one's credulity; it is only barely possible. In the context of the personal goodness of a person's life, it is surely entirely incredible. So I shall not depart from impartiality for the sake of discounting.

I accept temporal impartiality. This means all the weights in the value function (15.2.1) are the same. We can take them all to be one. A person's lifetime wellbeing can be represented by the total of her temporal wellbeing over her life:

$$(15.4.1) \qquad\qquad \Sigma_{t \in \Lambda} g_t.$$

Remember this conclusion is restricted to the possible lives of a particular person that occupy a particular span of time.

However, we can quickly extend the formula's application. When I set up a scale for lifetime wellbeing in chapter 5, I made it a universal scale of goodness for lives.[15] A person's lifetime wellbeing is in fact the goodness of her life, and a particular life is equally good no matter who lives it and when it is lived. (I am speaking of personal goodness; the general value of lives is another matter.) So the value function (15.4.1) allows us to compare all lives of the same length, lived by anyone at any time. We have arrived at:

> *Same-lifetime addition theorem.* Of any two lives that have the same length, one is better than the other if and only if it has a greater total of wellbeing over time.

This is a sort of personal utilitarian principle. The analogue for interpersonal aggregation is the same-number addition theorem stated on page 137. The same-lifetime addition theorem is part of my default theory of weighing lives.

The conclusion we have reached is in fact stronger than the same-lifetime addition theorem. I explained on page 219 that (15.4.1) is a cardinal representation of the value of a life, not merely an ordinal one.

Notes

1 *Reasons and Persons*, p. 275.
2 See *Weighing Goods*, p. 226.
3 See pp. 226–7.
4 pp. 232–6.
5 For example, see David Lewis's 'Survival and identity' and part III of Derek Parfit's *Reasons and Persons*.
6 *Reasons and Persons*, part III. *Weighing Goods*, pp. 236–7, explains more exactly how Parfit's arguments can be turned to support the premise.
7 See *Weighing Goods*, p. 79.
8 See page 100.
9 The two scales confront each other in practice in the measurement of the quality of life in health economics. Health economists need a cardinal scale quality of life for the purpose of evaluating alternative medical treatments. Different methods of measurement in practice give different cardinalizations. For a discussion of alternative cardinalizations, see my 'Qalys'.
10 See David Velleman, 'Well-being and time', and, for a contrary argument, Fred Feldman, *Pleasure and the Good Life*, chapter 6.
11 See Daniel Kahneman, 'The cognitive psychology of consequences and moral intuition', or Kahneman, Fredrickson, Schreiber, and Redelmeier, 'When more pain is preferred to less'.
12 The evidence is not conclusive. See Mancur Olson and Martin J. Bailey, 'Positive time preference' and the discussion in my *Counting the Cost of Global Warming*, p. 110 note 21.
13 For an exchange between economists on this point, see A. C. Pigou, *The Economics of Welfare*, pp. 29–30, and S. A. Marglin, 'The social rate of discount and the optimal rate of investment', p. 97.
14 See the Introduction to my *Ethics Out of Economics*.
15 See p. 95.

16

A life worth living

I am continuing to pursue intertemporal aggregation, following the analogy provided by interpersonal aggregation. In the analogue we are now up to chapter 10, where I examined the value of adding a person to the population. In this chapter I shall examine the value of adding a period to a person's life. Section 16.1 follows section 10.1, and section 16.2 follows section 10.2. In this chapter, it will emerge that we can shortcut a long segment of the analogous argument. After this chapter we shall be able to jump ahead to the analogue of chapter 13.

16.1 A neutral level for continuing to live

In section 10.1, I concluded that there is always a single neutral level of lifetime wellbeing for a person: a level such that the person's living at that level is equally as good as her not living at all. Her living at a higher level is better than her not living at all, and her living at a lower level is worse than her not living at all. Section 10.1 left open the possibility that the neutral level depends on the context: on which people are already living and what their wellbeing is. But in a given context, there is a single neutral level. It is neutral in terms of general value: the person's living at this level is generally equally as good as her not living.

For intertemporal aggregation, we can reach an analogous conclusion. Start from formula (15.1.1) on page 217. This formula tells us that a person's overall condition depends on her conditions at all times. If the person lives at all, the formula spelt out in more detail is:

(16.1.1) $g = g(\Omega, \Omega, \dots \Omega, g_l, g_{l+1}, \dots g_d, \Omega, \Omega, \dots \Omega)$,

where $g_l, g_{l+1}, \dots g_d$ are all numbers. l is the time of the person's birth, and d the time of her death. During her life, g_l, g_{l+1}, and so on indicate her temporal wellbeings. At times she is not alive, her conditions are all Ω.

Now think about changing the Ω that comes just after her life to a number measuring wellbeing. This change indicates the person lives one period of time longer, while her wellbeing during the rest of her life remains unchanged. Is this extension of her life a good thing or a bad thing for the person? Her lifetime wellbeing is now:

(16.1.2) $g = g(\Omega, \Omega, \ldots \Omega, g_l, g_{l+1}, \ldots g_d, g_{d+1}, \Omega, \ldots \Omega)$,

where g_{d+1} is now a number rather than Ω. Is g now greater or less than it is in (16.1.1)?

The answer will depend on g_{d+1}, the level of the person's wellbeing during her extra period of life. It turns out that there must be a single level of wellbeing such that living an extra period at this level is equally as good for the person as not living it and dying instead. I call this the 'neutral level for continuing to live'. An extra period at a higher level than this is better for the person than not living it, and an extra period at a lower level is worse for her than not living it. This neutral level is neutral in terms of the person's personal value: living an extra period at the neutral level is equally as good as dying, for the person herself.

I do not need to demonstrate the existence of a single neutral level, because the demonstration is exactly parallel to the one in section 10.1. Two of the assumptions it depends on are worth mentioning. The most crucial is that the person's individual betterness relation is complete. I made this assumption on page 82, when I assumed the person's betterness relation conforms to the axioms of expected utility theory. One of these axioms is completeness. Without completeness, I would not have been able even to define a quantitative notion of the person's wellbeing g.

A second assumption is the weak version of the principle of temporal good, which ensures that the function $g(\cdot)$ is increasing in each of its arguments.[1]

The neutral level for continuing to live may depend on the context. It may depend on how long the person has already lived, and on how well off she has been during her life. An eighty-year-old's neutral level, say, may differ from a twenty-year-old's. But in each context, there is only one neutral level.

I defined the neutral level for continuing to live in a forwards direction through time. We could also think about extending a person's life backwards, by adding a period at the beginning instead of the end. There will be a neutral level for backwards extension too. But the neutral level for extending a life backwards must be the same as the neutral level for extending it forwards; this is an easy inference from the same-lifetime addition theorem on page 231. So I do not need to distinguish these two neutral levels, and I can concentrate on extending life forwards.

We now have two neutral levels in this book. One is the neutral level for a person's existence; the other the neutral level for a person's continuing to live. The first is a particular level of lifetime wellbeing: the level such that a person's living a life at that level is equally as good as her not living it. It is neutral in terms of general value. The second is a particular level of temporal wellbeing: the level such that a person's continuing to live through an extra period at that level is equally as good for her as dying. It is neutral in terms of the person's personal value.

On page 67 I specified a temporal sense for the term 'a life worth living'. I rejected the lifetime sense as confused, but not the temporal sense. The neutral level of temporal wellbeing is the borderline between life that is worth living and life that is not worth living, in this temporal sense.

16.2 Is death typically neutral?

This brings us to the end of section 10.1 in the analogous development of interpersonal aggregation. In section 10.2, having shown that there is a single neutral level for existence, I then came up against the strong intuition that this is false: there is not just one neutral level, but a wide neutral range. The intuition is that a person's existence is ethically neutral as a general rule, and not just at one level of wellbeing. There are limits to the intuition. A person's existence is no doubt bad if her life goes badly, and perhaps her existence is good if her life goes very well, but at intermediate levels of wellbeing – neither bad nor very good – existence is neutral. That is the intuition.

An analogous view is that living an extra period of life is neutral as a general rule: it is neither bad for the person nor good for her. It is not neutral just for a single level of wellbeing, as I concluded in section 16.1. If you hold this view, you might set analogous limits to it. You might think it is bad for a person to live an extra period that is full of suffering. You might think it is good for her to live an extra period that is extremely good. But you will think that living an extra period is typically neither good nor bad for her but neutral: it is neutral at a wide range of intermediate levels of wellbeing – neither bad nor very good.

Whereas the view that existence is neutral is a common intuition, this analogous view is not intuitively very attractive. Most of us think it is typically better to live a longer rather than a shorter life. The view that living longer is neutral is more of a philosophical position than a natural intuition. But philosophers have taken this position, and I need to examine it.

It is more often expressed in the form of its mirror-image. When I say that living an extra period of life is neutral, I mean more precisely that a life containing an extra period is neither better nor worse for you than a life without the extra period. So a life without the extra period is neither better nor worse for you than a life that has it. That is to say, living a shorter life – shorter by one period – is neutral. More graphically, dying is neither better nor worse for you than continuing to live; it makes you neither better nor worse off. More graphically still: death is neutral. This is the form in which philosophers have usually expressed their belief in neutrality. It means the same: to say death is neutral means equivalently that continuing to live is neutral.

Epicurus apparently believed death is neutral. He says:

Become accustomed to the belief that death is nothing to us. For all good and evil consists in sensation, but death is deprivation of sensation ... So death, the most terrifying of ills, is nothing to us, since so long as we exist death is not with us; but when death comes, then we do not exist. It does not then concern either the living or the dead, since for the former it is not, and the latter are no more.[2]

'Death is nothing to us' may be taken to mean that death does not harm us. More precisely: a person's death does not harm the person who dies. I shall mention an alternative interpretation on page 238, but for the moment let us accept that one. Epicurus plainly thinks death does not benefit us, so his view seems to be that death is neutral.

This passage from Epicurus contains two separate arguments for the claim that death does not harm us. I shall take them in turn.[3]

The first is contained in the sentence, 'All good and evil consists in sensation, but death is deprivation of sensation.' This sentence starts by adopting hedonism as a premise. For the sake of argument, let us do the same: let us accept that the only good things in life are good sensations and the only bad things bad sensations. Granted that, in what ways can an event harm you? One way is to give you a bad sensation; another is to deprive you of a good one. So in pointing out that death deprives you of sensations, Epicurus goes no way towards showing it does not harm you. This is so even if we grant him hedonism as a premise. Hedonism has no tendency to suggest that death does not harm us.[4]

Epicurus forgets that the idea of harming involves a comparison. To harm someone you do not need to do something that is absolutely bad for her, whatever 'absolutely bad' might mean. You only need to make her less well off than she would otherwise have been. Death can have that effect.

So we may turn quickly to Epicurus's second argument. It is that 'so long as we exist death is not with us; but when death comes, then we do not exist'. The point seems to be that there is no time when death harms us. It does not harm us before we die, because then it has not yet occurred. It does not harm us after we are dead, because then we are not around to be harmed. Since there is no time when death harms us, it cannot harm us.

Of course, a person's death occurs at a time and, if her death harms the person at all, this is the time when the harm is caused. But Epicurus is not speaking of the time when harm is caused; he is speaking of the time when it is suffered. He argues that, since there is no time when the harm of death is suffered, there can be no such harm.

Evidently, Epicurus assumes as a premise that if an event harms a person, there must be a time when she suffers that harm. Should we accept this premise? It resembles the principle of temporal good, in its weak version that excludes uncertainty.[5] This principle implies that, if an event makes a person worse off than she would have been, there must be some time when she is worse off than she would have been. Its basis is part of the assumption of distribution, which is discussed in section 3.3. It is consistent with the existence of pattern goods, but it assumes there are no atemporal goods that do not appear anywhere in the sequence of a person's temporal wellbeings. I argued in section 3.3 that one might reasonably doubt this principle of temporal good, but that many reasonable doubts about it can be overcome.

However, the principle of temporal good is very different from Epicurus's premise in that it is explicitly restricted to lives that persist only over a particular stretch of time. It does not apply to changes that alter the length of a person's life. Possibly Epicurus's premise seems plausible because it would be plausible if it were restricted to events that do not alter the length of a person's life. But Epicurus means it to apply to events that do alter the length of a person's life. (In this application, it is the analogue of the 'person-affecting view' I mentioned on page 136.) And in this application, it is not plausible at all.

There is an obvious way for an event to harm you without harming you at any time: it only has to shorten your life. At first it might be surprising that you can be harmed without being harmed at any time, but by now we can see clearly how it can happen. If we compare (16.1.1) with (16.1.2), we can see that the person's lifetime wellbeing g may be less in (16.1.1) than it is in (16.1.2). Yet there is no time when she is worse off in (16.1.1) than she is in (16.1.2). This is not puzzling at all. Moreover, it is consistent with the assumption of distribution. The effects of death appear in a person's distribution of wellbeing.

An analogy might help. Suppose a book is altered by the editor before it is published. If the editor does not change the length of the book, at least one page of the published book will be altered. It will be different from what it would have been had the editor not made the alteration. However, if the alteration consists in cutting out the last chapter, no page in the published book will be altered. The book is altered but no page is altered. This is not puzzling at all.

We must reject Epicurus's premise, and with it his second argument.

Minding about death

Epicurus's arguments fail to establish that death does us no harm. They therefore give no support to the idea that death is typically neutral. However, Epicurus's purpose may be different. When he says 'Death is nothing to us', he may not mean death does not harm us. He may mean instead that we should not mind about dying. Perhaps we should not care about some of the harms we suffer, and perhaps the harm done by dying is one of those.

Dying may harm you by making your life as a whole less good than it would have been had you lived longer. But perhaps you should not care about your life as a whole. Instead, perhaps you should care only about things that benefit or harm you at some time. Since death does not harm you at any time, then you should not mind about dying. Perhaps this is Epicurus's point.

Wittgenstein makes a different suggestion. He says:

Only a man who lives not in time but in the present is happy. For life in the present there is no death. Death is not an event in life. It is not a fact of the world. If by eternity is understood not infinite temporal duration but non-temporality, then it can be said that a man lives eternally if he lives in the present.[6]

Wittgenstein recommends 'living in the present', and by that I assume he means caring only about the present. Certainly, if you care only about the present, you will never mind about dying. Since there is no time when death harms you, death does not harm you in the present, whatever time happens to be the present. More: it is not simply that you will not mind about dying; you will never even encounter the harm done by death among the things you care about.

Living in the present will save you from minding about death, but it is not a nice way to live. If your actions are governed by what you care about, and if you only care about the present, you will never take any steps to provide for yourself in the future. You will be entirely imprudent, so unless you are very lucky you will be in constant hunger, thirst and pain.

No doubt I am exaggerating Wittgenstein's meaning. To live in the present, I do not suppose he means you must not care at all about anything apart from the present. Perhaps you might care about your future in the way you care about other people. You might care in a special way about your present, but in a weaker way about other people and about your future. But in that case, why would you not mind dying, just as you mind if other people suffer a loss?

A possible answer is this. From the perspective of the present, you might treat living another period of life in the way you treat the coming into existence of a new life. It is the coming into existence of a new period, and your attitude to that period's being lived by yourself might be the same as your attitude to a life's being lived by someone else. Now suppose you subscribe to the neutrality intuition I described in section 10.2. Then you will not value the existence of a new life. You will not mind if a person who could have existed does not exist. Similarly, you might not value the existence of a new period in your life. So you might not mind dying when you could have continued living.

But if you take this attitude, you are making a mistake. You are accepting the neutrality intuition, which we now know to be mistaken.[7] No good reason not to mind dying can depend on this intuition. Living in the present can give you a good reason not to mind dying only if living in the present consists in the extreme attitude of caring exclusively for the present. And that is not a nice way to live.

A different, less extreme attitude would also save you from minding about death, and is more comfortable to live with. It has the benefit of living in the present with fewer costs. This attitude is to care only about things that benefit or harm you at some time, whether at the present time or at some other time. Epicurus may intend to recommend this attitude. It means you will care about having a decent life tomorrow (if you are still alive), since having a decent life tomorrow benefits you at some time, namely tomorrow. So you will be prudent. But you will not mind about dying. There will consequently be one lacuna in your prudence: you will do nothing to delay your death.

Perhaps this is the attitude Epicurus is recommending to us. Is he right to do so? Should we have this attitude? Fortunately, I do not need to answer. The subject of this book is good, not what we should care about. I have been considering what we should care about only because it offers a possible interpretation of Epicurus. So far as good is concerned, I had already said that Epicurus provides no sound arguments to support the idea that death is typically neutral.

Conclusion

The idea that death is typically neutral is not intuitively very attractive, and nor are there good arguments for it. Furthermore, it is incoherent, just as the analogous neutrality intuition is incoherent. I pursued the analogous intuition through several chapters before finally rejecting it on page 206. If I gave so much attention to the idea that death is neutral, the conclusion would be the same. But I do not need to give it so much attention, because it has fewer attractions in the first place. I shall leave it now, and accept the conclusion of section 16.1. There is only one neutral level for continuing to live: a level of temporal wellbeing such that living an extra period at this level is equally as good as not living it.

Notes

1 See p. 121.
2 Epicurus, *Letters to Menoeceus*, pp. 30–1.
3 My views on these arguments are similar to Fred Feldman's views, expressed in *Confrontations with the Reaper*, chapters 8 and 9.
4 In 'Death', his well-known commentary on Epicurus, Thomas Nagel concentrates on refuting hedonism. I think that was beside the point.
5 See section 15.1.
6 Wittgenstein, *Notebooks*, pp. 74–5.
7 I eventually rejected it on page 206.

17

The value of a life

Section 16.1 established that there must be a single neutral level for a person's continuing to live. This is a level of temporal wellbeing such that living an extra period at that level is equally as good for the person as dying. But so far, we have no reason to think this level is independent of the context. Section 17.1 in this chapter is concerned with whether it is. By the 'context', I mean how the person's life has already gone. The neutral level for continuing life might depend on how long the person has lived, and on how well off she has been during her life. Section 17.1 considers whether it does depend on these things.

This section corresponds to chapter 13 in the parallel development of interpersonal aggregation. But for intertemporal aggregation, I shall not be able to reach such a definite conclusion as I did in chapter 13. As a default, and without very solid grounds, I shall adopt the view that the neutral level for continuing to live does not depend on the context.

That quickly leads to a standardized total principle for aggregating across times within a person's life. Section 17.2 sets out this conclusion. In this, it corresponds to chapter 14 in the parallel development. Section 17.3 considers a couple of incidental matters: whether the badness of death might be relative to a time, and how far the neutral level for continuing to live is vague.

17.1 Is the neutral level for continuing to live constant?

Does the neutral level for continuing to live depend on the context? In chapter 13, I gave the firm answer no to the analogous question, with one qualification about small numbers of people. In this section I cannot be so firm. I shall start by mentioning two arguments that directly imply the neutral level is constant – independent of context. I would not like to rely on either. I shall then run through an argument analogous to the one in chapter 13, but with less definitive results.

It has happened before in this book that the available arguments are inconclusive. In those cases, my response has been to adopt a 'default' view, and move forward on that basis. If the default should turn out wrong, my conclusions will have to be adjusted, but at present no better alternative is available. In each case, I have chosen as the default a plausible, natural, simple view. In this section, I shall pick as my default the view that the neutral level is constant.

The metaphysical argument

I start with two arguments that, if successful, would directly support this default. The first stems from the metaphysical theory I described on page 221. This theory consists of two premises. One is a disuniting metaphysics, which says that a person has temporal parts. The second is that the unifying relations that hold between the temporal parts of a person are not axiologically significant. These premises imply that, if a period of life is to be lived, it is not axiologically significant whose life it belongs it. So, if a period is added to a life, the length and quality of the life it is added to can make no difference to the value of the period. If a period of a particular quality is neutral when joined to one life, it must be neutral when joined to any other. Therefore the neutral level is constant.

I said on page 222 that this metaphysical theory is open to doubt. One reason for doubting it is that it goes far beyond the conclusions we may want to draw from it. It implies the neutral level is constant but it also implies the doctrine I called separatism in section 7.3. In that section I described separatism as implausibly extreme. So I think it would be unwise to rely on the metaphysical argument.

Personal hedonism

A quite different theory also implies the neutral level for continuing to live is constant. It goes so far as to tell us what this level is. It is a version of hedonism: the most ordinary version, which I called 'personal hedonism' on page 208.

Personal hedonism is a theory of the personal value of a person's life. It implies (among other things) that this value is determined by the person's good and bad experiences only. Suppose a person's life is extended by adding to it a blank period: a period during which the person has no experiences. Then her life including this period contains exactly the same experiences as it would have contained had she not lived through the extra period. Therefore it must be equally good, according to personal hedonism. Adding this blank period is neutral.

The conclusion is that the neutral level is the level of a blank 'way of life', as I defined a way of life on page 102: a blank period of life. This is independent of context.

I can imagine a weaker version of hedonism that does not have this implication. It would be a temporally restricted hedonism, which confines itself to evaluating how a person's life is going at any time. It would avoid commitments about the value of a life as a whole. But I imagine most hedonists would accept personal hedonism, and so be committed to the conclusion that the neutral level for continuing life is at the level of a blank way of life. The general hedonism I considered on page 208 implies that the neutral level for existence is at the level of an entire blank life. But the general version is much more dubious, and many hedonists might reject it.

However, even though personal hedonism is more popular than general hedonism, it is very much open to doubt. Many of the doubts are so familiar that I do not need to mention them here. Some appear in Thomas Nagel's paper 'Death'. But in passing, Nagel mentions a view that casts a less familiar doubt on hedonism. Since he calls this view an 'allegation', I assume he is not committed to it himself. It is that:

There are elements which, if added to one's experience, make life better; there are other elements which, if added to one's experience, make life worse. But what remains when these are set aside is not merely *neutral*: it is emphatically positive.[1]

If this is correct, it rules out personal hedonism. It implies that a longer life is better than a shorter life that contains the same good and bad experiences. It implies that longevity has value, as well as good and bad experiences, and this hedonism denies.

The allegation may seem also to imply that a blank period of life is better than neutral, but it does not. It implies that a period of life without *good or bad* experiences is better than neutral. But 'what remains' after setting aside good and bad experiences may nevertheless be a way of life that contains experiences. This is the way of life Nagel is thinking of; he makes it clear he is not thinking of life in a coma.

In sum, we should not rely on the hedonist argument for a constant neutral level, any more than on the metaphysical argument.

What the neutral level might depend on

Section 13.2 showed that the neutral level for existence could depend only on the total number of people in existence, and on their average wellbeing. The argument was based on the same-number addition theorem. The same-lifetime addition theorem gives us an analogous conclusion: the neutral level for continuing life can depend only on how long the life has already continued for, and on its average level of temporal wellbeing. Since the analogy is precise, I do not need to go through the argument again. It means that, to decide whether this neutral level is constant, we have only to consider whether it can depend on either of these things. I shall consider each in turn, keeping one constant while considering changes in the other.

Length of life

Take length of life first. Compare two lives of different lengths: say a twenty-year life and an eighty-year life. Assume they both have the same average level of temporal wellbeing. Now consider adding a period of life to each of these lives. Suppose the added period has the same level of wellbeing in each case. Suppose this addition is neutral for one of the lives – let it be the eighty-year one. That is to say, the eighty-year life is equally good whether or not it has the addition. Is the added period necessarily neutral for the other life? That is the question we have to answer.

Several considerations seem to support the answer no, but they all turn out to be erroneous. One is the thought that more fresh experiences await a twenty-year-old, whereas an eighty-year-old has seen it all. In the extreme, a very long life will get boring. So extending the life of a twenty-year-old will do her more good than extending the life of an eighty-year-old will do her. All this may be true, but it is not relevant. Boredom or lack of it affects the wellbeing that a person has at a particular time. We are assuming that the period added to each person's life contains the same level of temporal wellbeing, so its boringness has already been taken into account.

Another thought is this. We commonly assume that most goods give diminishing marginal benefit. Small amounts of a good benefit us greatly, but the more we have, the less the benefit we gain from further amounts. There are various reasons why this should be so. One is that we naturally put our goods to use in the most beneficial way first. As we get more of them, we have only less beneficial uses left for further amounts. Another reason is that we can get bored of goods, so this thought is not entirely separate from the first. We might suppose that years of life have diminishing marginal benefit for reasons of this sort.

So an extra year brings more benefit to a twenty-year-old than to an eighty-year-old.

This is not a good answer to the question either. The idea of diminishing marginal benefit has to do with the contribution material goods – food, cars, medicine, and so on – make to our wellbeing. The more of these goods we have, the less will be contribution of further amounts. The idea does not apply to wellbeing itself. We know that the added period of life brings the same temporal wellbeing to the eighty-year-old as it does to the twenty-year-old. The problem is set up so the same amount of wellbeing is added in each case. There is therefore no room for a diminishing marginal contribution to wellbeing.

There is a response to this point. True, the same temporal wellbeing is added in each case. But we are interested in the contribution that temporal wellbeing makes to lifetime wellbeing. Temporal wellbeing might make a diminishing marginal contribution to lifetime wellbeing.

This is certainly possible, but the ordinary assumption of diminishing marginal benefit constitutes no reason for thinking it is true. There are reasons why a material good might make a diminishing marginal contribution to wellbeing; I just described some of them. But these reasons do not explain why temporal wellbeing should make a diminishing marginal contribution to lifetime wellbeing. If it does, we need a quite separate argument to show it does. Without an argument we have no reason to believe it.

A third thought is this. Suppose we were faced with a choice between giving an extra period of life to a twenty-year-old and giving it to an eighty-year-old. Suppose the one who does not receive this gift will die. Which would be the better choice? Giving it to the twenty-year-old, of course. So this is evidently the more beneficial thing to do. The period of life must bring the twenty-year-old more benefit than it brings the eighty-year-old. This argument stems from fairness or equality in the distribution of goods between people. Like the others, it is not a good argument, for two reasons.

First, if it is better to give the period of life to the young person, this is a matter of general value. But the benefits to the two people are personal values. Even if the benefits were equal either way, there might still be reasons why it would be generally better for the young person to receive the gift.

For example, some authors think that worse-off people should have priority: benefits that come to them should count for more in general value than benefits that come to better-off people.[2] The young person in our example is worse off in one way: she has had less of life. But if this is the reason why it is better for the young person to have the extra period to live, it does not show the benefit to her is greater. It shows the benefit to her counts more in general value, but it may still be the same benefit. That is to say, its personal value may be the same.

True, it is not so easy for me to rely on the point that personal and general value are different, because I have made various assumptions that connect general and personal value rather closely together. So the argument about general and personal value could go on. But to pursue it further would lead us into very tangled territory. We can circumvent it by turning to the second reason why the argument from fairness or equality is mistaken.

This argument is about the distribution of benefits between people. But our question is not about the distribution of benefits. It is about whether a particular added stretch of life is a benefit at all. It has to be a benefit before issues of distribution even come into play, so issues of distribution cannot determine whether it is a benefit.

We are comparing extending an eighty-year life with extending a twenty-year-life. I assumed the level of wellbeing is poor enough to be neutral for the eighty-year-old. This means the extension of her life would not benefit the eighty-year-old at all. Our question is whether, nevertheless, a period of life at this same level would benefit the twenty-year-old. This is obviously not a matter of fairness or equality between the eighty-year-old and the twenty-year-old. So the argument from distribution must be mistaken.

Those are three unsuccessful objections against my default position that the neutral level is constant. Specifically, they are arguments that the neutral level depends on the length of the person's life. The default survives these objections, and I can think of no others. So I think it is reasonable to assume – still simply as a default position – that the neutral level for continued life is independent of the life's length.

Average wellbeing

The next question is whether the neutral level is independent of the life's average level of wellbeing. To answer this, we should hold the length of the life constant. So take two lives that have the same length, but assume one has a greater level of average wellbeing. Imagine adding a period of life to each, at a particular level of wellbeing. Suppose the level is neutral for one. Is it necessarily neutral for the other?

It seems plausible to me that it may not be. Suppose one of the two lives we are considering is a poor one; its level of wellbeing is uniformly low. A period at only a modest, but better, level might improve this life. If the life contains a single period when the living is not so bad, that might be enough to make the life as a whole worthwhile. So for this poor life the neutral level is plausibly low. But suppose the other life is very good. Then a period of life at this modest level might spoil its value, viewed as a whole. For this life the neutral level is plausibly higher.

In saying this, I am not embracing the average principle for lives: the view that the goodness of a life is given by its average wellbeing. This is the intertemporal analogue of the average principle in interpersonal aggregation, which I examined in section 13.3. It implies that the neutral level for continuing to live is the average wellbeing of the life so far. The average principle is a feasible view, but surely too extreme to be credible. In section 13.3 I found serious faults with the interpersonal average principle, and the intertemporal version has worse ones. It gives value only to the quality of life and none to the length of life, whereas surely a longer life is better than a shorter one that has the same average quality. Length must count for something.

So we can reject the average principle. But we may still think the average wellbeing in a life may have some influence on its neutral level. The neutral level may not actually be equal to the average, but nevertheless still be affected by the average. I cannot confidently reject this possibility. I think it is a plausible objection to my default position. I believe the neutral level may not be constant, because it may depend on the average level of the life.

There is room for an alternative theory, different from my default but less extreme than the average theory. If one is developed, it might be a good replacement for the default. But at the moment I do not know of one, so I can do no better than stick to the default.[3]

Conclusion

From now on, I shall suppose that the neutral level for continuing to live is constant. Up to now, I have been dealing with one person only, so I mean only that the neutral level is constant for a particular person. The possibility remains open that different people might have different neutral levels. But my assumption on page 135 of impartiality between people immediately scotches that possibility. So I assume the neutral level for continuing to live is constant and universal.

17.2 The standardized total principle for lives

The universal neutral level gives us a more general formula for the value of a life than we have found so far. On page 231, I adopted the same-lifetime addition theorem as my default account of the comparative value of lives that have the same length. Its value function is (15.4.1) on that page. But this function does not fix the comparative values of lives of different length. Given a universal neutral level, we can apply algebra exactly parallel to my derivation of the standardized total principle in section 14.1. We shall emerge with a conclusion that is exactly analogous to (14.1.1) on page 201. In the notation I used in (15.4.1), it is:

$$(17.2.1) \qquad \Sigma_{t \in \Lambda}(g_t - \mu),$$

where μ is the neutral level for continuing to live, and Λ is the set of times when the person is alive.

This is the value function of the *standardized total principle for lives*, as I shall call it. To value a life according to this formula, we first calculate, for each time in the life, the amount by which its level of wellbeing exceeds the neutral level μ. We may call this amount 'standardized temporal wellbeing'.Then we add up all these amounts through the life.

I shall normalize the scale of temporal wellbeing by setting the neutral level μ at zero. I made this assignment informally on page 103; now I make it more formally. It means that I shall measure temporal wellbeing in its standardized form. The value function (17.2.1) may then be written simply as:

$$(17.2.2) \qquad \Sigma_{t \in \Lambda} g_t.$$

This formula says that the value of a life is simply the total of temporal wellbeing throughout the life. It is the same formula as (15.4.1) on page 231. But (15.4.1) represented only the comparative values of lives of the same length. (17.2.2) represents the value of any life.

Furthermore, we know from page 231 that it represents the value cardinally. That is to say, the goodness of a life is an increasing linear transform of (17.2.2). We may say (17.2.2) measures the goodness of a life cardinally. It measures the personal value of the life: how good it is for the person who lives it – her lifetime wellbeing. Remember I do not assign any personal value to not living at all. (17.2.2) allows us to compare the value of one life with the value of another, but it does not allow us to compare the value of a life with the value of not living.

For example, (17.2.2) tells us how much it benefits a person to have her life saved. Suppose you are threatened with death, but your life is saved. You would have lived a short life, but in fact you live a longer one. The benefit to you is the difference in value between the longer life you live and the shorter one you would have lived. Since (17.2.2) tells us that the value of your life is the total of temporal wellbeing you enjoy in your life. In simple cases the value of saving your life is the total of wellbeing you enjoy after you are saved. This may not be precisely correct. On page 46 I mentioned the possibility of backwards causation of wellbeing. Suppose your life is saved, and the result is that you finish the book you are writing. This achievement might add goodness to all the earlier years you spent on writing it. If it does, then the value of saving your life includes this retrospective benefit, which you would not have received had you died. But if we set aside the complicating possibility of backwards causation, then (17.2.2) implies that the benefit to you of saving your life is the total of wellbeing you afterwards enjoy.

17.3 The badness of death

In (17.2.2) we have a formula for the benefit you gain if your life is saved. Conversely, if your life is not saved and you die, it is the loss you suffer by your death. It is the badness of your death to you. To calculate the badness of your death, we compare how good your life was with how good it would have been had you not died when you did.

Time-relative badness

Jeff McMahan calls this account of the badness of death the 'life comparative account'.[4] He does not deny its truth. But he prefers an alternative, which he calls the 'time-relative interest account', because he thinks it better explains some of our intuitions. He argues that a person's interest in continuing her life depends on two factors. One is the amount of wellbeing that will be added to her life if she continues to live. This is what (17.2.2) measures. The other is how much this amount of wellbeing matters to her. McMahan points out that the psychological links that connect together the times in a person's life are not uniformly strong. He is thinking of links such as memory and intention. A person at any time is linked by her memory to herself at past times, and by her intentions to herself at future times. Taking his lead from Derek Parfit,[5] McMahan argues that the strength of these links determines how much the person's wellbeing, which she receives at particular times in her life, matters to the person. If at present her links to a particular future time are weak, at present she has only a weak interest in her wellbeing at that time; that wellbeing does not matter to her much at present. The life comparative account recognizes the first of the two factors, whereas the time-relative interest account recognizes both. It discounts the person's future wellbeing according to the strength or weakness of its links to the present.

One consequence of this account is that the death of an infant is not very bad – less bad than the death of a young adult. McMahan points out that an infant has very weak psychological links with later parts of her life. As an infant, she has few intentions for the future, and in the future she will scarcely remember her infancy. The weakness of these links dilutes her interest in continuing to live. So if she dies, she does not lose much by her death. On the other hand, a young adult is strongly linked to the rest of her life. Her death would therefore be very bad for her.

The time-relative interest account is relativist. It is supposed to be an account of the badness of a person's death, for the person. But because the badness depends on the links between a particular time and other parts of the person's life, we have to understand it as badness for the person, relative to that particular time. McMahan generally concentrates on the time when the person is threatened with death. He is concerned with the badness of her death relative to that time.

I gave up relativity in section 4.3, so I cannot adopt this sort of relative badness. It has no place in the nonrelativist theory of value I am pursuing. I have to adopt the life comparative account. The time-relative account might be useful nevertheless. Is it?

McMahan thinks it explains our intuitions about the badness of death at different ages. Intuitively, we think the death of an infant less bad than the death of young adult, and the time-relative interest account offers an explanation of why. Sometimes, it may also tell us how we ought to act. Suppose a doctor has a choice between saving a new-born baby and saving a young adult. According to the life comparative account, the baby's death is worse than the adult's. On the other hand, according to the time-relative interest account, the adult's death is worse than the baby's. It is intuitively plausible that the doctor should save the adult rather than the baby. If this is so, the time-relative interest account offers an explanation of why. It is plausible that, when we act, we ought to promote people's time-relative interests, relative to the time we act.

This plausible view is an instance of the relativist teleology I mentioned on page 74. Despite its initial plausibility, I am sceptical about it for the reason I gave on page 75: that following this relativist teleology leads us into incoherence. Here is an example of how.

Suppose the doctor has a different choice. As before, one of her patients is a new-born baby and another is a young adult. But in this example, neither is threatened with immediate death. Instead, each has a disease that will kill her in thirty years' time unless it is treated now. (In the intervening period she will live in good health.) The doctor has the resources to treat one of her patients, thereby saving that person's life in thirty years' time, but she cannot treat both. Which should she treat?

According to the time-relative interest account, treating the adult is better from the perspective of the present. The adult is now much more strongly linked to her life thirty years ahead than the baby is. So the adult now has a much stronger interest in having her life preserved thirty years from now. Relativist teleology therefore implies the doctor should save the adult. However, thirty years from now, things will be predictably different. By that time the baby will be a young adult herself. She will be strongly linked to her later life. But the present adult will be approaching old age, and have not many decades of life ahead of her. So evaluated from the perspective of thirty years ahead, saving the baby will be better than saving the adult. According to relativist teleology, if the doctor now acts to save the adult, in thirty years' time she should reverse that decision if she can. At that time, if she can, she should try to save the person who is now the baby, rather than the one who is now the adult. Yet now she should arrange for the opposite to happen. That is incoherent.

I shall continue with my nonrelative account.

Vagueness of the neutral level

When I normalized the scale of wellbeing to arrive at (17.2.2), I ignored the vagueness of the neutral level for continuing to live. I have no doubt this level is vague. Value in general is inevitably saturated with vagueness. Betterness relations are bound to be vague, and this neutral level must be vague too. I have ignored most of the vagueness of value throughout this book. For theoretical purposes, doing so is harmless. The theory that emerges will be true within each sharpening of each of its terms. The assertions made within the theory are general, so they will be true under each sharpening. Therefore, according to super-valuationism, they will be true. The vagueness makes no difference.

In our present context, let me describe a sharpening in more detail. Each sharpening of 'the neutral level' assigns a particular level of wellbeing to this term. Given my normalization, it also assigns zero on the scale of wellbeing to this level. Fixing the zero fixes all the rest of the scale. So a sharpening determines the whole scale: it assigns a number to each level of wellbeing. A different sharpening will reassign the whole scale; it will assign a different number to each level of wellbeing. That is how I am implicitly treating the vagueness of the neutral level for continuing to live. In practice, it allows me to ignore this vagueness.

The neutral level for existence is also vague, but in earlier chapters I treated its vagueness differently. The reason is that its vagueness plays an essential part in the account of weighing lives, as finally emerged on pages 213–14. It could not be ignored, and it needed to be made explicit. In section 14.2, I needed to consider different sharpenings explicitly. I did that by making each sharpening assign a different number to the neutral level v. I took the numerical scale of wellbeing to be the same in every sharpening. Each level of wellbeing had a fixed number assigned to it. In different sharpenings, different levels of wellbeing are neutral. Each sharpening assigns a different number to the neutral level.

What is the neutral level?

What is the neutral level for continuing to live, μ? I have already mentioned that the most standard version of hedonism – personal hedonism – implies it is the level of a blank way of life. But others might have a different opinion. For example, many people would think that, if a life ends with a blank period, such as a period in a coma, that damages the overall value of a life. These people believe the neutral level is above the level of a blank life.

I shall not try to go further in determining the neutral level for continuing to live. It is the boundary between life that is worth living in the temporal sense, and life that is not. It is a level of living such that it is equally as good to continue living at this level as to die. It is not an esoteric notion. It is within the domain of ordinary, not particularly philosophical, discourse. Some philosophical considerations contribute towards settling what it is, but I have mentioned all the ones I know.

Notes

1 p. 2, Nagel's emphasis.
2 This 'priority view' has come up in several places in this book. An important

source is Derek Parfit's 'Equality or priority?'.

3 In 'Social criteria for evaluating population change', Charles Blackorby and David Donaldson mention a value function that makes the neutral level proportional to average wellbeing, but not equal to it. They intend the function for the context of interpersonal aggregation, but it could be transferred unaltered to intertemporal aggregation. However, they do not find this function satisfactory.

4 *The Ethics of Killing*, p. 165–74.

5 *Reasons and Persons*, part 3.

18

The theory of weighing lives

This chapter puts together chapter 17's conclusion about intertemporal aggregation and chapter 14's conclusion about interpersonal aggregation. It will give us an integrated total principle. This is the final objective of this book. It is the integrated theory of value that I have been pursuing throughout. It is presented in section 18.1. Section 18.2 interprets it.

Section 18.3 considers briefly how we might develop the theory towards practical applications.

18.1 The integrated total principle

I shall now normalize the scale of *lifetime* wellbeing as well as the scale of temporal wellbeing. Call a life *constantly neutral* if it remains throughout at the neutral level for continuing to live. That is to say, if it remains throughout at the level I have now assigned zero to. All constantly neutral lives – however long – are equally good, because all of them have zero value according to (17.2.2). That is to say, they all have the same lifetime wellbeing. I shall now set this level of lifetime wellbeing to be zero on the scale of lifetime wellbeing. Zero is the level of wellbeing of a constantly neutral life.

With that done, (17.2.2) is more than a mere cardinal measure of a person's wellbeing. It is a measure on a *ratio scale*. In a ratio scale, the zero is fixed but the size of the unit is arbitrary. It is like a measure of length: length can be measured in feet or metres; the choice is arbitrary. Similarly the units of wellbeing – both temporal and lifetime wellbeing – are arbitrary. However, they are connected together through (17.2.2).

A person's lifetime wellbeing is given by (17.2.2), then. To express this fact formally, I shall restore the superscript 'p' as a reminder that we are dealing with a single person. I can say:

(18.1.1)
$$g^p = \sum_{t \in \Lambda^p} g_t^p.$$

In this formula, Λ^p is the set of times that constitute p's life.

This is a very convenient formula for lifetime wellbeing. Why have I waited till now to set the zeros of wellbeing in a way that makes it possible? These normalizations can only be made because we have a great deal of theory and a great many assumptions behind us. Only in my default theory is the neutral level of temporal wellbeing independent of context. I do not even insist that this default is correct, but without it I could not normalize the measures of wellbeing as I have. So even these normalizations belong to the default theory. If you do not accept the default theory, you cannot make them. I have to treat them as tentative, therefore.

The zero of lifetime wellbeing I have now fixed is the level of a constantly neutral life. But a constantly neutral life is not necessarily what I called on page 142 a neutral life. I apologize for the risk of confusion created here by my terminology, but I can find no good way round it. A neutral life is a life such that its being lived is equally as good as its not being lived, from the point of view of general good. It might be either better or worse than a constantly neutral life. I defined the neutral level for existence as the level of lifetime wellbeing in a neutral life. So the neutral level for existence is not necessarily zero on my new normalized scale of lifetime wellbeing.

As before, let us continue to use the symbol v for the neutral level for existence. It is now measured relative to the new zero of lifetime wellbeing. We can now encapsulate our whole default theory of value in a single formula. The value of a distribution of wellbeing is:

(18.1.2) $$\sum_{p \in \Pi} \left(\left(\sum_{t \in \Lambda^p} g_t^p \right) - v \right).$$

This is (14.1.1) and (18.1.1) combined. It is the standardized total principle for interpersonal aggregation combined with the standardized total principle for lives. The v appears in the formula just because the two standardizations do not necessarily coincide: a neutral life is not necessarily a constantly neutral life.

I shall call (18.1.2) the *integrated standardized total principle*. It is the integrated formula for aggregation across people and lives that I have been looking for throughout this book. It is only a default theory. I am reasonably confident of the standardized total principle for aggregating across people; it is based on fairly solid arguments. But there are several good reasons why one might doubt the corresponding total principle for aggregating across times within a person's life. I have mentioned many of them. Still, I hope the integrated total principle is a useful starting point, even if it needs to be rejected in the end.

If the neutral level is vague, as it surely is, (18.1.2) is the formula for the value of a distribution within a particular sharpening. Different sharpenings will have different values for v.

Possible amendments

Some of the reasons one might doubt (18.1.2) are set out in section 15.3. The formulae (15.3.1) and (15.3.2) introduced two transformations $h(\cdot)$ and $f(\cdot)$ into the aggregation of temporal wellbeing across a life. I said these transformations seem plausible. They can in fact be carried directly through into our universal formula for value. Instead of (18.1.2), we end up with the more complicated version:

(18.1.3) $$\sum_{p \in \Pi} (h(\sum_{t \in \Lambda^p} f(g_t^p)) - v).$$

I shall not run through the derivation of this formula. I mention it only to fulfil a promise I made in section 15.3, that I would show some of the amendments that can be made to the default theory.

18.2 Separatism and complete utilitarianism

What does the integrated standardized total principle mean? What implications does it have? Let us start with the special case where v, the neutral level for existence, is zero. This is the case where what I called a constantly neutral life is also what I called a neutral life. That is to say, a life that is, throughout, just on the borderline of being worth continuing is, taken as a whole, just on the borderline of being better lived than not lived.

In that case, the formula (18.1.2) amounts to complete utilitarianism. I defined complete utilitarianism on page 110. It is the theory that the value of a distribution is the total of all the temporal wellbeing it contains, aggregated across people and across times.

It is a separatist theory. Separatism is the view that only amounts of temporal wellbeing matter in determining the value of a distribution. It does not matter whereabouts in the distribution they appear. It does not matter whom they come to, or how they are packaged together into the lives of individual people. I said in section 7.3 that separatism seems to me implausible but defensible. It is implausible just because it seems that the packaging of wellbeing should matter. One of its implications is that longevity is not valuable: several short lives are just as good as one long life. That too seems implausible.

But separatism is defensible. I outlined a metaphysical defence in section 15.2. At that point I was only interested in the principle of temporal good, and this principle does not imply separatism. But the metaphysical argument I described goes much further and does imply separatism.

I can also now mention a further defence of separatism. Any argument for complete utilitarianism is an argument for separatism, and we now have another argument for complete utilitarianism. It follows from all the assumptions that brought us to (18.1.2), together with personal and general hedonism. Remember from page 242 that personal hedonism implies the neutral level for continuing to live is the level of a blank way of life: a way of life without experiences. An entire life without experiences is therefore constantly neutral. By my normalization, it follows that a blank life has zero wellbeing. Remember from page 209 that general hedonism implies that the neutral level for existence is the level of a blank life. So the neutral level is zero. Setting the neutral level v to zero in (18.1.2) gives us complete utilitarianism.

It is not surprising that general hedonism should support separatism. General hedonists value good experiences simply as good things to have in the world; they do not value them because they contribute to making any particular person's life good. They therefore do not care whose life the experiences occur in. How experiences are packaged together in a life is immaterial.

However, I said from the start on page 209 that general hedonism is not very plausible, precisely because it does not care who experiences any particular experience. So I do not find it a convincing basis for defending separatism. Separatism remains defensible but implausible.

Separability of times again, and the value of longevity

For any value of v besides zero, (18.1.2) is inconsistent with separatism. This is an important feature of it. The theory we have eventually arrived at, simple though it is, can give value to longevity. It does not imply separability of times, and is not subject to the objections I raised in chapter 7 to separability of times.

It is worth seeing why not. Look at table 9 on the next page. If we compared the distributions in this table in a snapshot fashion, looking only at each time separately, we would have to conclude that A is better than B if and only if C is better than D. This is the implication of separability of times. Here is the demonstration. Compare A with B, first looking only at times 1 and 2. At those times A and B are identical. So

Table 9

		Times							Times			
		1	2	3	4				1	2	3	4
People	p	1	1	1	1		People	p	1	1	1	1
	q	Ω	1	Ω	Ω			q	Ω	Ω	Ω	Ω

Distribution A   Distribution C

		Times							Times			
		1	2	3	4				1	2	3	4
People	p	1	1	Ω	Ω		People	p	1	1	Ω	Ω
	q	Ω	1	1	1			q	Ω	Ω	1	1

Distribution B   Distribution D

according to separability of times, the difference in value between *A* and *B* can only arise from the difference at times 3 and 4. Similarly, the difference in value between *C* and *D* can only arise from the difference at times 3 and 4. But the difference between *A* and *B* at times 3 and 4 is exactly the same as the difference between *C* and *D* at those times. So *A* is better than *B* if and only if *C* is better than *D*.

However, this is not what (18.1.2) says. First use it to compare distributions *A* and *B*. The difference between them is that two periods of life belong to *p* in *A* but to *q* in *B*. Between *A* and *B* they are shifted from one person to the other. (18.1.2) says these two distributions are equally good.

Now compare *C* and *D*. Again the difference between them is that two periods of life belong to *p* in *C* but to *q* in *D*. However, in this case the result is that *q* exists in *D*, whereas she does not exist in *C*. *D* has a greater population than *C* does. According to (18.1.2), the value of *C* is (4 – v) and the value of *D* is (4 – 2v). So *C* and *D* are equally good only if v is zero. If the neutral level v is positive, *C* is better than *D*. This conclusion satisfies the intuition I called on on page 108, that longevity is valuable. Both *C* and *D* contain the same amount of temporal wellbeing. The difference is that in *C* it is contained in one long life, whereas in *D* it is contained in two short ones. If we value longevity, *C* is better.

A positive neutral level for existence v gives the right result in this case, then. It is also independently plausible. The zero of temporal wellbeing is the neutral level for continuing to live. It is the level of life that is equally as good as dying. That is surely a very poor life, perhaps as bad as life in a coma. The zero of lifetime wellbeing is the level of a whole life lived at this zero level – perhaps as bad as a life lived in a coma throughout. Very plausibly, it would be better if such a life was not lived at all. Although, once started, it is just on the borderline of being worth continuing, it would plausibly be better if it never started. If this is right, this life that has zero lifetime wellbeing is below the neutral level for existence. It follows that the neutral level for existence is above zero.

I think this is the assumption we should make: that the neutral level for existence is positive, once the zero of lifetime wellbeing is normalized at the level of a constantly neutral life.

For a further illustration of the implications of the integrated standardized total principle, look back to figures 8 and 9 in chapter 1. Figure 8 depicts the question of whether or not it is better for parents to have a second child, even at the cost of some loss of wellbeing to their existing child. The answer given by the integrated standardized total principle (18.1.2) is that it may be. It is better if the second child's lifetime wellbeing is sufficiently above the neutral level. The difference between it and the neutral level must be greater than the loss of wellbeing suffered by the existing child.

Figure 9 depicts the different question of whether or not it is better to save the life of a second child, as a very young baby, even at the cost of some loss of wellbeing to her sibling. The answer given by the principle to this question is also that it may be, but the condition under which it is better is different. It is better if the wellbeing that will be enjoyed by the baby in the rest of her life is greater in total than the loss of wellbeing suffered by the existing child. The neutral level does not come into it.

Provided the neutral level is positive, the second question is much more likely than the first to have the answer yes. On page 10 I mentioned that the small extra blip of existence in figure 9 seems to most people to make all the difference. The integrated standardized total principle agrees with most people, if the neutral level is positive. The effect of a positive neutral level is to make it more beneficial to extend the life of an existing person than to bring a new person into existence, when the amounts of wellbeing are the same either way. This confirms most people's strong intuitions.

18.3 What next?

At the beginning of this book, I said I hoped to develop a theory that could give a basis to practical decision making in problems involving weighing lives. I have now completed the theoretical work. The outcome of it is the integrated standardized total principle, which is expressed in the simple value function (18.1.2). To reach this conclusion, I had to make several assumptions that were not well supported. Particularly in chapters 15, 16 and 17, where I dealt with intertemporal aggregation within a life, I found myself developing a default theory rather than one I firmly believe to be correct. The default is a simple theory that can at least serve as a starting point for practical decisions. There may be good reasons to amend it. To illustrate some of the amendments that might be needed, in (18.1.3) I showed a generalized version of the formula.

If the theory is to be applied, we need a practical way to measure the various quantities it contains. It we stick to the default, we need three things. First, we need a cardinal scale of temporal wellbeing, which assigns a quantity of wellbeing to each way of life. Second, we need to fix a zero on this scale, which is to say we need to identify a way of life that is neutral for continuing to live. Third we need a value for the neutral level for existence.

So far as the scale of temporal wellbeing is concerned, I have gone about as far as I can on the basis of *a priori* theory. On the basis of theory, I have attacked the problem of aggregating wellbeing across time and across people. But now we have come to what is aggregated: the quantity of a particular person's wellbeing at a particular time. For this, we need some empirical input.

A person's wellbeing is made up of various components: her health, her access to material goods, her social relations and so on. Each of these is itself a complex good, with components of its own. All of these components need to be aggregated together somehow to determine how well off the person is at a time. Philosophers have offered some thoughts about this type of aggregation, based on theoretical considerations. For example, some have argued that all the different components ultimately boil down to a single good such as pleasure. Others have distinguished higher and lower goods, and so on. But none of that philosophy helps much in the concrete task of measuring how well off a person is at a particular time. The relative weights of all the different components of her wellbeing cannot plausibly be determined *a priori*. They seem more plausibly to depend on our contingent nature. For this reason, we need empirical input.

Qalys

Health economists have some experience of this type of work. They have undertaken to answer some of the practical questions I posed in chapter 1. In answering them, they commonly measure the benefits of treatment in terms of 'quality-adjusted life years', or *qalys*.[1]

A person's quality-adjusted life years are the number of years she lives, adjusted for their quality. 'Quality' refers to the quality of the person's health only. For example, a quality of life might be: in constant slight pain and unable to walk. Another might be: deaf. A year in good health counts as one qaly. A year in less good health counts as less than one qaly; its value is reduced by a 'quality-adjustment factor'. If a particular quality has an adjustment factor of .7, a year of life at that quality would be valued at .7 of a qaly, equivalent to .7 of a year in good health. To calculate a person's qalys, we add up across the years of her life, counting each year at its quality-adjustment factor.

Take the example of figure 1 on page 2. Aggressive treatment will lead to the patient's having some number of qalys, and palliative treatment to her having a different number. A health economist would favour the treatment that leads to the greater number of qalys.

A person's qalys are formally parallel to the total of her temporal wellbeing, added up through her life. The difference is that in qalys wellbeing is replaced by health, and health is measured by quality-adjustment factors. In practice, these factors are elicited in one way or another from the judgements people make about the badness of various states of health. The data come from surveys and focus groups.[2] As I say, we need empirical input, and these may be good ways to get it.

However, in health economics the data are concerned with health only. A person's health is a component of her wellbeing, but not all of her wellbeing. So in using qalys, health economists are deliberately attending to only one part of wellbeing.

I think they are wrong to do so.[3] But I mention qalys because I think they represent something like the right approach to the problem of weighing lives. The approach would be exactly right if wellbeing were substituted for quality of life as health economists understand it. Qalys simply need to be generalized. We need wellbeing-adjusted life years instead of quality-adjusted life years.

Moreover, in setting up an empirical scale for quality of life, health economists have experience with some of the problems that come up in measuring wellbeing. On page 226, I mentioned that temporal wellbeing might be cardinalized in two alternative ways. Quality-adjustment factors may be cardinalized in either of the same two ways, and different scales result. This is a recognized problem within health economics.[4]

Moreover again, the empirical scale of qalys has a zero. Some qualities of life are rated zero on the scale, and these are the ones that are empirically rated as bad as death. That is to say, they are such that continuing to live at that quality is equally as good as dying. This is the neutral level for continuing to live, as I defined it. I normalized my more general scale of temporal wellbeing by assigning zero to this level. So my zero for temporal wellbeing coincides with the zero of qalys. On page 252 I said that philosophy can make only a limited contribution to determining what is the neutral level for continuing to live. A useful contribution might come from empirical methods.

I suggest that the experience of health economics with qalys, and with measuring qualities of life, might be a good starting point for developing a scale of temporal wellbeing and fixing its zero. The method needs to be generalized from health to all of wellbeing. Since the measurement of wellbeing is becoming a serious subject for economics,[5] perhaps this might be achieved in time. I do not pretend it will be straightforward.

Willingness to pay

There is a cultural divide within economics between two very different approaches to the value of life. I have mentioned the approach of health economics, using qalys. Other economists use an approach they call 'willingness to pay'. When they want to assess the value of extending people's lives, they do so by finding out how much money people are willing to pay to have their lives extended. To be more exact, they generally find out by various empirical methods how much people are willing to pay to increase their chances of living longer.[6] Suppose you are willing to pay £100 to reduce your chance of dying in the course of next year by one in ten thousand (say from three in ten thousand to two in ten thousand). Then the willingness-to-pay measure of the value of your life will be £100 multiplied by ten thousand: £1,000,000.

A great advantage of this approach is that economists are used to measuring all sorts of values in terms of money, by means of willingness to pay. So willingness to pay could in principle be a useful way of weighing the value of lives against other good things. However, it also has severe disadvantages.

One is that it does not provide a good basis for comparing together benefits that come to different people. Money to one person does not have the same value as money to another. For one thing, money is worth more to poor people, who can use it to satisfy urgent needs, than it is worth to rich people, whose urgent needs are already satisfied. In the context of weighing lives, another factor is also important: money is worth less to people who are near death. If you are likely to die soon, you have less chance of being able to use money than other people have, so you will value it less. If a rich person, or someone near death, is willing to pay more than other people to extend her life, that does not show her life is especially valuable.

For example, suppose Americans on average are willing to pay about fifteen times as much as Bangladeshis to reduce their risk of dying.[7] It does not follow that American lives are worth fifteen times as much as Bangladeshi lives.

It is possible to make adjustments to willingness-to-pay measures of value, in order to correct for people's differing values of money.[8] But the corrections are difficult, and I have never seen willingness-to-pay measures of the value of life adjusted in this fashion. Consequently, at present these measures are badly inadequate.

They suffer from another major defect. To make a good assessment of the value of a person's life requires some theory. Yet the willingness-to-pay approach applies no theory. For example, it makes no presumption that extending a person's life by thirty years is more valuable than extending it by one year. Instead, it leaves it entirely to people as individuals to judge how much their lives are worth, and display their judgement in their willingness to pay to reduce risk. But there is good empirical evidence that we are very bad at making judgements of this sort. Our preferences about risks are often plainly irrational. Here is just one example, taken more or less at random. In a survey, M. W. Jones-Lee, G. Loomes, and P. R. Philips found that 37% of the people surveyed were willing to pay no more to gain a large reduction in their risk of suffering an accident than to gain a much smaller reduction. 9.4% of the people were willing to pay more to gain a smaller reduction than a larger one.

Valuing lives is a complex matter. It involves issues of aggregation, which have taken up a substantial amount of space in this book. The work is not particularly easy. It would be foolish to rely on people's own untheoretical judgements to get these valuations right. People cannot be expected to be good at making these judgements in the market or in responding to surveys, and the evidence is that they are not.

I think it is foolish to try to value lives without some theoretical background.[9] I do not think willingness to pay at present offers a satisfactory approach to weighing lives.

The neutral level for existence

There remains the problem of fixing the neutral level for existence. The neutral level is bound to be vague, so the problem is to set limits to its vagueness. This seems to me appallingly difficult, but I have a little to say about it.

At the very end of chapter 14, I drew together various intuitions that constrain the neutral level. The upper limit to its vagueness must be fairly high to prevent the positive repugnant conclusion from being repugnant. The lower limit must be fairly low to prevent the negative repugnant conclusion from being repugnant. On the other hand, the vagueness must not be very extensive, because if it is we reach a different implausible conclusion. We can find that subtracting people from the population, and adding people to the population at the same level of wellbeing, can both cancel out badness.

These constraints are tight. It seems that whatever we do, some implausibility will remain. We need to minimize it. I suggest this is the right approach to determining the neutral level. The upper and lower boundaries of its vague borderline must be such as to leave us with the most credible consequences.

Notes

1   For example, see Alan Williams, 'The value of qalys' or 'Economics, society and health care ethics', or Joseph Pliskin, Donald Shepard, and Milton Weinstein, 'Utility functions for life years and health status'. The World Health Organization favours a variant of the qaly called the 'disability-adjusted life year' or 'daly'. See Christopher Murray, 'Rethinking DALYs'.
2   See the discussion in Christopher Murray, 'Rethinking DALYs', pp. 27–43.
3   See my 'Measuring the burden of disease'.
4   In 'Utility functions for life years and health status', Joseph Pliskin, Donald Shepard, and Milton Weinstein explicitly transform one scale to the other. See the discussion in my 'Qalys'.
5   For example, see Bruno Frey and Alois Stutzer, *Happiness and Economics*.
6   See M. W. Jones-Lee, *The Economics of Safety and Physical Risk*.
7   Figures in 'The social costs of climate change' by David Pearce and others show this proportion.
8   See Jean Drèze and Nicholas Stern, 'The theory of cost-benefit analysis'. These authors take Bernoulli's hypothesis for granted. I have adopted Bernoulli's hypothesis as part of my definition of a cardinal scale of wellbeing.
9   This point is more fully developed in my 'Structured and unstructured valuation'.

Bibliography

Aristotle, *Nicomachean Ethics*.

Arrhenius, Gustaf, *Future Generations: a Challenge for Moral Theory*, Uppsala University, 2000.

Arrhenius, Gustaf, 'An impossibility theorem for welfarist axiologies', *Economics and Philosophy*, 16 (2000), pp. 247–66.

Arrow, Kenneth, 'Extended sympathy and the possibility of social choice', *American Economic Review Papers and Proceedings*, 67 (1977), pp. 219–25, reprinted in his *Collected Papers Volume 1: Social Choice and Justice*, Blackwell, 1984, pp. 147–61.

Arrow, Kenneth, *Social Choice and Individual Values*, Second Edition, Yale University Press, 1963.

Arthur, W. B., 'The economics of risks to life', *American Economic Review*, 71 (1981), pp. 54–64.

Atkinson, Anthony B., and Joseph E. Stiglitz, *Lectures on Public Economics*, McGraw-Hill, 1980.

Barry, Brian, 'Rawls on average and total utility: a comment', *Philosophical Studies*, 31 (1977), pp. 317–25.

Bernoulli, Daniel, 'Specimen theoriae novae de mensura sortis', *Commentarii Academiae Scientiarum Imperialis Petropolitanae*, 5 (1738), translated by Louise Sommer as 'Exposition of a new theory on the measurement of risk', *Econometrica*, 22 (1954), pp. 23–36.

Blackorby, Charles, Walter Bossert, and David Donaldson, 'Birth-date dependent population ethics: critical-level principles', *Journal of Economic Theory*, 77 (1997), pp. 260–84.

Blackorby, Charles, Walter Bossert, and David Donaldson, 'Critical level utilitarianism and the population-ethics dilemma', *Economics and Philosophy*, 13 (1997), pp. 197–230.

Blackorby, Charles, Walter Bossert, and David Donaldson, 'Intertemporal population ethics: critical-level utilitarian principles', *Econometrica*, 65 (1995), pp. 1303–20.

Blackorby, Charles, Walter Bossert, and David Donaldson, 'Population ethics and the existence of value functions', *Journal of Public Economics*, 82 (2001), pp. 301–8.

Blackorby, Charles, Walter Bossert and David Donaldson, *Population Issues in Social Choice Theory, Welfare Economics and Ethics*, Cambridge University Press, forthcoming.

Blackorby, Charles, Walter Bossert, and David Donaldson, 'Quasi-orderings and population ethics', *Social Choice and Welfare*, 13 (1996), pp. 129–50.

Blackorby, Charles, and David Donaldson, 'Pigs and guinea pigs: a note on the ethics of animal exploitation', *Economic Journal*, 102 (1992), pp. 1345–69.

Blackorby, Charles, and David Donaldson, 'Social criteria for evaluating population change', *Journal of Public Economics*, 25 (1984), pp. 13–33.

Broome, John, 'A comment on Temkin's trade-offs', in *'Goodness' and 'Fairness': Ethical Issues in Health Resource Allocation*, edited by Daniel Wikler and Christopher J. L. Murray, World Health Organization, forthcoming.

Broome, John, 'Are intentions reasons? And how should we cope with incommensurable values?', in *Practical Rationality and Preference: Essays for David Gauthier*, edited by Christopher Morris and Arthur Ripstein, Cambridge University Press, 2001, pp. 98–120.

Broome, John, *Counting the Cost of Global Warming*, White Horse Press, 1992.

Broome, John, 'Deontology and economics', *Economics and Philosophy*, 8 (1992), pp. 269–82.

Broome, John, 'Equality versus priority: a useful distinction', in *'Goodness' and 'Fairness': Ethical Issues in Health Resource Allocation*, edited by Daniel Wikler and Christopher J. L. Murray, World Health Organization, forthcoming.

Broome, John, *Ethics Out of Economics*, Cambridge University Press, 1999.

Broome, John, 'Extended preferences', in my *Ethics Out of Economics*, pp. 29–43.

Broome, John, 'Fairness', in my *Ethics Out of Economics*, pp. 111–22.

Broome, John, 'Is incommensurability vagueness?', in my *Ethics Out of Economics*, pp. 123–44.

Broome, John, 'Kamm on fairness', *Philosophy and Phenomenological Research*, 58 (1998), pp. 955–61.

Broome, John, 'Measuring the burden of disease', in *'Goodness' and 'Fairness': Ethical Issues in Health Resource Allocation*, edited by Daniel Wikler and Christopher J. L. Murray, World Health Organization, forthcoming.

Broome, John, 'Qalys', in my *Ethics Out of Economics*, pp. 196–213.

Broome, John, 'Representing an ordering when the population varies', *Social Choice and Welfare*, 20 (2003), pp. 243–6.

Broome, John, 'Some principles of population', in *Economics, Growth and Sustainable Environments*, edited by David Collard, David Pearce and David Ulph, Macmillan, 1988, pp. 85–96.

Broome, John, 'Structured and unstructured valuation', in my *Ethics Out of Economics*, pp. 183–95.

Broome, John, *Weighing Goods: Equality, Uncertainty and Time*, Blackwell, 1991.

Bykvist, Krister, 'Violations of normative invariance: some thoughts on shifty oughts', typescript.

Carlson, Erik, 'Broome's argument against value incomparability', *Utilitas*, 16 (2004).

Carlson, Erik, *Consequentialism Reconsidered*, North-Holland, 1995.

Carlson, Erik, 'Mere addition and two trilemmas of population ethics', *Economics and Philosophy*, 14 (1998), pp. 283–306.

Cowen, Tyler, 'Consequentialism implies a zero rate of intergenerational discount', in *Justice Between Age Groups and Generations*, edited by Peter Laslett and James S. Fishkin, Yale University Press, 1992, pp. 162–8.

Cowen, Tyler, 'What do we learn from the repugnant conclusion', *Ethics*, 106 (1996), pp. 754–75.

Dasgupta, Partha, *An Inquiry Into Well-Being and Destitution*, Oxford University Press, 1993.

Dasgupta, Partha, 'Lives and well-being', *Social Choice and Welfare*, 5 (1988), pp. 103–26.

Dasgupta, Partha, and G. M. Heal, *Economic Theory and Exhaustible Resources*, Cambridge University Press, 1979.

Diamond, Peter, 'The evaluation of infinite utility streams', *Econometrica*, 33 (1965), pp. 170–7.

Drèze, Jean, and Nicholas Stern, 'The theory of cost-benefit analysis', in *Handbook of Public Economics, Volume II*, edited by Alan J. Auerback and Martin Feldstein, North-Holland, 1987, pp. 909–89.

Ellsberg, Daniel, 'Classic and current notions of "measurable utility"', *Economic Journal*, 64 (1954), pp. 528–56.

Epicurus, *Letter to Menoeceus* (edited by Whitney Oates), New York, 1940.

Fehige, Christoph, 'A Pareto principle for possible people', in *Preferences*, edited by Christoph Fehige and Ulla Wessels, de Gruyter, 1998.

Feldman, Fred, *Confrontations with the Reaper: a Philosophical Study of the Nature and Value of Death*, Oxford University Press, 1992.

Feldman, Fred, *Pleasure and the Good Life: Concerning the Nature, Varieties, and Plausibility of Hedonism*, Oxford University Press, 2004.

Fine, Kit, 'Vagueness, truth and logic', *Synthese*, 30 (1975), pp. 265–300.

Frey, Bruno S., and Alois Stutzer, *Happiness and Economics: How the Economy and Institutions Affect Human Well-Being*, Princeton University Press, 2002.

Graff, Delia, 'Phenomenal continua and the sorites', *Mind*, 110 (2001), pp. 905–35.

Griffin, James, *Well-Being: Its Meaning, Measurement and Moral Importance*, Oxford University Press, 1986.

Hammond, Peter, 'Interpersonal comparisons of utility: why and how they are and should be made', in *Interpersonal Comparisons of Well-Being*, edited by Jon Elster and John Roemer, Cambridge University Press, 1991, pp. 200–54.

Harsanyi, John C., 'Cardinal utility in welfare economics and in the theory of risk-taking', *Journal of Political Economy*, 61 (1953), pp. 434–5, reprinted in his *Essays on Ethics, Social Behavior, and Scientific Explanation*, Reidel, 1976, pp. 3–5.

Harsanyi, John, 'Cardinal welfare, individualistic ethics, and interpersonal comparisons of utility', *Journal of Political Economy*, 63 (1955), pp. 309–21, reprinted in his *Essays on Ethics, Social Behavior, and Scientific Explanation*, Reidel, 1976, pp. 6–23.

Harsanyi, John, *Rational Behavior and Bargaining Equilibrium in Games and Social Situations*, Cambridge University Press, 1977.

Hurka, Thomas, 'Value and population size', *Ethics*, 93 (1983), pp. 496–507.

Jones-Lee, M. W., *The Economics of Safety and Physical Risk*, Blackwell, 1989.

Jones-Lee, M. W., G. Loomes, and P. R. Philips, 'Valuing the prevention of non-fatal road injuries: contingent valuation vs standard gambles', *Oxford Economic Papers*, 47 (1995), pp. 676–95.

Kahneman, Daniel, 'The cognitive psychology of consequences and moral intuition'. Tanner Lecture on Human Values, University of Michigan, 1994.

Kahneman, Daniel, B. L. Fredrickson, C. Schreiber, and D. A. Redelmeier, 'When more pain is preferred to less: adding a better end', *Psychological Science*, 4 (1993), pp. 401–5.

Kamm, Frances, *Morality, Mortality: Vol I, Death and Whom to Save From It*, Oxford University Press, 1993.

Kamm, Frances, *Morality, Mortality: Vol II, Rights, Duties and Values*, Oxford University Press, 1996.

Kripke, Saul, 'Outline of a theory of truth', *Journal of Philosophy*, 72 (1975), pp. 690–716.

Lewis, David, *On the Plurality of Worlds*, Blackwell, 1986.

Lewis, David, 'Survival and identity', in *The Identities of Persons*, edited by Amelie O. Rorty, University of California Press, 1976, pp. 17–40, reprinted with additions in his *Philosophical Papers*, Vol 1, Oxford University Press, 1983, pp. 55–77.

Lucretius, *On the Nature of the Universe*, Penguin, 1951.

Marglin, S. A. 'The social rate of discount and the optimal rate of investment', *Quarterly Journal of Economics*, 77 (1963), pp. 95–111.

McGee, Van, and Brian McLaughlin, 'Distinctions without a difference', *Southern Journal of Philosophy*, 33 Supplement (1994), pp. 203–51.

McKerlie, Dennis, 'Equality and time', *Ethics*, 99 (1989), pp. 475–91.

McMahan, Jeff, *The Ethics of Killing*, Oxford University Press, 2002.

McMahan, Jeff, 'Problems of population theory', *Ethics*, 92 (1981), pp. 96–127.

McMichael, Anthony, and Andrew Githeko, 'Human health', in *Climate Change 2001: Impacts, Adaptation and Vulnerability*, Intergovernmental Panel on Climate Change Working Group II, Cambridge University Press, 2001, pp. 451–85.

Moore, G. E., *Principia Ethica*, Cambridge University Press, 1903.

Murray, Christopher J. L., 'Rethinking DALYs', in *The Global Burden of Disease*, edited by Christopher J. L. Murray and Alan D. Lopez, Harvard University Press, 1996.

Nagel, Thomas, 'Death', in his *Mortal Questions*, Cambridge University Press, 1979, pp. 1–10.

Narveson, Jan, 'Moral problems of population', *The Monist*, 57 (1973), pp. 62–86, reprinted in *Ethics and Population*, edited by Michael D. Bayles, Schenkman, 1976, pp. 59–80.

Narveson, Jan, 'Utilitarianism and new generations', *Mind*, 76 (1967), pp. 62–72.

Ng, Yew-Kwang, 'Social criteria for evaluating population change: an alternative to the Blackorby-Donaldson criterion', *Journal of Public Economics*, 29 (1986), pp. 375–81.

Nozick, Robert, 'Moral complications and moral structures', *Natural Law Forum*, 13 (1968), pp. 1–50.

Oddie, Graham, and Peter Milne, 'Expectation and the representation of moral theories', *Theoria*, 57 (1991), pp. 42–76.

Olson, Mancur, and Martin J. Bailey, 'Positive time preference', *Journal of Political Economy*, 89 (1981), pp. 1–25.

Parfit, Derek, 'Equality or Priority?', The Lindley Lecture, University of Kansas, 1991, reprinted in *The Ideal of Equality*, edited by Matthew Clayton and Andrew Williams, Macmillan, 2000, pp. 81–125.

Parfit, Derek, *Reasons and Persons*, Oxford University Press, 1984.

Parsons, Josh, 'Axiological actualism', *Australasian Journal of Philosophy*, 50 (2002), pp. 137–47.

Pearce, D. W., W. R. Cline, A. N. Achanta, S. Fankhauser, P. K. Pachauri, R. S. J. Tol, and P. Vellinga, 'The social costs of climate change: greenhouse damage and the benefits of control', in *Climate Change 1995, Volume III: Economic and Social Dimensions of Climate Change*, Intergovernmental Panel on Climate Change, Cambridge University Press, 1996, pp. 179–224.

Pigou, A. C., *The Economics of Welfare*, Fourth Edition, Macmillan, 1932.

Pliskin, Joseph S., Donald S. Shepard, and Milton C. Weinstein, 'Utility functions for life years and health status', *Operations Research*, 28 (1980), pp. 206–24.

Qizilbash, Mozaffar, 'The mere addition paradox, parity and critical-level utilitarianism', *Social Choice and Welfare*, forthcoming.

Rachels, Stuart, 'Counterexamples to the transitivity of *better than*', *Australasian Journal of Philosophy*, 76 (1998), pp. 71–83.

Rachels, Stuart, 'A set of solutions to Parfit's problems', *Noûs*, 35 (2001), pp. 214–38.

Rawls, John, *A Theory of Justice*, Harvard University Press, 1972.

Raz, Joseph, 'Value incommensurability: some preliminaries', *Proceedings of the Aristotelian Society*, 86 (1985–86), pp.117–34.

Regan, Donald, 'Against evaluator relativity: a response to Sen', *Philosophy and Public Affairs*, 12 (1983), pp. 93–112.

Roberts, Melinda A., *Child versus Childmaker: Future Persons and Present Duties in Ethics and the Law*, Rowman and Littlefield, 1998.

Sartre, Jean-Paul, 'The humanism of existentialism', in his *Essays in Existentialism*, Citadel Press, 1968, pp. 31–62.

Scanlon, T. M., *What We Owe to Each Other*, Harvard University Press, 1998.

Scheffler, Samuel, (ed.) *Consequentialism and Its Critics*, Oxford University Press, 1988.

Scheffler, Samuel, *The Rejection of Consequentialism*, Oxford University Press, 1982.

Schumm, George F., 'Transitivity, preference and indifference', *Philosophical Studies*, 52 (1986), pp. 435–7.

Sen, Amartya, 'Rights and agency', *Philosophy and Public Affairs*, 11 (1982), pp. 3–38.

Sidgwick, Henry, *The Methods of Ethics*, Seventh Edition, Macmillan, 1907.

Skorupski, John, 'Quality of well-being: quality of being, in his *Ethical Explorations*, Oxford University Press, 1999, pp.106–33.

Strotz, R. H., 'Myopia and inconsistency in dynamic utility maximization', *Review of Economic Studies*, 23 (1955–6), pp. 165–80.

Sugden, Robert, 'Why be consistent? A critical analysis of consistency requirements in choice theory', *Economica*, 52 (1985), pp. 167–83.

Temkin, Larry S., 'An abortion argument and the threat of intransitivity', in *Well-Being and Morality: Essays in Honour of James Griffin*, edited by Roger Crisp and Brad Hooker, Oxford University Press, 2000, pp. 263–79.

Temkin, Larry S., 'Aggregation and problems about trade-offs', in *'Goodness' and 'Fairness': Ethical Issues in Health Resource Allocation*, edited by Daniel Wikler and Christopher J. L. Murray, World Health Organization, forthcoming.

Temkin, Larry S., 'A continuum argument for intransitivity', *Philosophy and Public Affairs*, 25 (1996), pp. 175–210.

Temkin, Larry S., 'Health care distribution and the problem of trade-offs', in *'Goodness' and 'Fairness': Ethical Issues in Health Resource Allocation*, edited by Daniel Wikler and Christopher J. L. Murray, World Health Organization, forthcoming.

Temkin, Larry S., 'Intergenerational inequality', in *Justice Between Age Groups and Generations*, edited by Peter Laslett and James S. Fishkin, Yale University Press, 1992, pp. 169–205.

Temkin, Larry S., 'Intransitivity and the mere addition paradox', *Philosophy and Public Affairs*, 16 (1987), pp. 138–87.

Thomson, Judith Jarvis, 'Imposing risks', in *To Breathe Freely*, edited by Mary Gibson, Rowman & Allanheld, 1985, pp. 124–40.

Vallentyne, Peter, 'Gimmicky representations of moral theories', *Metaphilosophy*, 19 (1988), pp. 253–63.

Vallentyne, Peter, and Shelley Kagan, 'Infinite value and finitely additive value theory', *Journal of Philosophy*, 94 (1997), pp. 5–26.

Velleman, David, 'Well-being and time', *Pacific Philosophical Quarterly*, 72 (1991), pp. 48–77.

Voorhoeve, Alex, and Ken Binmore, 'Defending transitivity against Zeno's paradox', *Philosophy and Public Affairs*, 31 (2003), pp. 272–9.

Wagstaff, Adam, 'QALYs and the equity–efficiency trade-off', *Journal of Health Economics*, 10 (1991), pp. 21–41.

Wakker, Peter, *Additive Representation of Preferences*, Kluwer, 1989.

Williams, Alan, 'Economics, society and health care ethics', in *Principles of Health Care Ethics*, edited by Raanan Gillon, Wiley, 1993.

Williams, Alan, 'Intergenerational equity: an exploration of the "fair innings" argument', *Health Economics*, 6 (1997), pp. 117–32.

Williams, Alan, 'The value of qalys', *Health and Social Service Journal*, 18 July

1985, pp. 3–5.

Williams, Bernard, 'The Makropulos case: reflections on the tedium of immortality', in his *Problems of the Self*, Cambridge University Press, 1973, pp. 82–100.

Williamson, Timothy, *Vagueness*, Routledge, 1994.

Wittgenstein, Ludwig, *Notebooks 1914–16*, Blackwell, 1961.

Index